KU-773-166

MUIRHEAD LIBRARY OF PHILOSOPHY

An admirable statement of the aims of the Library of Philosophy was provided by the first editor, the late Professor J. H. Muirhead, in his description of the original programme printed in Erdmann's *History of Philosophy* under the date 1890. This was slightly modified in subsequent volumes to take the form of the following statement:

'The Muirhead Library of Philosophy was designed as a contribution to the History of Modern Philosophy under the heads: first of different Schools of Thought—Sensationalist, Realist, Idealist, Intuitivist; secondly of different Subjects—Psychology, Ethics, Aesthetics, Political Philosophy, Theology. While much had been done in England in tracing the course of evolution in nature, history, economics, morals and religion, little had been done in tracing the development of thought on these subjects. Yet "the evolution of opinion is part of the whole evolution".

'By the co-operation of different writers in carrying out this plan it was hoped that a thoroughness and completeness of treatment, otherwise unattainable, might be secured. It was believed also that from writers mainly British and American fuller consideration of English Philosophy than it had hitherto received might be looked for. In the earlier series of books containing, among others, Bosanquet's *History of Aesthetic*, Pfleiderer's *Rational Theology since Kant*, Albee's *History of English Utilitarianism*, Bonar's *Philosophy and Political Economy*, Brett's *History of Psychology*, Ritchie's *Natural Rights*, these objects were to a large extent effected.

'In the meantime original work of a high order was being produced both in England and America by such writers as Bradley, Stout, Bertrand Russell, Baldwin, Urban, Montague, and others, and a new interest in foreign works, German, French and Italian, which had either become classical or were attracting public attention, had developed. The scope of the Library thus became extended into something more international and it is entering on the fifth decade of its existence in the hope that it may contribute to that mutual understanding between countries which is so pressing a need of the present time.'

The need which Professor Muirhead stressed is no less pressing today, and few will deny that philosophy has much to do with enabling us to meet it, although no one, least of all Muirhead himself, would regard that as the sole, or even the main, object of philosophy. As Professor Muirhead continues to lend the distinction of his name to the Library of Philosophy it seemed not inappropriate to allow him to recall us to these aims in his own words. The emphasis on the history of thought also seemed to me very timely; and the number of important works promised for the Library in the near future augur well for the continued fulfilment, in this and other ways, of the expectations of the original editor.

H. D. LEWIS

MUIRHEAD LIBRARY OF PHILOSOPHY

General Editor: H. D. Lewis

Professor of History and Philosophy of Religion in the University of London

The Analysis of Mind. By BERTRAND RUSSELL. 8th Impression.

Analytic Psychology. By G. F. STOUT. 2 Vols. 5th Impression.

Coleridge as Philosopher. By J. H. MUIRHEAD. 2nd Impression.

Contemporary American Philosophy. Edited by G. P. ADAMS and W. P. MONTAGUE.

Contemporary British Philosophy. Edited by J. H. MUIRHEAD.

Contemporary Indian Philosophy. Edited by RADHAKRISHNAN and J. H. MUIR-HEAD.

Contemporary British Philosophy. Third Series. Edited by H. D. LEWIS.

Development of Theology Since Kant. By O. PFLEIDERER.

Dialogues on Metaphysics. By NICHOLAS MALEBRANCHE. Translated by MORRIS GINSBURG.

Ethics. By NICOLAI HARTMANN. Translated by STANTON COIT. 3 Vols.

The Good Will: A Study in the Coherence Theory of Goodness. By H. J. PATON.

Hegel: A Re-Examination. By J. N. FINDLAY.

Hegel's Science of Logic. Translated by W. H. JOHNSTON and L. G. STRUTHERS. 2 Vols. 2nd Impression.

History of Aesthetic. By B. BOSANQUET. 4th Edition. 5th Impression.

History of English Utilitarianism. By E. ALBEE.

History of Psychology. By G. S. BRETT. Edited by R. S. PETERS. Abridged one-volume edition.

Human Knowledge. By BERTRAND RUSSELL. 3rd Impression.

A Hundred Years of British Philosophy. By RUDOLF METZ. Translated by J. W. HARVEY, T. E. JESSOP, HENRY STURT. 2nd Impression.

Ideas: A General Introduction to Pure Phenomenology. By EDMUND HUSSERL. Translated by W. R. BOYCE GIBSON. 2nd Impression.

Indian Philosophy. By RADHAKRISHNAN. 2 Vols. Revised 2nd Edition.

The Intelligible World Metaphysics and Value. By W. M. URBAN.

Introduction to Mathematical Philosophy. By BERTRAND RUSSELL. 2nd Edition. 8th Impression.

Kant's First Critique. By H. W. CASSIRER.

Kant's Metaphysic of Experience. By H. J. PATON. 2nd Impression.

Know Thyself. By BERNADINO VARISCO. Translated by GUGLIELMO SALVADORI.

Language and Reality. By WILBUR MARSHALL URBAN.

Matter and Memory. By HENRI BERGSON. Translated by N. M. PAUL and W. S. PALMER. 6th Impression.

Modern Philosophy. By GUIDO DE RUGGIERO. Translated by A. HOWARD HANNAY and R. G. COLLINGWOOD.

The Modern Predicament. By H. J. PATON.

Moral Sense. By JAMES BONAR.

Natural Rights. By D. G. RITCHIE. 3rd Edition. 5th Impression.

Nature, Mind and Modern Science. By E. HARRIS.

The Nature of Thought. By BRAND BLANSHARD. 2nd Impression.

On Selfhood and Godhood. By C. A. CAMPBELL.

Personality and Reality. By E. J. TURNER.

The Phenomenology of Mind. By G. W. F. HEGEL. Translated by SIR JAMES BAILLIE. Revised 2nd Edition. 3rd Impression.

Philosophical Papers. By G. E. MOORE.

Philosophy and Political Economy. By J. BONAR. 4th Impression.

Philosophy of Whitehead. By W. MAYS.

The Platonic Tradition in Anglo-Saxon Philosophy. By J. H. MUIRHEAD.

The Principal Upanisads. By RADHAKRISHNAN.

The Problems of Perception. By R. J. HIRST.

Reason and Goodness. By BRAND BLANSHARD.

Some Main Problems of Philosophy. By G. E. MOORE.

Time and Free Will. By HENRI BERGSON. Translated by F. G. POGSON. 6th Impression.

The Ways of Knowing: or The Methods of Philosophy. By W. P. MONTAGUE. 4th Impression.

E
L

EDINBURGH UNIVERSITY LIBRARY
WITHDRAWN

30150   002403068

The Muirhead Library of Philosophy
EDITED BY H. D. LEWIS

THE THEOLOGICAL FRONTIER OF ETHICS

G61/2008

THE THEOLOGICAL FRONTIER
OF ETHICS

AN ESSAY

*Based on
the Edward Cadbury Lectures in the
University of Birmingham 1955–56*

BY

W. G. MACLAGAN

*Professor of Moral Philosophy
in the
University of Glasgow*

LONDON: GEORGE ALLEN & UNWIN LTD

NEW YORK: THE MACMILLAN COMPANY

EDINBURGH UNIVERSITY LIBRARY
WITHDRAWN

FIRST PUBLISHED IN 1961

This book is copyright under the Berne Convention. Apart from any fair dealing for the purpose of private study, research, criticism, or review, as permitted under the Copyright Act, 1956, no portion may be reproduced by any process without written permission. Enquiries should be addressed to the publisher.

© *George Allen & Unwin Ltd, 1961*

PRINTED IN GREAT BRITAIN
in 11 on 12 pt Imprint type
BY UNWIN BROTHERS LIMITED
WOKING AND LONDON

PREFACE

This work is a long-delayed outcome of the invitation given me to deliver the 1955–56 series of Edward Cadbury Lectures in the University of Birmingham. It is my first and very pleasant duty to thank those responsible for that invitation for the privilege accorded me, and my Birmingham hosts and audience for their kindness and forbearance. Part of the material of the lectures was later used in three special University Lectures in Theology given at King's College, London, in January 1958. I am grateful for the opportunity and incentive thus provided to review and rearrange my thoughts.

It is obvious that a book with such an origin will be in some sense theological, even though its theology is exceedingly amateurish. Whether it also deserves to be called philosophical is another question; on which, however, I am content to accept the verdict of the Editor of the Muirhead Library. What I am sure of is that the issues it discusses are important, that philosophers should concern themselves with them, and that, if they do so, they must be willing to speak in ways that may offend the taste of those whose austere ideal it is to seem to hold no form of creed while analytically contemplating all. I therefore make no apology for the general character of this work, whatever may be its more specific faults of substance or style.

Isaac D'Israeli justly observed that titles of books 'are generally too prodigal of their promises'; but he conceded that many authors are not, after all, so vain as they appear, for magnificent titles 'have often been given from the difficulty of forming any others'. I acknowledge the truth of the first of these propositions in the present instance and plead the truth of the second. It is in order to emphasize the very restricted purpose of my book that I describe it as 'an essay'. I shall be exploring the *relation between* theism and a certain type of ethics, not (save to a very meagre extent) theism and that kind of ethics themselves. Such a limitation is surely defensible when, as here, both terms in the relation answer to widely-held, and not manifestly foolish, convictions. (It is of secondary importance that I personally share one of these convictions and at least strongly incline to the other; though, doubtless, but for that fact I should not have chosen to write on this subject myself.) But the essay has limitations additional to the one just mentioned. Certain difficult problems that emerge in the course of it (such as, notably, that of the epistemology and ontology of 'value') are indicated but not enlarged upon. This is not from any lack of interest on my part, nor even altogether from a lack of ideas. But I have preferred to present one fairly straightforward and fundamental thesis, on our attitude to which much else will depend, with a minimum of elaboration and complication. Such a treatment can provide no more than a beginning to reflection on these matters: but it is important that (whether it be by acceptance or rejection of the thesis) we should get the beginning right. I am perhaps not mistaken in believing that simple and central truths are easily lost in a tangle of premature subtleties.

I am indebted to a number of friends for valuable advice and help. I must in particular mention my colleague Professor C. A. Campbell, who has endured with great patience and good-humour the worst consequences of our propinquity. My readers, like myself, have every reason to be grateful to him for his unfailing readiness to adopt my perplexities as his own, and to lavish on them a fatherly care. I have profited much also from the understanding criticism of Professor R. C. Cross, Professor H. D. Lewis and Professor D. M. MacKinnon; and it is no fault of theirs that I have not profited more. Finally, I must thank my colleague Mr. R. S. Downie for preparing the Index and for help with the preparation of the Table of Contents and with proof-reading. Mr. Downie also contrived to mitigate the clumsiness of my English at a number of points, and could undoubtedly have done so at many more. Unfortunately, this was a case of the doctor being summoned too late.

NOTE

An obscurity in the statement of my views was brought to my notice only after the proofs had been corrected and returned to the printer. I appear to treat moral choice and responsibility as 'non-episodic' on p. 46, but as 'episodic' on p. 195. It is the language of the latter passage (and in particular the expression 'occasions of action') that is careless. Although a distinction must be drawn between moral and non-moral choices I do not really think of these as co-ordinate species of choice. *All* occasions of choice are *moral* occasions (involving, fundamentally, the issue of 'volitional sincerity'); and the term 'non-moral choice' refers, strictly, only to an abstracted aspect of such concrete occasions. There may well be other passages besides those mentioned where it will be important to bear this in mind.

CONTENTS

'duty-consciousness', but consciousness of absolute demand postulates an objective 'order of values'. Thus the question whether the fact that we have duties admits of or requires interpretation in theological terms invites discussion both of the authority of duty and of the being of values.

§3: Theological concepts may be said to elucidate the authority of the moral law in either of two ways, 'contextual' and 'aetiological'. These explanations may each be offered either with a view to sustaining the sense of duty or with a view to analysing it.   §4: The contextual explanation may take a crude form in which appeal is made to the hypothesis that the good man will be rewarded. This turns morality into self-interest.   §5: A more refined form of contextual explanation says that a man cannot be expected to do his duty unless he believes the universe to be 'friendly' towards the realization of moral ideals. But however hostile the universe may appear the moral demand is still felt as authoritative.   §6: The tendency in such a case to regard our situation as 'absurd' arises precisely from the fact that we cannot doubt the authority of duty. Moreover, to say 'absurd' rather than 'hateful' seems to beg the theistic question. But moral experience may carry with it, though it does not presuppose, a conviction of the 'friendliness' of the universe.   §7: The moral demand must be taken as authoritative in itself: so taken, it may be an index of what we mean when we speak of 'God'.

§8: The aetiological theory interprets duty as God's command or will for us. Complication here arising from the distinction between objective and subjective duty is common to all theories of obligation.   §9: The theory has a less radical form according to which there is one underived duty, to obey God, other duties being determined by this. Objections to this view. In its more radical form the theory admits no obligation whatever that is not a product of the Divine Will. This has the merit of consistency but is not an improvement in any other respect.   §10: To say that God commands the right as being right makes the command hypothesis ethically superfluous and at the same time raises theological difficulties. Yet the proposal to leave God out of the account altogether may be resisted for various reasons. §11: One consideration is that 'moral law' may seem to imply God as Lawgiver. But this is to misunderstand what is meant by 'moral law'.   §12: The contention that duties imply corresponding claims and these in turn a Divine Claimant must likewise be rejected.   §13: It is in fact impossible to frame the required concept of 'Divine Claimant'. This follows from the distinction between goodness and a person's good or interest: rights relate only to the latter.   §14: Kant spoke of reverence for the moral law, and it is argued that there can be reverence only for that which is personal. But this cannot be substantiated, nor is it what Kant himself held.   §15: If the moral law is neither independent of God nor dependent on God we must say that it *is* God. This is not to deny that 'God' has a wider meaning than 'moral law'.

IV. THE MORAL RESPONSE *Page* 95

more and more difficult. §12: Reply to the criticism that
the 'bare will' whose freedom we are safeguarding is a vicious
abstraction. The criticism fails, but it supports the view that
there can be no empirical assurance of the will's purity.
The lack of this assurance may give rise to a sense that what
we seek to be assured of is itself impossible. §13: The
ideal condition of the will must be distinguished from the
ideal condition of the whole person. It is not claimed that
we can of ourselves attain to the latter, and confusion of
the two may lead to disbelief of our ability to achieve the
former. §14: Although the moral response conceived as
dutifulness can be accounted for without help from
theology it may be that dutifulness is a corrupt or defective
ideal and that the proper excellence of the will is to be
described in some other way.

V. DUTY, LOVE AND PRAYER   *Page* 133

§1: Pursuit of dutifulness as an ideal has been criticized as
self-frustrating.   §2: The criticism misconceives the
character of dutifulness, which is essentially outward-
looking. §3: Neither the philosopher's emphasis on the
quality of the will as distinct from its objective nor the
agent's desire not to lose his self-respect by wrongdoing is
inconsistent with this outward-looking character, though
each has its dangers. §4: Discussion of the objection that
whereas we condemn ourselves for wrong actions we should
not praise ourselves for right ones. §5: The life of worship
can become as self-centred as a degenerate moral life.

§6: Is the ideal of a life based on love superior to that of
one based on dutifulness? This cannot be true of our love
for our fellow-men whether in the form of natural affection
or of respect for them as persons. §7: For the same reasons
it cannot be true of love for God, in so far as God is conceived as a person. §8: If God is identified with the moral
law the love of God is not a motive superior to dutifulness
but is identical with it. §9: But can dutifulness in itself ever
deserve the name of love? The argument that it can do so
will at the same time dispose of a final objection to the
denial of constitutive grace. The problem will be approached
indirectly.

§10: What does religion require by way of a doctrine of
grace? §11: A doctrine of grace is analytically involved in
the theist's conception of God. §12: Is grace in any sense
an empirical fact? §13: It is in prayer, if at all, that we
should expect to be aware of ourselves as subjects of grace.
§14: The claim that such awareness occurs is full of difficulty, but will here be conceded. §15: Granted that prayer
as petition is valid in principle, can any account be given
of prayer for the enablement of the will without the admission of constitutive grace? Proposal to consider first the
prayer for forgiveness, which will be found to be analogous
in important respects. §16: Discussion of the nature of
forgiveness. The concept of God's forgiveness has meaning

in so far as God is thought of as person; but, unless we misrepresent His nature, the prayer for forgiveness is not strictly petition but is penitence expressed as petition. §17: We must, however, distinguish between injury and sin. The concept of forgiveness fails us altogether in regard to sin. Once again what appears as petition must be understood as an activity whereby we reconstitute ourselves. §18: The prayer for enablement is similarly not petition but resolution. §19: In moral crises this may gain indefinitely in intensity and become a passionate loyalty of will. §20: Two points to be noted: (*a*) Not all occasions exact this intensity, but even without it a man may have a 'readiness' that could be called love of the right. (*b*) It is more appropriate to speak of 'love' in connection with 'good' than in connection with 'right', but the sense of duty is inseparable from some consciousness of the values that are the source of the duty. §21: We conclude that what appears as the petition for constitutive grace is in fact a willed attentiveness to the claim upon us. This may yield what might be thought of as a love that transcends dutifulness but is really dutifulness itself in its supreme form.

§1: Theism conceives of God in personal terms, but the nature of the moral demand requires that Deity (if admitted at all) be conceived as impersonal. §2: The second of these propositions may be attacked as resting on the false assumption that there is no *via media* between impersonalism and anthropomorphism. But the concept of person cannot be purged of anthropomorphism and still retain the positive content on which its explanatory value depends. §3: Rejection of the view that the concept of person is not derived from experience of human beings but is *a priori* and relates primarily to the perfect personality of God. §4: Rejection of the view that although the concept is empirically derived we can use it to speak of God not univocally but by analogy. §5: If Deity must be represented as both personal and impersonal these features cannot be regarded as simply coexisting. §6: Yet it seems impossible to frame any idea of God that integrates the two. Postulating an uncomprehended unity we may apply to it the term 'supra-personal', so long as we bear in mind that this no more means merely 'personal *plus* . . .' than it is a mere synonym of 'impersonal'.

A morality of conventional decencies is possible without religion, but is not genuinely moral. Genuine morality may be described as religious in its very nature as morality, but it is not essentially dependent on religion in any sense of 'religion' that distinguishes it from morality. (This is not to say that true religion is nothing but morality, nor to deny that in so far as it is more it can have 'moral utility'.) The insistence that morality depends (extraneously) on religion debases both; it may rather drive men from morality than bring them to religion; and (if the safeguard of a 'blessed inconsistency' failed) it could even lead to the corruptest forms of fanaticism.

CHAPTER I

MORALS AND RELIGION:
THE QUESTION DEFINED

(1)

'Morals without religion'—what sort of morals can we have on these terms? Does morality depend on religion or does it not? People debate the matter with considerable heat. And the first thing it might reasonably occur to one to ask in this connection is why, in the whole tangled problem of the relations between religion and morality, it is this question in particular that rouses such passion. We might equally well enquire whether religion can exist or thrive without morals; but in fact people in general do not ask this, and if it is asked it strikes us as somewhat academic. This is not to say that it has no interest, but any interest it has seems to be of the cool theoretical kind that does not touch our business and bosoms.

Both questions alike, of course, could be dealt with in a way that robs them of excitement. They could be decided by definition. One might, for example, without any study of facts or careful concern for the natural use of words, elect to say that nothing should count as morality that was not saturated with the feelings and beliefs constitutive of an attitude that could be called an attitude of worship; or again that nothing should count as religion that did not embody a recognition, a practical and operative recognition, of a difference between right and wrong in conduct. Such decisions would no doubt give rise to further questions that really would be questions of substance: but the questions 'Morals without religion?' and 'Religion without morals?' would have been deprived of all importance in themselves. If they are to be important, as one at least of them commonly seems to us to be, they must be handled in a different way.

Suppose, then, that we are not to settle simply by definition whether religion is independent of morality. Suppose that, for example, we identify religion with the holding of certain express beliefs about a being that transcends and somehow sustains the whole context of human affairs, and with the employment in

B

association with these beliefs of certain distinctive ritual pro-
cedures; or at least identify it with certain distinctive practices in
which beliefs of the sort indicated are implicit. Can religion so
understood exist altogether apart from *some* kind of morality? It
is a different question, of course, whether a *particular* sort of
religion goes with, and owes its distinctive character to, a *particular*
sort of morality; but let us pass that by. Confining myself to the
more fundamental question, I confess that I can see no reason
a priori why practices and beliefs that are religious in the sense
just suggested—a possible enough sense whether or not a satisfactory one—should not be detachable from all moral concern.
On the other hand it is very doubtful whether in fact they are
ever to be found in this detachment. And putting these considerations together we might plausibly conclude that while it may be
true that we cannot have religion without morality this signifies no
direct essential tie between the two, but is simply a special case
of the general truth that we can have nothing in human life
without morality, that the moral concern is inseparable from our
human nature. Certainly if any evidence is to be adduced to the
contrary, it seems that we must ask the anthropologists to provide
it, hunting it out for us from remote times or places; and we can
afford to wait for their answer with that merely speculative interest
to which I have already referred. In our day and society the existence of a moral concern, however feeble its energy and however
perverse its forms, seems to be something we can take for granted.

Far otherwise is it with the question whether morality can exist
or thrive apart from religion. Setting aside all those who exhibit
merely a practical indifference to religion, there are very many
among us—and, significantly, they include in their number some
who, by any test that does not beg the question, are among the
most intelligent and serious-minded—who expressly disclaim
religious belief, who dismiss it as superstition, even as dangerous
superstition. It could be their honest hope that all should come
to share their disbelief; nor is it a quite fantastic hope. It is easy
to see how these should have a passionate two-fold interest in the
issue; a concern, taking an anti-religious form, for truth, and a
concern to satisfy themselves and their fellows that they are not
the enemies, perhaps are even the best friends, of morality. It is
equally easy to see why this passion should be reciprocated, and
honourably so, on the side of those who uphold the claims of

religion. For them not only truth is at stake but the supreme quality of human living, which is not to be described in merely moral terms. And if they believe that morality itself is in danger when religion is threatened, their insistence on this will at one and the same time express the moral passion that they may share with their opponents and be a legitimate and powerful defence of those religious convictions that are the most precious of all their possessions.

It is therefore not at all perplexing that the general question of the relation between morality and religion should tend to become concentrated into the narrower form of a dispute whether morality depends on religion or is independent of it, and that in this narrower form it should be a theme of heated popular debate, not simply of calm social-historical or sociological or philo-sophical enquiry. But even in this narrower dispute the issues are far from clear, and if we may assume that, though truth is not the only thing that matters, truth does matter, and that neither party wishes simply to bind it as a victim on the Altar of Victorious Prejudice, we must ask for calm here also. Our business is not to slay truth with sacrificial knives but to save it by the scalpel of analysis, using a steady mind for the surgeon's steady hand. That one has no hope of more than partial success in the operation will not excuse a refusal to attempt it.

(2)

What is it, then, that we affirm or deny when we debate the dependence of morality on religion? It is probable that most people who suppose this dependence to be a fact have chiefly in mind that at a given time there is a certain well-established norm of decent behaviour (it is not necessary to particularize about the moral rules that constitute it) and that those social groups and those epochs in which religious conviction is strong come at least nearer to living up to their standard than do those groups and epochs the religious life of which is feeble. The most generally available criterion of religious conviction is the habit of public religious observances; in the case of Christianity therefore (with which in all this matter we may take ourselves to be primarily concerned) the main criterion is regular church-going. Reflective Christians would of course admit that the existence of this habit provides weaker evidence of the presence of religious conviction than the non-existence of the habit does of its absence. But, subject to this limitation, the test proposed seems fair enough in view of the nature of Christian doctrine about the Church. If morality really is supported by religion, then where the Church is weak the level of moral practice should tend to be lowered.

Now the question whether this is in fact so is an empirical question, a social-historical one; it is not to be answered by philosophical reflection. It is thus a purely 'lay' opinion that I express when I say that there seems to me to be at least a considerable measure of truth in the contention. On the other hand it cannot be pretended that there is no noble living among agnostics and avowed atheists; and the suggestion often put forward that this is possible only within certain limits of time, and only because (to use a dangerously easy and unexamined metaphor) they are drawing on the accumulated 'capital' of an earlier age of faith, must be looked at very sceptically. The suggestion has some force, I think, with reference to the persistence of the norm itself, to the persistence, that is to say, of the accepted *ideal* of conduct. But as regards actual practice I should question whether the vital religion of the past can have any direct relevance at all, in distinction from such indirect effects on conduct as are produced by the very fact that a certain ideal continues to be held up to us. What can, and what no doubt in some degree does, *directly* affect the actual moral practice of unbelievers is rather the actual practice of religious people not in the past but in contemporary society. But this again is only possible up to a certain point. Speaking broadly, it will only happen so long as the body of religious people is strong enough to provide what we could call the 'dominant ethos' of the society. For up to that point the desire to be at one with one's group, expressing itself in a concern for what is really just 'good form', will be effective; but beyond that point not.

Those who maintain the essential dependence of morality, in the sense of the level of moral *practice*, on religion may of course perfectly well admit this; it is precisely what in their view makes the need for religious revival so urgent. What reflects adversely on the truth of their contention is not the fact simply that some agnostics and atheists live what are overtly morally good lives but the fact that the inner quality also of these lives is genuinely moral and not mere 'conformism'. And surely this is sometimes the case; to go no further back than the last century, one might confidently ask whether it was not the case with, say, John Stuart Mill or George Eliot. Surely too (though it is not necessary to my argument to make the point) it is bound to be so in any instance of agnosticism or atheism in which the avowed principles and overt practice are of a quality 'out of key with' and, we should judge, actually finer than the prevailing modes, whether these be the modes of a nominally religious society or not. It would of course be a precarious matter to adduce illustrations of this last contention without the most careful scrutiny of the particular case. For though it might not be too hard to find negative instances to refute those who would make the best morality of an epoch invariably dependent on some *particular* religious faith (the Christian religion, say), it would be difficult and perhaps impossible to show, where religious faith in any and every form is not expressly disclaimed, that it was not in *some* form operatively present. To cite but one example: how should we view the morality of classical Stoicism? Are we to regard it as religious or non-religious? But about the possibility of a genuinely agnostic moral practice that rises even above the level of its time and place I cannot pretend to entertain any serious doubt.

Now of course none of all this, no biographical truths about the finer agnostics, can do anything to upset the social-historical generalization (which, as I have said, I judge to have some force) that a decay of religion tends to be associated with a depression of the level of actual conduct. It could still be true that, apart from religion, the agnostic *élite* would find themselves to be *rari nantes in gurgite vasto*. None the less there are some highly important questions that the existence of such an *élite* does raise. It raises, first and most importantly, the question whether, even granted that religion has some sort of moral relevance, moral practice can be said to depend on religion in any *essential* way; and indeed it suggests that the answer to this question must be negative. And this is important because in the end, surely, both sides in the dispute over non-religious morality take themselves to be concerned with something more than contingent psychological and historical facts. They regard themselves as maintaining a view about the very nature of morality which the empirical facts merely indicate or illustrate or tend to confirm. The existence of an agnostic *élite* raises also, and by the same token, the question

of the real moral status of such good conduct as does apparently
depend on religion. And, finally, it raises the question how far,
in any concomitant rise and fall of religious faith and the quality
of conduct, it is the rise and fall of the former that determines
the latter and not the other way round. There seems to be only
one method by which these questions might even appear to be
foreclosed in favour of what for the sake of brevity I call the
religious thesis. This is the method of claiming that even the most
explicit and sincere professions of agnosticism on the part of those
who take the moral life seriously are based, and necessarily so,
on self-delusion, that those who utter them must still be possessed
of religious faith without knowing it, and could not be concerned
about morality in the way they are were it not for that faith. But
even this device does not really serve its purpose. There may
indeed be a sense, perhaps an important sense, in which the hypothesis proposed is a sound one: on that I need not here commit
myself either way. The issue at present is not whether the
suggestion is true, but whether its truth can be established
empirically; and it seems plain to me that it cannot. It is possible
that empirical grounds should exist for suspecting that one or
another agnostic or atheist is in fact deluded in his profession,
that his operative beliefs are other than he himself supposes. But
the claim under consideration goes, as to be effective it must go,
further than the assertion that there are such cases, with the mere
possibility annexed that all cases may in fact happen to be such.
It is the claim that any atheistic or agnostic profession on the part
of the morally serious *must* be mistaken. And how is this to be
shown? Must we not say that the question whether this is the
truth of the matter has to be considered as an aspect of the first
and most fundamental of the three questions that the affirmation
that it is the truth was supposed to obviate? It surely need not
be the truth if the essential nature of morality is not such as to
require a religious foundation, and it cannot be the truth if the
essential nature of morality is such as to preclude such a
foundation.

And at this point the philosopher can claim that we have left
the territory of history and positive science and entered what is
properly his province. The question has become a question of
the concepts involved in the definition of morality and of the
theological concepts involved in the religious interpretation of

morality, and of the relations, whether of entailment, mutual indifference, or exclusion, that hold between the two. It should further be noted that in undergoing this transformation the question of the relation between morality and religion has at the same time become what may intelligibly be termed a metaphysical question; that is to say, in language appropriate to the context of theistic religion, to which I here restrict myself, it is at bottom a question of the relation of man's moral experience to *God*. It is our answer to this question that defines for us what relation, if any, holds essentially, and not merely contingently, between moral experience and *religion* considered as itself a mode of experience.

(3)

I have so far taken the problem of the relation between morality and religion to be concerned with the quality of our practical response to acknowledged ideals, our success or failure in living up to whatever is the approved norm of conduct. This, I am sure, is the aspect that is primarily in mind in the more popular debates on the subject. But the position is essentially the same when we turn to the question of the adoption of the norm itself and the recognition of its authority for us. Indeed as regards the recognition of its authority, the consciousness of 'moral demand' as such (considered in abstraction from all the various particular beliefs about what is demanded), I do not find that there is anything at all in the conclusions already reached that requires to be retracted or modified. Nor is this surprising; for so far as our practical loyalty to our standards can properly be said to be explicable *conduct* the explanation of it must lie precisely in our awareness of the *authority* that those standards possess. So the one body of contestants will say that a real and effective sense of this authority can only be provided by religion; and there will be a large amount of empirical evidence that appears to support them. But once more, as the other party will be quick to point out, we are faced by the problem posed by the existence of the morally serious agnostic or atheist. And if we wish to clear our minds we shall again have to have recourse to a philosophical consideration of the ethical and theological concepts an assumption of whose mutual relatedness, or lack of it, underlies the entire argument.

It is of course another question whence we derive the particular *content* of the code by which we feel bound to live. For the religious man this will doubtless include requirements that do depend essentially not only on his being religious but on the particular religion to which he adheres, requirements of specifically religious practice. But that is altogether irrelevant in the present connection; it is only a special case of the general truth that what we think it right or necessary to do or to abstain from doing will depend on what we take the facts to be, without this constituting any reason whatsoever for holding that the facts are so. In just the same way our moral codes might be expected to alter in certain respects if we supposed plants to be persons or stocks and stones to be sentient. But if we except the case of specifically religious practice, what in the detail of our codes can plausibly be said to have come to us from religion?

A full and considered answer to this question would require a thorough scrutiny of the history of religion and of moral ideas. Here I must content myself with the easier but riskier procedure of giving simply the general impression made on me by my own desultory reading. Yet I cannot feel that the risk is great if one says merely that it is at most *some* moral beliefs that can reasonably be regarded as arising from specific developments in religion. Consider then one such belief, a very fundamental one, which we might with some plausibility be said to owe to Christianity; or perhaps to Judaism and Christianity together, though it can hardly be questioned that it is to the New Testament rather than the Old that we must go for the emphatic assertion of it. I refer to the principle indicated by such a formula as that we must 'respect persons as persons', or, more warmly, by the command to love one another. Let us suppose for the sake of argument that it is indeed true that this principle did, as a matter of history, come into our ethical tradition through the Christian religion; that it is not to be found in the pre-Christian world or in any non-Christian societies that have not been subject to Christian influences. Perhaps this is not true;[1] but let us suppose that it is. What then? The crucial question surely is not that of the historical context in which the principle emerged but whether, once brought before our minds, it convinces of itself or is acceptable only as part and parcel of a religious attitude. If it commends itself, must it not be accounted a matter of natural (or, if you will, 'mere')

---

[1] What of Stoicism? See, for instance, Rashdall, *Conscience and Christ*, p. 242.

morality? What should we think of a person who took what we considered a very clipped view of what morality involved and who, when his attention was called to some Stoic valuation (let us say) that demanded a less ignoble conception of the attitudes proper to the natural man, retorted 'But that's not just "morality"; that's Stoicism'? Is the case really different with a Christian contribution to our moral inheritance? 'Mere' morality is not to be circumscribed within the limits of what is allowed to be right and good at some particular stage in human history, so as to exclude the insights of a later day. It embraces whatever we can and do acknowledge as our standard at any time independently of any religious associations it may have. It would of course be of great interest if it could be shown that some moral principle that now shines for us by its own light could not have been seen in the first instance save by the light of some special religious revelation. But even in this case (and I am not at all sure that it makes sense to suppose it possible) the question of importance in the present connection would be whether the idea once come by really can maintain itself by its own authority, instead of depending for its continued vitality on the continuance of the faith in which it had its birth. The circumstances of its birth would not as such matter to us. Now what shall we say of our persuasion that persons are beings such that it is a condition of all proper action that affects them that we should treat them with respect—'never simply as a means but always at the same time as an end'—and should even positively seek out ways of expressing and sustaining this relationship between us and them? It does appear to me that this belief is one that is as capable of maintaining itself in the absence of Christian or other religious convictions as is the belief (which could almost be regarded as defining what is properly to be called a moral attitude) that there are claims on us at all that run or could run counter to our self-interest. It seems to me quite untrue to say, for instance, that the *substance* of our thought when we speak of the brotherhood of man necessarily presupposes a conviction of the fatherhood of God, although it may be the case that this language would not naturally, or even could not properly, be used in the *expression* of our thought except in association with such a conviction. And this verdict on the status of one particular moral principle could, I believe, be generalized.

It might of course be suggested that it is not after all a question just of this or that element in our moral convictions but of the whole body of them; that we are to suppose that so far as there is any health in them at all they are all alike 'revealed', and that the reception of the revelation is always in fact, even when it is not recognized as such, a religious experience. But this is once again to have recourse to a hypothesis that evades empirical tests; and once again the ascertainment of even the possibility of its truth depends not only (as it certainly does) on our ability to establish the truth of religion itself but also on the successful prosecution of an enquiry into the relations that can be supposed to hold between God and the moral life of man.

(4)

It is such an enquiry that I propose now to undertake, but with its scope restricted within fairly narrow limits. I propose to explore only certain stretches of what might be termed the theological frontier of ethics. Ethics of course has frontiers other than the theological one. The integrity of its province needs defence against teachings of a 'naturalistic' character that expressly or by implication (sometimes an unintended implication) deny that there is a human experience possessed of those features that are, in my view, essential to its deserving the title 'moral experience' at all. On the present occasion, however, I shall simply ignore this task and assume the adequacy of the defence. I confine my attention to the theological frontier. My purpose is to protest against certain 'frontier-incidents' for which I believe theologians rather than moralists must take the blame. I do not insist that all theologians are open to my criticisms; they are certainly not all equally so. But I cannot attempt to go into the detail of the differences between one and another, even to the extent of my own slender knowledge of them. I aim at securing only a general view of the disputed territory.[1] It is enough for me to be satisfied that I am not attacking 'men of straw', and that outside the ranks of scholars the views to which I object have a wide currency which churchmen seem at least not eager to discourage.

[1] For this reason I have thought it not only permissible but even advisable to cite certain compendious and more or less 'popular' statements of Christian doctrine while fully recognizing their insufficiency as examples of theological *argument*.

CHAPTER II

SIN AND THE NATURAL MAN

(1)

At the very outset of our enquiry we are confronted by a major difficulty. The task I have set before myself is that of a secular philosopher. I mean by this that whoever undertakes it must, in the nature of the case, argue from the standpoint of a religiously uncommitted moralist, with reliance on the natural light of reason and on the validity in principle of the moral insights of the 'natural man'. There are, however, certain theological positions that would appear to rule out the possibility of this; to rule it out by denying the authority of such 'reason' and 'insight' on the ground that they are functions of our unredeemed nature, which is corrupt. It is necessary to say something on this matter before we can proceed.

The type of theology to which I refer is that which is so powerfully advocated in our time, with a broad similarity of emphasis despite their far from unimportant disagreements, by such men as Barth and Brunner and Reinhold Niebuhr. How far this theology is truly faithful to that of the first great continental theologians of the Reformation from which it claims descent is a question I must leave for those to answer who have the necessary scholarly equipment. But whatever conclusion they may reach it will not solve the paramount issue, which is whether it is acceptable doctrine. For myself, while acknowledging that I may have misunderstood it, I feel bound to say that it seems very far from being acceptable. It seems indeed in some respects as absurd as it is terrible; and perhaps more interesting, though not more important, than the question of its truth would be the question how it has come to be believed, what factors, dogmatic, psychological and historical, give it its appeal.[1] I cannot seriously doubt

---

[1] An obvious dogmatic motive would be the belief that only such a doctrine does justice to the majesty of God and to the magnitude of Christ's saving work. But it is to be enquired how far it glorifies the Creator to denigrate the creature, and whether the creature, in this account, is such that the concept of salvation can still be given a spiritual, not magical, sense.

that many Christian thinkers share this view of it. One may wonder why they do not more often express their opinion with something of the energy of condemnation judged proper in the case of the professed enemies of religion. Does a difference of profession, however sincere, suffice to rid of their hatefulness the perversions of religious thought itself? We might do well to remember Plutarch's pungent observation on the subject of atheism and superstition, and much else beside in that essay of Bacon where it is quoted.[1] We should remember also, of course, that what is in question is the character and tendency of certain views, and not the personal stature of those who hold them.

I ought perhaps to content myself with merely recording a protest against a theological dogma that (being itself *ex hypothesi* unarguable) affirms the incompetence of the only faculty to which its critics can have recourse; all the more so since those who might wish for a fuller treatment of the subject may be referred to what has been said by (among others) Professor H. D. Lewis and Professor N. H. G. Robinson.[2] I would ask the interested to study their arguments for themselves, and to attend especially to Professor Robinson's criticisms, despite and even because of my own greater sympathy with the views of Professor Lewis. Professor Robinson's discussion is particularly valuable since, besides combining the qualifications of the trained theologian and the trained philosopher, he handles his theme with a patience and sympathy that I (and perhaps also Professor Lewis) cannot hope to emulate, and in the end adopts a position that still, I think, shows traces of the defects he censures. His testimony to the ethical, and logical, inadequacies of the doctrines he examines is the more impressive for that reason. Having said this I might be well advised to leave the subject. But I shall venture to add a little on my own account, asking that it be considered as addition merely, and not as a substitute for what earlier critics have written. I wish to touch on a question which I personally find very perplex-

---

[1] Bacon, *Of Superstition.*

[2] H. D. Lewis, *Morals and the New Theology,* and certain of the essays in *Morals and Revelation*: Robinson, *Faith and Duty,* more especially (for criticism of the theology in question) the first three chapters. This last work may be supplemented, but cannot be replaced, by the same author's subsequent volume *Christ and Conscience.* See also Paton, *The Modern Predicament,* Chapter III.

ing, and which is connected with the dissatisfaction I feel with regard even to Professor Robinson's own standpoint.

(2)

The heart of the theology to which I am objecting is, as I understand it, the doctrine of *sola gratia*, the doctrine that what may be called 'natural man', man apart from the work of grace, lacks the capacity to live as he should. This incapacity of 'natural man' affects at once his insight and his will; he cannot of himself discern any more than he can enact the good. And the incapacity is absolute. Any weakening on this point, any hedging about its extent (here Barth would seem to be justified against Brunner) would be in effect a surrender of the whole position.

Verbally this thesis is clear enough. But it cannot be said to be clear in substance unless it is perfectly plain what (over and above the formal negation of 'grace') is meant by speaking of 'natural man'. Who *are* in a state of mere nature—what is it to be in such a state? In somewhat the same way it is a clear enough statement that those who fail in a certain university examination will not qualify for a degree; but one might reasonably want to know what constitutes failure, what sort of characteristics in the performance give this result, and 'not passing' would be an unacceptable answer. Now in point of fact it is far from plain how (the negation of 'grace' apart) we are to conceive of 'natural man'. To be more specific, there is, I think, a crucial ambiguity about the expression 'natural man', to which the use of the term 'matter' by Aristotle and in Aristotelian scholasticism, in the doctrine of 'matter' and 'form', affords a parallel. And perhaps it may be helpful to some, as I believe it has helped me, if I employ this analogy.[1]

Aristotle tells us that physical objects (we can here ignore the problem of the non-physical) are, from whatever point of view and at whatever level of analysis, a combination or complex of matter and form. Thus, for example, a statue has a form which the sculptor imposes on his material, and relatively to this form the marble is the matter of the statue. But it is only relatively to this

---

[1] I mention Aristotelian scholasticism because it is in scholastic philosophy that the matter-form antithesis is most fully worked out. But for the simplified version that is sufficient for my purpose we need not go further than Aristotle himself.

form that the marble can be considered simply as matter: taken in itself the marble too is at once both matter and form. It is only as form that it has the characteristic nature that distinguishes it from, say, bronze or flesh. Pure or mere matter, conceived of as what lacks, and is to be contrasted with, form of any kind would *eo ipso* lack also all distinctive character. 'The matter and form of physical things, it must be noted, are elements distinguishable by thought but inseparable in reality. Matter never exists bare but always informed. It exists with at least so much form or definite character as is implied in its being either aether or fire or air or water or earth; these are the simplest "natural bodies".'[1] Accordingly what Aristotle called 'first matter'—matter in an absolute and not merely relative sense—is not itself a thing; it is an abstraction from the total nature of any physical thing. It is, so to put it, what would be left if, *per impossibile*, all form were removed. Now this is certainly not matter at all in our ordinary meaning of the word, though what Aristotle intends is not therefore nonsensical. Matter, for the plain man, is always some concrete physical thing, like the stone that Dr Johnson kicked by way of refuting Berkeley. For Aristotle, on the other hand, this is already *informed* matter, matter and form together.

Now just as there are here two quite different meanings of 'matter', a common-sense one and a metaphysical one in which it signifies the bare correlate of all that is form, so, it seems to me, there may be two possible and quite different conceptions of 'nature' and of 'the natural man'. Analogous to the metaphysical concept of 'first matter' there may be a concept of 'natural man' that refers to no actual individual at all but only to a purely hypothetical being; that is to say, to man as he *would* be were it not for the grace of God, but (the theologian might wish to add) as in fact he never is, since this is God's world which He has not abandoned. If grace be opposed to nature in this sense one could perfectly well affirm that all good is of grace (as, in the analogous case, all positive being is by form) without prejudice to any estimate whatsoever that we may feel constrained to frame of men as they actually are. The affirmation would signify no more, though also no less, than that man, whatever be his empirical character, is to be 'metaphysically *interpreted*', if I may so express it, in terms of theistic doctrine.

[1] Ross, *Aristotle*, p. 66.

But then, of course, there is the possible alternative meaning of 'natural man', analogous to the everyday meaning of 'matter', according to which 'natural man' would certainly not be a mere abstraction, a hypothetical entity, but on the contrary a very common actuality. He would, I suppose, be man as he is apart from the Christian revelation, and indeed as he is apart from the 'appropriation' of the revelation in Christian faith, however this 'appropriation' is to be understood. He would be 'fallen' man as we actually find him in ourselves and in our fellows; fallen and not yet raised, as it were, above himself by grace, like the marble block (if that is not too honorific an illustration) that the sculptor's skill has not yet glorified.

Now if, speaking of 'natural man' in this second way, we still treat 'natural' and 'of grace' as contrasting and opposed characterizations, it is simply a question of fact whether in 'natural man' there is any goodness at all and, correspondingly, whether there is a goodness that is not of grace. And I cannot see how, on those terms, we can in reason avoid answering both questions affirmatively. But we may without absurdity, if we please, affirm both that there is some good in man in his condition as natural and also that all good is of grace, treating grace here as *constitutive* of what is, in this second sense, natural, and not simply as contrasted with it. This dual affirmation is possible if, in effect, we give the term 'grace' the wide range of application appropriate to it as contrasted with 'nature' in the first of our two senses of 'nature' while at the same time using the term 'nature' itself in the second sense. Nor is there any real harm in doing this (though it could be accused of inviting misunderstanding) so long as we are clear what it is we are doing. But the position is very different if, using 'nature' in the second sense and at the same time restricting 'grace' to signify what is not of nature in this sense but is antithetic to it, we reiterate the doctrine that apart from grace there is no health in us. This would be to affirm of the whole antithesis of 'nature' and 'grace' consistently employed in one sense something that can only reasonably be maintained with reference to the whole antithesis when consistently employed in the other sense. For now, and simply as a result of this confusion, we shall no longer be accepting, as in principle sound, our actual human estimates of men as they are, and then going on to suggest a theological interpretation of their being as they are; on the contrary, we shall be denying that things are as, in our most careful and, in the ordinary use of the word, enlightened reflection, they obstinately seem to us to be. This is the point at which human reason and human moral judgment are put 'out of court'. Can it be that those who reject their witness do so (or, having other motives for doing so, are helped to believe that such a rejection is defensible) by reason of this confusion the possibility of which I have been trying to explain?

(3)

I have spoken of putting human reason and human moral judgment 'out of court'. But it may perhaps be said that in fairness I should have spoken, more cautiously, of the 'mere' or 'secular' reason and moral judgment. For after all it is still, in a sense, human faculties that are being employed when, from the vantage ground of faith, we make what is claimed to be the *true* assessment then for the first time possible of man's natural condition and of merely human ideals. But to grant this will not obviate any of the real difficulties of the position. We shall still have to choose between saying, on the one hand, that what is upheld by the 'natural man' is essentially and in principle coincident, so far as it goes, with what we are enabled by faith to affirm and, on the other hand, saying that there is some significant difference of content between the pronouncements that are possible at these two levels respectively. Now if we choose the former of these alternatives, what precisely becomes of our insistence on the incompetence of the natural light? If we still maintain that it is involved in man's very status as 'natural' that his thinking and doing are corrupt, must we not then regard soundness of mind and action as constituted by a sort of, empirically unobservable, *transubstantiation* in respect of his faculties? I confess I should be unable to make any sense of such an idea, and I ask myself in vain what any one who asserted it as fact could really be thinking. At least there would be no point in pretending to debate any further with him. But suppose, alternatively, that it is held that, as regards their content, the pronouncements of faith and of the natural light respectively are in conflict with one another, and that only the former can claim validity. What then? It may be that the alleged 'conflict' is illusion, generated by some misrepresentation of what the 'natural man' really judges, or is capable of judging, to be the case. But if not—well, the two 'authorities' conflict; and the natural reason can only dismiss the asseverations of the rival authority as dangerous dogmatism. It would have to do so equally whether the spokesman of that authority were a Christian theologian or, say, a Rosenberg; for by what criterion that the Christian theologian has not already, *ex hypothesi*, repudiated could one hope to discriminate between the two? If this dismissal does not amount to a refutation of the theological views under consideration (it would be question-begging to claim that it does), that is only because those views exclude the very conditions of any possible refutation, if not indeed the concepts of demonstration and refutation themselves.[1] But again one cannot but wonder what a man could really be thinking who said that he believed what natural reason, in himself no less than in others, is bound to repudiate.

(4)

I have been distinguishing various possibilities, and I must admit that (partly because of my own ignorance, but partly also, I believe, because of ambiguities and hesitancies in the presentation of the doctrine of human corruption itself) I do not know which of them it is most proper to regard as actualized in the views of particular theologians.[2] But if all the possibilities alike are an offence, perhaps this uncertainty does not greatly matter. At least—and this is the vital point—it would seem fairly clear that the representatives of the type of theology that is here under criticism must be agreed in understanding by 'natural', and accordingly corrupt, man, with vision blinded and in his action

---

[1] I need hardly say that I am aware that here (as at other points in this essay) the whole problem of the concept of revelation is involved, and that volumes might be written about that. This, however, is not to be one of them.

[2] Thus, for example, Luther in his *De Servo Arbitrio* (English translation by Packer and Johnston, under the title of *The Bondage of the Will*, pp. 251–3) seems to me simply to misrepresent the possibilities of pagan nobility—'They did it all for their own glory'—though of course what he says is widely true of all human beings. (Fame is the last infirmity of noble mind.) But I am not sure whether he consistently and clearly holds to this position as distinguished from what I called the 'transubstantiation' view; or again from a third view, namely that even genuine moral nobility is not to the point, what matters being 'faith' in a sense that is not essentially connected with quality of moral life at all.

C

sinful, man concrete and actual, as he is in fact to be found in the world. How in the first place could Barth and Brunner dispute, as they have disputed,[1] about the *extent* of man's corruption were they referring only to man as he *would* be were God non-existent or inoperative? Much less extreme theologies than theirs would rebel against the supposition that God Himself (not simply the saving knowledge of God by faith) might be deleted without a total collapse of man's spiritual being. Nor is it surely to a mere hypothesis or abstraction that they address themselves when they use language like that of the prophets of the Hebrews crying out to a backsliding people. Nor could the contempt and disregard of secular philosophy, both in the field of ethics and in that of natural theology, find a warrant otherwise: it is not by abstractions that moral theories or 'proofs' of God's existence are excogitated and discussed. But again I ask whether it may not be that the adoption of such a doctrine of man's corruption, and indeed the mere willingness to consider it seriously, is at least assisted by confusion with the other reading of the nature-grace antithesis in which 'nature' signifies simply an unrealized logical possibility, unrealized and, from a theistic viewpoint, by definition unrealizable.

It may be presumptuous in me to voice such a suspicion; and in fact I should not have dared to do so had I not thought that it gained some support from a passage in Professor Robinson's presentation of his own view. It is a passage that, to my mind, plainly exhibits the difficulty that even the soberest thinker must experience when he tries to keep a clear head in this theological *Walpurgisnacht*. Having done his best to reconcile our moral insights with the essence of the religious insight that he takes Barth, Brunner and Niebuhr to be defending, Professor Robinson very curiously (as it seems to me) concludes his book[2] with the admission that 'what has been under consideration is perhaps to a large extent an abstraction'. He goes on: 'The abstraction in question is natural man, for although man inhabits a world which affirms itself as a human concern, he at the same time inhabits a world which God so loved that He sent His only begotten Son, a world in which God has placed His Church, and in which He

---

[1] The tracts published in English under the title *Natural Theology* illustrate their differences in a compact and convenient form.

[2] *Faith and Duty*, pp. 146–7.

has never left Himself without a witness. Does this mean that natural man as he has been described in these pages is not what any man is, but what any man would be without the grace of God? In other words, is natural man the logical presupposition but never the chronological antecedent of Christian man? . . . It may be so, but these are questions which lie beyond the scope of this enquiry.' This conclusion I confess I find surprising. To me they appear to be questions that lie at the very foundation of the enquiry, since they govern the meaning to be given to terms that are basic in it. As a matter of fact, it had not occurred to me until I reached this final paragraph of Professor Robinson's book that for him 'natural man' *might* be just an abstraction, so strongly did the whole atmosphere of the discussion suggest the contrary. And even at the end I remain perplexed; for I cannot see clearly what it is, on the 'abstraction' view, to which the secular philosopher is bound to object, and yet the case is argued as though he were certain to do so. But whatever may be true of Professor Robinson's own position, I am unable to believe that this milder teaching could be the effective purport of the views of the distinguished theologians on whom he has commented. The most I could say in their case is that the very fact that this more defensible interpretation of the doctrine of natural corruption is available as an alternative may have had some influence as a confuser of the issues. It was to illustrate this possibility that I called Professor Robinson in evidence.

(5)

I shall add no more here about the theology of radical corruption, beyond repeating that what I have said is offered not as systematic critique but merely as supplementary gloss on earlier criticisms. But this theology is only the extreme or limiting case of an emphasis on human sinfulness that is characteristic of Christian thought generally. And since this emphasis is by no means equally characteristic of philosophical ethics, it will be well to indicate my attitude towards it. I am concerned, of course, only with uses of the term 'sin' to which the possessives 'my', 'your' 'our' would be appropriate. If there are any other legitimate uses they are not of primary interest to the moralist.

I do not wish to insist that 'sin' should be restricted to cases of conscious disloyalty to the right as we see it; that is to say, to what is sometimes technically denominated 'actual' sin and, what is more, 'actual' sin in the 'formal' mode, as contrasted with the evilness of actions that are 'materially' wrong though not thought by the agent to be so. There is perhaps nothing to be said in favour of describing 'materially' wrong action as sinful when it results from ignorance of fact merely, and much to be said against so describing it. In this case 'wrong' has only the force of 'mistaken'; the action is 'wrong' much as a sum in arithmetic might be. But the case is very different where it is a man's values that are wrong. Even here, it is true, it may be a misdescription to speak of the values as 'perverted'. Need they, in many cases, be worse than 'immature'? The two things are not the same; the sapling is not a deformed tree. Still, though it may baffle us to draw the line empirically, there certainly could be a positive perversion, as contrasted with a mere infancy, of value-consciousness; and it may well deserve to be called perversion no matter how we conceive of its origin, and, in particular, regardless of whether its antecedents do or do not include a volitional failure on the part of the individual in question. Now such positive perversion, at least, may intelligibly be described as a sinful condition, no less than the condition of the man who is guilty of sin 'actual' and 'formal'. Both alike may be represented as 'alienation from God', both the darkened conscience and the acting against conscience. Only we must take care that, if 'sin' is used to name both these things, we do not allow the ethically vital distinction between material and formal sin to become blurred thereby. Whereas the latter is rightly a matter for reproach the former is not, except in so far as it arises from the latter, from volitional disloyalties.

On the other hand, merely being *tempted* to actual sin (whether formal or material) is not as such sin in any useful sense of the word; and Christian theologians, with the Gospels in front of them, will scarcely wish to suggest the contrary. Thus the fact that, simply in virtue of our having desires at all, we are, I suppose, at all times liable to the temptation to put 'what we want' in the first place, and in that very wide sense of the term to be selfish, is not itself the sin of selfishness.

We must, however, be careful not to misread this truth in such a way as to deny one or both of two possible modes of what can significantly be called sin. In the first place, although temptation

is not as such sinful, certain particular temptations may understandably be so described, even while they remain mere temptation; those, namely, in which what solicits or prompts us is evil
in itself, as hunger and sexual desire are not but jealousies and
envyings are. These, like the perversions of our values, may be
called sinful irrespective of whether we admit any personal
responsibility for their upsurge in us, or attribute them (for
instance) wholly to 'social conditioning' or to some other source
outside ourselves the nature of which we do not pretend to
understand.[1]

Secondly, although temptation is not sinful simply as temptation, there is a risk that we may describe as 'merely being tempted'
what in fact goes beyond that, inasmuch as we permit ourselves
to 'savour' or 'nourish' an impulse to act wrongly. Certainly from
one point of view this 'savouring' is still to be called mere temptation; as compared, that is, with the enactment of what we thus
toy with in idea. But from another point of view it is already
itself inward act; and it is sinful accordingly, in the mode of
actual sin, even when the impulse is not itself intrinsically evil.
Arnold Bennett's account of Sophia's feeling towards Chirac in
the Paris restaurant is a good enough illustration of the point.[2] It
is in this sense that 'lusting after' may be said to be the sin of
adultery, even though sexual desire is not in itself sinful. We
have to distinguish in principle between the natural psychical or
psycho-physical urge as it is external to, and as much a part of
the *context* of, the moral will as an onset of giddiness would be,
and the same urge when half-accepted by us, accepted as it were
in play though not yet in earnest. By this acceptance it ceases
to be merely a sort of pressure from without and becomes a
positive velleity within the citadel of the self. We are then a
Troy that has too carelessly, too unfearfully, admitted the Greek
gift. Troy may not in the end go down: the velleity is still not
full commitment, and it may yet be resisted. But, whatever the
eventual outcome, two things are true. First, this velleity is a
spiritual, not merely natural evil; and, second, it is an evil we
have brought on ourselves—it does not come by any merely
natural breakdown, like a drowning swimmer's failure of strength

---

[1] Webb, *Problems in the Relations of God and Man*, pp. 116–29, is suggestive
in this connection, though not, I think, altogether clear.
[2] *The Old Wives' Tale*, Book III, Chapter VI, Section 5.

—and we must take responsibility for it accordingly. If we are to speak of sin at all, then, we may rightly speak of it in this case. It is not the same sin as that of full commitment, but it is sin in the same sense. And I think we must add that even if we refrain from the full commitment we can only do so, so long as this inner infection is not purged, with what is in a manner a divided will, a will exhibiting a characteristic strain and loss of energy. If the concept of the sinlessness of Jesus is to be understood in an ethical sense it would, I should suppose, be best taken to signify something more than the fact that, whatever civil warfare there may have been in his nature, the right forces always as a matter of fact triumphed; and also something less than that he was not even capable of sin. (The latter would amount to saying that, however plagued and afflicted, he was not really *tempted*.) It would best be taken to signify his possession of the undivided will, the inner integrity of the man whose velleities were pure even though the solicitations to which he was subject might be as powerful (and some of them as evil in themselves)[1] as any to which his fellows have been a prey.[2]

I do not wish then, to restrict 'sin' to signify only the wickedness of 'formally' evil actions (in the ordinary sense of 'action') for which we are ourselves responsible. Velleities, as distinguished from actions in this sense, may similarly be sinful; and, though in a different mode, so also may be certain passions and desires as they arise even in one of whom it could be said that 'he had absolutely no truck with them'. And as these occurrent features of our life are sinful, so also are any dispositions of which they are the intermittent expression. 'Spiritual blindness', again, when the light that is in us is darkness, may legitimately be included in our sinfulness. All this can be allowed, the concept of sin can be given all this range of application, so long as the common name

---

[1] A pang of envy, for example, or an impulse to hurt? If we refuse to admit this, was he in *all* points tempted like ourselves? If however we do admit it, and at the same time call these things *in themselves* 'sin', then *in that sense* we must speak of him too as sinful.

[2] What I have said here should be taken in conjunction with my later remarks (Chapter IV, Sections 5 and 10) on total dutifulness. The Appendix on 'The Sinlessness of Jesus' in L. W. Grensted, *The Person of Christ*, is well worth attention (see especially pp. 278–81). J. S. Whale's statement that Jesus 'was able to sin, and . . . even desired to sin, but did not' (*Christian Doctrine*, Fontana edition, p. 95) seems to me at least misleading. How precisely are we to understand 'desired'?

is not permitted to obliterate the diversity of types and, more particularly, is not used as a cover for the ascription to sin in all its modes of that character that belongs distinctively to the volitional failure to live up to one's own standards. If those who talk of human sinfulness cannot be trusted to respect this condition, then certainly it would be better to do as some would in any case prefer, and use 'sin' simply as the theological equivalent of 'actual and formal' moral failure.

(6)

Of sin as predicable simply and solely of individual persons I do not wish to say more. But groups and societies, and indeed (and, in theology, especially) the entire human race may also be spoken of as sinful, much as particular groups or societies may be described as peace-loving or aggressive. What are we to make of such language?

It could be that when we speak of groups or societies in these ways we intend only that all or most *members* of the society have the characteristics in question; or, alternatively, that certain members of the society who are in some way especially representative of it have these characteristics. In that case no new problem arises regarding the meaning of the predicate term. But it must be allowed that if, groups or societies have in some sense a real being of their own, if that is to say, there are facts about the functioning of social institutions that cannot be reduced to facts about individuals taken as isolates (as I believe there are),[1] then to ascribe a certain character to a society may not be simply an abbreviated and disguised way of ascribing that character to a number of individual persons. Naturally, in admitting this we need not fly to the other extreme and suppose that societies themselves are individuals of a larger growth and that, accordingly, we can correctly speak of them in just the same way in which we speak of their constituent individuals. Were we to do so there would, of course, once again be no new problem about the meaning of our *predicate* terms; no new problem, for example, about the meaning of 'sinful' when we call a society sinful. But we should undoubtedly be indulging in fantasy as regards what our *subject*

---

[1] See, for a discussion that brings out well the character of the problem, Gellner, 'Explanations in History' (*Proc. Ar. Soc.* Suppl. Vol. XXX (1956)).

term signifies, and a dangerous fantasy at that. Societies, whatever they are, are not like individual persons; and if we speak of a society as sinful, in other than the 'shorthand' sense of the expression earlier referred to, we cannot possibly be saying anything strictly in parallel with 'Smith is sinful' or 'Higgins is sinful'. What then shall we be saying? I wish I knew. I do not doubt that if 'sinful' in such a case means anything at all it must mean something that stands in a very intimate relationship to that in the life of the individual for which we employ the same word. Perhaps we should even hold that in a sense it means the very same thing in the two contexts but that in one of them this meaning is, as it were, consciously misapplied. That is to say, we may be speaking of the society *as though* it were an individual while recognizing that in fact it is not, and accordingly in calling it 'sinful' we at the same time make a sort of 'corrective mental gesture' the precise import of which is the x of our problem.[1]

But, whatever the precise analysis to be given of such an assertion, I allow the formal possibility that societies, and even the whole human race, might meaningfully be described as sinful in a sense that does not reduce to any complex of assertions about individual men and women. Whether in fact this is one of the things that can be meaningfully (not to say truly) said about societies in this irreducible way I really do not know. But, supposing it to be so, at least we must insist that the sinfulness of a society is a fact of a different order from the sinfulness of a man, and that the term 'sin' cannot be univocal in the two cases. More particularly we must insist that, in its application to society, the term 'sin' cannot properly have the force of 'sin actual and formal': only an individual person can be sinful in that sense.

Now this, as it seems to me, is a consideration that is insufficiently regarded in many characteristic theological utterances about man's 'solidarity in sin', about each man's 'sharing' in the sin of his society or of the race. For it looks as though the 'share' of each was being supposed somehow to consist in and constitute the individual's own sinfulness; and this is a confusion of 'orders'. It is rather like speaking of an electron, as one might of bodily tissue, as infected by and sharing in some organic disease. It looks moreover as though the individual sinfulness in such a case was

---

[1] Compare this with what is said later about the use of anthropomorphic language in speaking of God (Chapter VI, Section 2).

thought to include, or to be capable of including, guilt in the ordinary meaning of that term, a meaning that ties it to *actual* sin. Is not this the implication of such language as asserts that 'an Englishman today may feel that he has a share in the guilt of the nation which burnt Joan of Arc or which took a leading share in the slave trade'?[1] It is not necessary to deny that an Englishman may *have* such a feeling: the question is whether it could be anything other than a mere pathological *malaise*. If it is something other or more, its precise nature is still to seek; but at least it cannot be correctly represented by the language I have quoted. That language would, it is true, seem more plausible were it used of participation in a society's contemporaneous evil-doing; for instance, if one were to speak of an individual German's share, in 1938, in the sin of his nation's treatment of the Jews. But this should do nothing to remove suspicion of the ways of thought of those who do not carefully and expressly restrict the concept of 'sharing' to such instances. And why, as a matter of fact, is the use of the concept more plausible within these limits? Surely the natural explanation is that here we can regard ourselves as employing simply an idiomatic alternative to speaking of the strictly *personal* guilt of one member of a society all the members of which are in varying degrees guilty *as individuals*, though the fact and consequences of their guilt cannot be identified and traced in each individual case. Now this, of course, would not be to treat group-sinfulness as a fact other than, and somehow constitutive of, individual sinfulness; rather it would be the other way round. To say this is not to deny, but on the contrary almost explicitly to admit, the validity of the idea of collective responsibility in one sense. It admits it in the sense that 'every one of us has been an active participant in an uncountable number of good and bad things of which he does not have, and indeed cannot have, any knowledge, and for which he is none the less co-responsible before God'.[2] What has to be avoided is confusion of this perfectly sound meaning of 'co-responsibility' with other

---

[1] *Doctrine in the Church of England* (The Report of the Commission on Christian Doctrine appointed by the Archbishops of Canterbury and York in 1922), 1938, p. 67.

[2] The quotation is from Scheler's *Vom Ewigen im Menschen*, as rendered by Stark in his introduction (p. xxx) to the English translation of the same author's *The Nature of Sympathy*. I do not know if Scheler himself keeps rigorously to this interpretation of 'collective responsibility'.

meanings in which the elements of 'collectivity' and 'responsibility' are at war with each other.

(7)

It has not been my purpose in what I have said simply to attack the concept of race sinfulness, of man's solidarity in sin, in every form, any more than it has been my purpose positively to commend it, understood in some particular way, as a useful, or indispensable, tool of thought. My concern has been to keep the concept of personal sin, and above all of sin as the guilt of responsible wrongdoing, intact and clear. But I have to note that even so I must again, with all respect, part company with such a moderate and careful thinker as is Professor Robinson. The limitations I have felt bound to impose on the use of the ideas of race sinfulness and of collective responsibility are not limitations that he would accept. The issue is sufficiently important to excuse my devoting a few paragraphs to explaining the difference between us.[1]

Notwithstanding his dissatisfaction with views of Barthian colour Professor Robinson has no intention of surrendering the doctrine of the solidarity in sin of the human race and of the equal sinfulness of all men. This doctrine he regards as an affirmation of 'the Christian consciousness', which appears to be considered, in this connection, as a faculty at once inerrant and unambiguous in its pronouncements. He believes, however, that (even when full account is taken of criticisms of the concept of collective responsibility such as those urged by Professor Lewis)[2] it is possible to combine the theological doctrine, as he grants it must somehow be combined, with the acceptance as valid of the judgment of our ordinary moral consciousness. How, then, does he propose to effect this synthesis?

The doctrine of total *sinfulness*, we are asked to note, is not the same as the doctrine of total *moral corruption*. Morally, men are not wholly corrupt, nor are they all, as is the case in regard to their sinfulness, on one and the same level. What then is the essence of their sinfulness, as distinguished from their moral

[1] For what follows see the constructive half (i.e. Chapters IV and V) of Robinson, *Faith and Duty* (supplemented by the later volume, *Christ and Conscience*). A pertinent review of *Faith and Duty* by Professor H. D. Lewis will be found in *Philosophy*, July 1951.

[2] Lewis, *Morals and Revelation*, Chapter V.

defect; a sinfulness whose universality, of course, is of no merely *de facto* and contingent character? Here precisely is where the concept of racial solidarity has its place, but it must be understood in terms that do not in effect depersonalize the individual; that is to say, it must be understood in terms of collective *responsibility*, in some legitimate sense of that last expression. Now collective responsibility in a perfectly proper sense of the words is to be found, Robinson tells us, in any genuinely joint enterprise; and in such an enterprise all the partners can be said also to have an *equal* responsibility. 'If . . . the moral consciousness could be confronted by partners who were thoroughly of the one mind, and equally committed to the joint enterprise, the fact that within it they all played different parts would be of no importance'; and supposing the enterprise to be evil 'the moral consciousness would surely judge all the agents involved as equally blameworthy'. Now all men are in fact partners in one comprehensive joint enterprise; that, namely, of the 'world' conceived of as 'a *human* concern in which the human will is law'. We all 'constantly accept, affirm, and acquiesce in the one world as a human enterprise'.[1] It is this leaving of God out that is sin; and it is a quite different thing from all the various forms and degrees of moral failure of which men may be guilty *within* the framework of this, universal and equally shared, sinful attitude. At the same time (we are given to understand) men can no more disclaim *responsibility* for this sinful affirmation and acquiescence than they can disclaim responsibility for their specific moral failures.[2]

It would require a very lengthy discussion to present and criticize Robinson's argument in all its complexity. Perhaps to reprint it with a running commentary would be the only satisfactory method. Suspecting that I have not at every point understood it, I can but express the hope that in the observations I shall make I at least fix on, and do not distort, what is central in it. In this spirit of hesitancy I offer the following comment.

To assert that all men as such, and equally, are guilty of affirming the world as a purely human enterprise seems to me to contradict plain fact; unless (and here I recur to a point on which

---

[1] *Faith and Duty*, pp. 137–9. See also *Christ and Conscience*, pp. 26–32.

[2] The sin of 'leaving God out' is essentially the sin of pride, which is thus in one sense *the* sin (*Christ and Conscience*, pp. 32–4. Cf. J. S. Whale, *Christian Doctrine*, Fontana Books, p. 73: 'Mere moralism is a form of pride'). *Within* morality, so to put it, *the* sin (or the general form of sin) is selfishness.

I touched earlier) we mean, by 'man', 'natural' man so conceived that the statement becomes a tautology. But, then, 'natural' man so conceived is simply an abstraction from actual man in his empirical wholeness. Even accepting Robinson's account of what sin essentially is, must we not then be content to say not that all men *are* sinners but only that they all *would be* sinners if, as is not in fact the case, they were in the sense indicated merely 'natural'? I am not at all clear what importance there would be in the thesis of human solidarity in sin were it so interpreted; but it seems in any event certain that this is not how it is ordinarily intended or understood. Perhaps we could get back to the obviously important categorical form of the assertion of universal and equal sinfulness by insisting that what *appears* as a transcendence, in particular individuals, of the purely secularist or humanist view of human life is not really such. But how can we avail ourselves of that possibility without at the same time implying that none of us, not even a theologian, can claim to know what an affirming of the world as *God's* world would be, what the language which spoke of such an affirmation could mean?

Anyhow, as I read him, this is not a path that Robinson himself follows. On the other hand, it is not clear to me what path he positively does follow. 'Even in the loftiest moments of *most* Christian people the world is still affirmed,' he tells us[1]—affirmed, that is, as a purely human concern. Here it is obvious that we are dealing with man in his empirical concreteness, and (it seems) allowing, as regards man thus understood, some breach in the sinful solidarity of humankind. This might encourage one to suppose that it is only with reference to 'natural' man in what we may call the abstract and hypothetical sense that the doctrine of quite universal and equal sinfulness is asserted. But at the same time is there not discernible some anxiety to represent the breach (not quite convincingly) as only a very little one? And this anxiety would surely be superfluous if what it is important to retain is only the doctrine of the essential sinfulness of 'natural' man in that abstract sense. I seem to detect a note of apologetic illogicality in Robinson's 'most' that is reminiscent of the 'exiguum' in the 'exiguum clinamen' of Lucretius. The uncertainty whether, in speaking of man and his sinfulness, Robinson has in mind man 'in the concrete' or an abstraction is indeed frustrating; yet, as

[1] *Faith and Duty*, p. 140 (my italics).

I have already noted,[1] so far from trying to clear this up Robinson apparently regards it as quite irrelevant to his argument. I may add (although the force of the remark can only be appreciated in the light of views that I have still to expound) that I should question whether any genuinely moral attitude can fairly be said to affirm the world as a purely human concern, true though it is that such an attitude need not be associated with conscious acceptance of the distinctive tenets of Christianity, or indeed of theism in any form. And if morality as such turned out to be, in some good sense of the expression, world-transcending, then merely to be genuinely moral in one's attitude might be held to constitute escape from the trammels of sin, as 'sin' is understood by Robinson in the present connection. There is room at least for debate about this; and perhaps Robinson, like other theologians, is able to rest with full conviction in his view that mere morality is something essentially inadequate only because of an essential and question-begging inadequacy in his conception of what mere morality is.[2]

(8)

I have criticized Robinson's presentation of the doctrine of universal and equal sinfulness by questioning whether there is any useful sense in which it is true that all men are by nature such that they take the world as a purely human joint enterprise. But it might further be asked whether, supposing they do all so take it, their being in this condition should properly be called 'sin'.

I have myself earlier allowed that the term 'sin' need not be restricted to refer only to imputable fault; so that even a simple ignorance of God, and a corresponding 'affirmation' of the world as a purely human concern, may intelligibly be spoken of as sinful—at least (a point that invites further discussion) if this ignorance can be regarded as having the quality of 'value-ignorance', and is not just the unawareness of a fact. But to speak of sin, in the present connection, merely in this sense would be to agree with Robinson only in words, one might surmise, and not in substance. For sin so understood could not warrant the employ-

---

[1] Above, p. 35.
[2] To cite a single fairly precise indication of what is, I think, a pervasive bias, *Christ and Conscience*, p. 73, seems to me question-begging in this way.

ment of the particular tone of voice in which he refers to it. That tone of voice implies, what Robinson in any case expressly asserts, the sinner's responsibility for his condition: and if Robinson's language is to be justified the sin must surely be sin actual and formal. That is to say, it must be constituted by a conscious and voluntary repudiation of, a *choosing* to repudiate, the claim of God recognized as such. But surely it is a quite fantastic notion that all actual men do in *this* way affirm, if one may so put it, the irrelevance of God. While as for the abstract and hypothetical 'natural man', he least of all, supposing him actualized as a totally corrupt real individual, would be capable of such sin: he would not be good enough potentially to be bad in this particular way actually. The universal sin of mere moralism, then, even if it be a fact, is not something for which man bears *responsibility*.

So one might argue. But Professor Robinson would not agree. And the reason why he would not agree is that he does not believe, what I have treated as axiomatic, that responsibility involves choice between alternatives. This comes out most clearly in his criticism of certain contentions of Professor C. A. Campbell.[1] But, though the issues involved are by no means all of them simple, the central truth does seem to me perfectly plain, that whatever be the account we are to give of choice the sheer denial of its occurrence on any occasion entails denial of responsibility also on that occasion. Robinson maintains that to tie responsibility to choice is to make responsibility an episodic, spasmodic feature of human life in a way that is totally unplausible. But clearly this will be so only if choice itself must be understood as something episodic. Possibly Campbell does so understand it; I am not concerned to adjudicate on this. If he does, Robinson is urging a quite effective *argumentum ad hominem*. But the importance of the argument will lie not in its showing that there can be responsibility without choice but in its showing that we must give a non-episodic interpretation of choice, viewing it primarily as a *continuum* of active process. And this I believe is not only a perfectly possible but also the right interpretation to give.[2]

[1] See *Christ and Conscience*, p. 34, and following.

[2] I should make it clear that the contrast of 'episodic' and 'non-episodic' is drawn with reference to those periods only of our biological existence that can be regarded as 'moral life' at all. Our moral life itself everyone would take to be 'episodic' relative to the whole duration of biological existence. Cf. Chapter IV, Section 2, below; and see also my paper 'On Being Sure of One's Duty',

It is true that Campbell regards the thought of duty as a necessary condition of moral choice and that Robinson claims that there may be responsible action when there is no thought of duty, 'when, for example, a person allows himself to be led by some violent desire'.[1] If both these views are sound, it must after all be possible to have responsible action without choice. Now Campbell's view, in my opinion, is sound; but it is not necessary to admit Robinson's claim. Certainly his example, which I have quoted, does not support it. The word 'allows' is surely important if the flavour of responsibility is not to be removed. But what can it mean, if we take it seriously, unless it indicates a choice occurring in a context impregnated by some sense, however vague, of an 'oughtn't to'? The fact is that we can concede to the thought of duty the same measure of continuity that we ascribe to choice. The thought of duty is not to be regarded as absent, any more than is the reality of choice, merely because it is not clear-cut; and nothing that Robinson has said entitles us to suppose that there is or could be moral responsibility where that thought is altogether lacking.

Nor do I think that Robinson is at all helped by his treating, correctly, the field of 'strict moral responsibility' as congruent with that of 'remorse'.[2] It seems plain to me that whatever, and however intense and painful, our feelings may be when we survey the evil we have done, we should not describe those feelings as 'remorse' unless they were combined with the belief that at the moment of action it was open to us to take another course. To feel remorse is at the same time to set aside every plea that rests on a supposition of our mere innocent thoughtlessness or of our being blindly driven by passions that we could neither prevent nor master. A satisfactory phenomenology of moral experience is undoubtedly a very difficult thing to achieve. But its difficulties at no point suggest, what appears to me impossible, that the *concepts* of choice and responsibility can be disjoined; and the attempt to saddle mankind with *responsibility* for their supposed universal sinfulness fails accordingly.

Philosophical Quarterly, October 1950, pp. 47–8. Hampshire (*Thought and Action*, p. 116) speaks similarly of action as a continuum 'which may later be divided into separate individual actions in many different ways'.

[1] *Christ and Conscience*, p. 44.   [2] *Op. cit.*, pp. 48–50.

(9)

But let me turn from negative criticism to summary affirmation. Briefly, my own attitude as a moralist towards assertions of man's natural sinfulness is this. If we are content to say that all men, by their human constitution, are liable to formal sin, that they all do in fact thus sin, that their minds, moreover, are in greater or lesser degree darkened, and that they are subject to feelings and impulses that are (in another sense) sinful even when resisted, we have a picture of the human condition that need not offend any secular moralist, even though the word 'sin' itself is not in his vocabulary. It is true that this account includes no recognition of a positive natural bias towards sin. But the existence of feelings and impulses that are as such sinful may be regarded as justifying even the language of bias, so long as the equally manifest good feelings and impulses for which we can claim no merit are treated as being not of nature but of grace. How far this particular use of the antithesis of nature and grace is a helpful one is another matter. Further, if formal sin is a universal fact this too might be spoken of in terms of a positive tendency to sin, as (if the comparison will be forgiven) batsmen might be said to have a tendency to get out although we can see no 'must' about it. The mere temptation to formal sin, however, which its actual occurrence presupposes, is not itself properly to be described as a bias towards sin. The temptation constitutes, of course (by definition), a certain 'pull', of which we are conscious, in a sinward direction; somewhat as the driver of a car with a mechanical fault may feel it pulling off the road. But then we must not regard man as being like the car and not the driver. Rather we should treat him as analogous to car and driver in one. And if we treat car and driver as a complex unity, what reason have we to say that this unitary being has a tendency to swerve any more than that it has a tendency to go straight? In different respects it has both tendencies: as a whole it has neither. It is no doubt quite natural that the moral reason, taking no notice of itself, should think in terms of our having a bias specifically towards what is evil. We have just got to be careful not to let this mislead us.

I do not presume to say that all this goes far enough to satisfy Christian theologians. Yet I do not see how we are to go any further in principle, though much might be said by way of

CHAPTER III

THE MORAL DEMAND

(1)

Considered as comment from the standpoint of ethics on the theological concept of sin, the discussion just completed is itself a part of our main theme. It was initially undertaken, however, only as a ground-clearing operation, and that is how the first half of it at least should still be primarily viewed. I had said that we were to proceed on the assumption (since without it we could not proceed at all) that the moral philosopher as such, starting with no theological presuppositions, is competent to tell us what morality is. His account, however it may be supplemented, is to be accepted so far as it goes, not just dismissed as necessarily a perversion of the truth. But I observed that since this assumption has been challenged it was essential that I should at least state plainly how I myself regard the challenge, how incapable I find myself of taking it seriously except in the sense in which all influential irrationalism must be taken seriously; namely, as a distressing social phenomenon. Having now performed this task as well as I can, I may be allowed to take up the question originally propounded; the question, that is, of the relationship between the concepts involved in moral theory and certain theological concepts that have a manifest relevance to morality, theological concepts that are thought to be in one way or another interpretative of the moral life.

I said, earlier on, that I should confine the enquiry within fairly narrow limits. I meant by this that I should concentrate attention on what seemed to me the central issues. And if now I am asked what *are* the central concepts in moral theory, I reply that there are two facts that I take to be fundamental for any experience that is properly called moral experience; first, that we have duties, and, secondly, that we can elect either to respect or to ignore these in our practice. These two facts relate to what may be termed the moments of moral demand and of moral response in our experience, respectively. It is proper and needful to distinguish these moments, and I shall discuss them separately.

elaboration, unless we are to allow that man is sheerly impotent of himself to avoid moral failure. This, I may be told, is just what I should go on to allow: but whether I ought to do so or not is precisely one of the cardinal issues that fall to be discussed in the pages that follow.[1] For the time being we can let the matter rest.

[1] See Chapters IV and V.

But it is of course quite as necessary to insist that they do not actually occur in separation, any more than do action and reaction within a physical system. Any consciousness of demand is already in some form or other a responsive consciousness; and response, again, is distinctively a moment in personal living, something other than sub-personal reaction, only as it encloses an awareness of the demand that it either meets or evades. The abstraction my discussion requires need not be vicious, but it must be remembered that it is abstraction.

It may be objected that the characterization of moral experience, as, essentially, the having of duties and the choosing whether to perform them or not is both very crude and very narrow. Certainly it is the former; brevity can only be had at this price. But something at least of the desiderated refinement will be added as we proceed. As to the charge of narrowness, I am not of course to be understood as denying that moral experience is a much richer and more complex thing than my formula describes. Just so the human body is much more than its spinal column. But then my present interest is precisely in what one might call the spinal column of morality, and I maintain that the formula quite correctly indicates what is the nature of that. Much criticism of so-called 'duty-ethics' rests, I consider, on sheer misunderstanding either of what its proponents intend or of morality itself. I must be content here with barely asserting that morality itself is misunderstood by any who do not recognize that the concept of duty is cardinal in the interpretation of it. On the other hand, I am misunderstood if my saying this is taken to signify that I think of the morally good man as one in whose ears the 'Voice of Duty' is continually sounding and whose life has the sourness of aspect that this painful consciousness would naturally generate. I shall have a little more to say about this when I come to consider specifically what I have called the moral response. That is the more appropriate context for my comment. But, anyhow, it is to be noted that (for better or worse) it is simply with this two-sided feature of our experience, duty, and our response to it, that I shall be directly concerned, taking each aspect in turn and asking how theology is relevant to the account of it.

As to what is to be understood by 'theology', it is only necessary to say that although I do not mean by the term specifically

EDINBURGH UNIVERSITY LIBRARY
WITHDRAWN

Christian theology, but rather such a doctrine of God as is appropriate to any theistic religion, it is naturally Christian formulations that I shall have primarily in mind.

(2)

Our first question, then, concerns the fact that we have duties. We are to ask whether this fact admits of interpretation in theological terms, or perhaps even requires the use of theological concepts for its proper description or elucidation. But before we begin on an answer let me be a little more explicit as to what the expression 'the fact that we have duties' signifies. Is having a duty, though of course it is precisely like nothing else, more like having red hair (in the sense that the duty can be there apart from our consciousness of it, something that we may either notice or fail to notice), or is it more like having a disagreeable time (in the sense that it is of its very essence to be a mode of our consciousness)?

Surely in one, perfectly proper, sense it is more like having red hair. For example, it is perfectly natural and proper to say of a man that he has a duty to make some particular sacrifice to help others who are in distress, even though he himself fails to see that this is so. All of us, from time to time, both seek and give advice as to what we ought to do; and this implies that there *is* something we ought to do of which, none the less, we may as yet be unaware.

But it is equally clear that this is not the only sense in which we use the word 'duty'. We also use it in such a way that there is no duty laid upon us until our conscience challenges us. Our duty, in this sense, is to act in whatever way our own conscience directs, not as even the wisest and soundest advice from another may suggest to us: and its existence presupposes that we have somehow, and no matter with how questionable a result, terminated our search for enlightenment regarding our duty in the former, or 'red hair', sense. In this second sense of 'duty', to speak of having it is to speak of being in a certain state of mind. The duty is itself at the same time a duty-*consciousness*: and a man does not even *have* a duty to sacrifice his comfort, for example, for another's sake except as he himself sees the moral necessity of doing so.

Much more would require to be said about the distinction between these two uses of the word 'duty' were it my purpose fully to explain it and to guard against all misconception. But I cannot think that there is any difficulty in the bare recognition of it. (It is indeed precisely what underlies the theological distinction, earlier mentioned, between 'material' and 'formal' sin.) I have drawn attention to it here only in order to point out that it is duty in the second of these two senses[1] that I have primarily in mind when I speak of the having of duties as an essential—or the essential—and central feature of moral experience.

This duty is moral duty, of course, only inasmuch as a man regards himself as *categorically* required to act in a certain way. There may be a variety of reasons why he so regards himself. If he is asked 'Why is this, rather than that, to be done?' he should, up to a point, be able to justify his judgment. It is true that it can be only 'up to a point'. There must in the nature of things be a last term in any series of explanations, and, some might even say, it would be silly to ask 'Why?' at all if it would be sensible to ask it forever. Still, within limits a man may be expected to defend his judgment. But it remains true that in doing so he will be defending his view of the content of his duty; he will be trying to explain why the particular thing in question is what he 'absolutely must' do. At no point will he be trying to get behind the 'absolutely', to justify the quality of his obligation as distinct from its content. If he once lost the sense of this 'absolutely' his consciousness, so far as concerned that particular occasion, would thereby cease to be a *moral* consciousness altogether.

The moral demand, then, comes to us in the form of a duty-consciousness that imposes an absolute claim on our lives. But no such consciousness could arise unless there were, however little articulated and reflected upon, some sort of valuation on our part of alternative possibilities of action, a preferring, in judgment, of one to another. The moral demand, that is to say, must after all have its material aspect of determinate content as well as its formal aspect of categorical requirement; and though we may

[1] It has been called 'putative duty'; not altogether happily, however, since the term is liable to suggest that there is really no duty there, in the same way that to speak of an 'imaginary animal' is to indicate that there is really no animal there. 'Putative duty', on the contrary, is not merely real duty but even (I should hold) is what best deserves that title, if we are unwilling that the title should be shared.

distinguish these two they cannot be separated. Our moral consciousness is not simply a consciousness of being 'under obligation' in a quite general and empty way, though no doubt there are pathological anxiety-conditions that simulate this state of affairs. There is always some specific 'this' rather than 'that' that we should do or seek after. Now implicit in this comparative valuation of the 'this' and 'that', if our preference is even to seem to ourselves to have the constrained and authoritative character that belongs to *judgment*, there is the assumption of what may be called, loosely and vaguely but still, I think, quite properly and intelligibly, an objective 'order of values':[1] and with this the former of the two senses of 'duty' that I have distinguished comes back into the picture. I do not see how without this assumption of an objective 'order of values' we can suppose that the fundamental valuations of different persons (conflict between which is at least conceivable) could be said to be capable of rectification, as distinct from mere alteration, true though it is that correction properly so called might still be possible *within* a valuational system, in the form of a replacement of incoherence by consistency. And neither do I see how, without a belief in corrigibility as contrasted with mere changeability, any of us could, as we do, take seriously the task, which is sometimes an anxious and exacting one, of attaining (as we very naturally express it) a *right* judgment of where our duty lies.

I am well aware that what I have just said constitutes a brusque disagreement with a large body of contemporary philosophical thought, and on a question that I grant to be exceedingly difficult, as well as quite fundamental. I am taking what is certainly an unfashionable line. But so long as it is recognized that I am not ignorant of this I am content, on the present occasion, simply to

---

[1] *Pace* Mr Kai Nielsen (*Philosophical Quarterly*, April 1959), to cite but one recent and forthright exponent of the contrary view. But is Nielsen's dismissal of the concept of a 'value realm' perhaps just a natural concomitant of a failure to take seriously enough the concept of the 'categorical'? (Cf. his article 'Is "Why should I be moral?" an absurdity?' in *Australasian Journal of Philosophy*, May 1958). The question may apply to others besides him. I am more perturbed by Ewing's change of view regarding the 'non-natural', reported in his *Second Thoughts in Moral Philosophy*, pp. 50–3; for he is certainly as insistent as I could wish on the objectivity of moral judgments, though I do not myself think he can secure it on his terms. I am not perturbed at all by Nowell-Smith's blunt, and perhaps unconsidered, assertion that 'the use of the word "values" as a noun is a pernicious barbarism'. (*Mind*, January 1952, p. 129).

state my position, which is after all not a peculiar one.[1] Only I
would stress that in assuming it I am making no claim that the
'objective values' postulated are 'given' to us in some clear and
direct 'intuitive apprehension'. What in fact I believe is rather
the reverse of this: namely, that they are, as Plato said of the Good,
what the soul at best 'inkles', dimly divining their existence.[2] But
the epistemological problem is too complicated to be dealt
with in an aside; it would need an article, if not a volume,
to itself.

In the light of this account of what is involved in having a duty
it appears that the question before us, whether a theological
interpretation of the fact of duty is either necessary or even possible, presents two aspects. On the one hand we have the problem
of the absoluteness of the moral demand, its unquestionable
authoritativeness. On the other hand we have the problem of the
nature of that objective 'order of values', belief in whose reality
is presupposed in every endeavour to determine correctly the
changing content of our duty in the changing circumstances of
our lives. It may be that in the end these two problems coalesce;
I mean, it may turn out that the only way of understanding the
authoritativeness of the demand is to view it as a function of the
absolute importance of what is demanded. But if this is true, at
least it is not a truth 'of the first look'. On the contrary, it could,
I suspect, only be explained in terms of a sort of moral eschatology,
for which the various secular concerns that yield the content of
our duty are morally urgent, are in fact *duty*, only through their
'participation' in and 'relevance' to a different and non-secular
order. The vital words 'participation' and 'relevance' here serve
merely to signal a perplexity, which I must leave unresolved. But
if, as I propose to do, we remain at a more common sense, and
superficial, level we must certainly say that while every duty is
as such absolutely *binding* it is very far from true that every duty
is, in respect of its manifest content, equally and absolutely
important. Many duties indeed seem trivial—like sweeping a room,
let us say, choosing that example deliberately for the sake of the

[1] I am in general sympathy in this matter with the position of Professor
Everett W. Hall, as set out in his 'Practical Reason(s) and the Deadlock in
Ethics' (*Mind*, July 1955). See also Mr King-Farlow's energetic protest in
Philosophical Quarterly, April 1957.

[2] *Republic*, 505E. I have made use of Cornford's rendering of ἀπομαντευομένη
τι εἶναι.

overtones it owes to George Herbert.[1] We therefore may, and
here we must, take separately the two problems I have distinguished, of the authority of duty on the one hand and the being
of values on the other.

(3)

Consider first, then, the authoritativeness of what is called 'the
moral law' as that makes impact on us in our consciousness of
duty. Do concepts of a theological nature do anything to elucidate
this? Here I think we must differentiate between two sorts of
ways in which they may be supposed to do so. I label these
respectively the *contextual* and the *aetiological* explanations of the
claim of duty. They are not mutually exclusive: on the contrary,
it is very natural, though not I think strictly necessary, to combine
them. They are different kinds of explanation none the less.

On the one hand it may be held that the claim of duty upon us,
when it is considered, with a Kantian austerity, simply in
itself, is a sort of absurdity: but that if we can suppose that the
universe is somehow 'friendly' to moral obedience, then it makes
sense, as it otherwise would not, to expect this obedience from
us. The supposition of a friendly universe is naturally, even if
not inevitably, given a theistic form: our concern, anyhow, is
with it only in that form. It is because this is God's world and
only because it is God's world that it is reasonable to follow the
path of duty, without condition or reservation, wherever it may
lead. This is the pattern of what I call the contextual explanation
of the claim of duty. The aetiological explanation, on the other
hand, treats our sense of duty as a kind of 'hearing God addressing
and commanding us'. The claim on us is authoritative and absolute
because and only because God is its source. However independent
of our recognition of this fact our sense of the claim may be it
remains a sort of absurdity until it is understood in these terms.

It is to be noticed that each of these explanations could in turn
have either of two different intentions. The first intention would
be this. The sense of duty, it may be supposed, however it
originates, can only sustain itself in us as rational creatures, once
we reflect, if we are able to interpret it in one or other of the two

[1] Herbert, *The Elixir*: 'Who sweeps a room, as for thy laws, Makes that and
the action fine.'

ways I have distinguished. The validity of the explanation, in this case, has a direct practical importance; it is relevant to the quality of our actual living, in so far as we are not protected by mere thoughtlessness or benign error. But a second view would be that our sense of duty is perfectly self-sustaining, only it is in itself very puzzling; and that no one will ever get rid of his intellectual worries about it until he finds himself able to accept the theistic account. In brief we might say that the intention in the first case is to give support to the moral claim, while the intention in the second case is to give a satisfying analysis of its nature.

I think these two intentions are sometimes confused together in the minds of those who urge the need for a theistic account of the claim of duty, whether in the contextual or in the aetiological form. And it must be allowed that, as a matter of psychology, intellectual dissatisfaction in a matter of this kind can hardly be without effect on practice. A man is always in danger of losing his grip on the fact of duty itself from a feeling of persistent inability intellectually to 'make sense of it'. Yet the intentions are in principle distinct; and I think it is correct to say that the contextual explanation is more apt than the aetiological to be used with the purpose of supporting the moral claim and not merely interpreting it. Just for that reason I regard it as constituting the more radical moral heresy; and I take it first in order to emphasize at the outset the vital thesis that the claim of acknowledged duty, whatever may be its nature and origin, neither requires nor admits of *justification* by reference to what is other than itself.

(4)

The contextual explanation of the claim of duty—the postulate that the universe must be friendly to the doing of our duty if there is to be any sense in doing it—may assume either a crude or a more refined form. Consider first its very familiar crude form, a form in which its purpose is most plainly to give practical support and not just to elucidate. The good man, it is said, will be rewarded and the evil punished. The universe, in fact, is friendly to the performance of duty in the sense that it looks after the interests of the dutiful.

Now it could of course be true that this is the way of things, and it is perhaps perfectly natural and innocent to hope that virtue will have other rewards than itself. But, whether it be true or not, to find in the belief of it a necessary condition of its being reasonable to do one's duty (meaning by that, a condition of its being fair to expect a reasonable man to do it) is to deny the very morality one claims to be supporting. A moralist who appealed to men in these terms would be not unlike a priest for whom the case for the worship of God rested on the fact that (by divine appointment) it ministered to our own satisfaction. I say this in the hope that any priest would scent a blasphemy here. If we can see that this conception of the nature of worship contradicts the very spirit of religion, can we not equally well see that the appeal to reward contradicts the very spirit of morality—that theists themselves must condemn it as recommending (in an excellent phrase from *II Clement*) a 'training ourselves in commerce and not in godliness'?[1]

It may be claimed that such criticism can be fairly urged only against a reward theory in which 'reward' is interpreted with insufficient 'spirituality', and is regarded as somehow artificially annexed to the practice of morality instead of as the 'rewarding-ness' of that practice itself. And of course there is some merit in this plea. There are coarser and finer conceptions of the motive of reward, and the difference between them is not to be denied. But the point of principle remains. Either moral practice and its reward can be distinguished or they cannot. If they cannot be distinguished the language of reward is empty: if (no matter precisely how) they can, then the language of reward—employed, that is, not simply as 'promise' but as 'bribe'—is inept. No one is being asked to pretend that he is quite unconcerned about his happiness in this world or another: but he is asked to recognize that this is not the *moral* concern, even when it is another world that he has in view. Morality is not to be identified with even the most refined and the most comprehensive form of egoistic pru-dence.[2] It is surely significant of the strength of our conviction

[1] II Clement, XX, 4. Tr. Kirsopp Lake. (*The Apostolic Fathers*, in the 'Loeb Classical Library' series, Vol. I, pp. 160–1.)

[2] This of course is the sort of jejune insistence on the duty-interest dis-tinction for which Prichard, whose work in ethics is so dominated by it, has been severely castigated (e.g. by Hawkins in *Philosophical Quarterly*, April 1951, p. 242 and following). I cannot see, however, that its validity and importance are in the slightest degree affected by the fact that there is a great deal *more* to be said about the relation between 'happiness' and 'the good life', though it may be regretted that Prichard himself did not go on to say it.

that this is so that many Christian thinkers, committed to the view that Jesus is supreme in his moral perception, have found in His use of language that has the appearance of an appeal to the motive of reward not the guarantee that such an appeal is defensible but a problem of interpretation.[1] In the case of others, unfortunately, this language, whatever its proper interpretation may be, is likely to have played some part in obscuring the ethical fact.

About this crude form of the contextual explanation of the claim of morality we must say, then, that it simply explains it away. And though it would be optimistic to suppose that the view has lost its popular appeal, it certainly does not have the status in philosophical thinking that at one time it had. Paley's famous definition of virtue (as 'the doing good to mankind, in obedience to the will of God, and for the sake of everlasting happiness')—a definition published, by a nice irony of history, in the same year as Kant's *Groundwork of the Metaphysic of Morals*—is, at least as regards its final clause, generally felt to strike a false note. Yet the idea expressed remains insidious, and it is not impossible to cite contemporary thinkers of deserved reputation who have at least toyed with it.[2] But I shall not here consider it further. Let us turn to the second, which I called the refined, form of the contextual theory. It is much the more interesting of the two.

[1] See for instance Kirk, *The Vision of God*, Lecture III, Part IV, and Garrard, *Duty and the Will of God*, Chapter X.

[2] This seems to me to be true, for instance, of W. R. Matthews, *Studies in Christian Philosophy*, Lecture IV, Part III. It would be plainly unfair to put 'self-realization' theories also in this same class along with Paley; to do so would be to attach no significance whatever to the difference between the language of 'eudaemonism' and that of 'hedonism'. I think, nevertheless, that in the end such theories are simply a confused compromise between egoistic hedonism on the one hand and on the other hand a doctrine of obligation to realize *values*, such that the *self*-realizing character of our action is, so to say, morally accidental and 'not of the essence'. This is of course matter for argument; but if I am correct there is no need to give separate consideration to the ethics of self-realization in the present context. It is, however, necessary to say that it seems to me a complete mistake to suppose that the moral law can be authoritative for us only if it is self-imposed in a sense that involves the principle of self-realization; as, for example, Matthews, in the passage to which I have referred, Baillie, *Our Knowledge of God*, p. 245, and perhaps also Tillich, *Systematic Theology*, Vol. I, p. 312, would hold.

(5)

This second form of the theory allows that a man may be expected to devote himself without thought of personal advantage to what he conceives as duty; only, it holds, he cannot be expected to do so unless he believes the universe to be friendly to the realization of moral purposes and ideals. But though such a view certainly is more refined than that already considered, still it is, I think, only a more refined error; as is likewise the closely related suggestion that we might even *define* morality in terms of what the universe is friendly towards.[1]

It is certainly true that some degree of tolerance of our moral efforts on the part of the universe is a necessary condition of our engaging in them. If it were possible to suppose that no actions of ours ever made a difference for better or worse in the world it would certainly not be possible to combine with that supposition the will to achieve the better. Moral devotion, then, requires belief in a universe friendly to the extent that in *some* measure our ideals can be realized in it; and it is an empirical fact, not just a venturesome faith, that it is thus friendly. But what is intended by those who look for friendliness in the universe as a condition of the reasonableness of the moral demand is clearly more than this. They are demanding something that can be questioned, something that *is* a postulate of faith.

It is not easy to state the postulate in positive terms, but its nature may at least be indicated as follows. Suppose that man, with his rational and moral nature, were an emergent 'accident' in a blind world-process, unique in the universe, inhabiting a tiny corner of it and enduring, as a race, for (let us say) a mere million years or so, a speck-like oasis of intelligence and devotion, though imperfect in both, in what is else an unbounded cosmic Sahara; suppose that the good he can achieve, though real, is transient, and that when he and it pass away there is nothing, no one, even to regret their passing; suppose there is no power not himself, let alone an omnipotence, making for righteousness and co-operating with his labours; suppose all this, and then try to suppose also

[1] 'Some attitudes and actions run along the grain of the universe, and others run contrary to it; this is really what is *meant* by describing some attitudes and actions as moral and others as immoral.' Stephen Neill, *Christian Faith To-day* (Penguin Books 1955), p. 42. My italics.

that he stands under an absolute obligation to do his best, here and now: *this*, it is suggested, is just what we cannot do.

What shall we say in reply? Without necessarily assenting to the view that, in the sense indicated, the universe is indifferent to morality we must surely allow that this pessimistic hypothesis has been entertained and credited, persistently by some and, I suspect, intermittently by most or all of us. How for such men or at such moments does the moral demand look? Is the reaction one of 'Nothing really matters: let us eat, drink and, if we can, be merry'? It may be so. Psychologically, there is strong temptation to make it so. Moral debacle may then set in for those for whom this 'pessimism at the metaphysical level' is a matter of deep feeling and not simply of superficial intellectual acknowledgement; just as it tends to set in, even with less reflective people, and perhaps especially with them, in times of famine or pestilence or civil chaos. But surely it does not always do so; and surely we cannot, when we stop to think about it, regard its doing so as justified and exempt from censure. The claim of the better, however exiguously better it be, is still to be heard: the 'I ought' is as authoritative as ever it was, though it may no longer have the ring of a *sursum corda*. We still know the difference between acting worthily and acting unworthily; and (surely a crucial test) we still 'hope with our moral reason', if I may so put it, even against all impulses of natural affection, that those for whom we care most should act worthily, at whatever hurt to themselves, if only (should it come to the worst) as the crew of a doomed vessel and not as the rats it harbours in its hold. To urge all this is only to echo the conclusion of a famous essay by Bertrand Russell.[1] Critics may be right who find in its rhetoric, as in that of Henley's well-known poem, a certain shrillness. Let me confess that the tones of Arnold's *Dover Beach* please me better. But literary likes and dislikes do not affect the truth of the matter. To borrow an image from another, and a gentler, essayist, even if human life is only a Goshen in Egyptian darkness the resolution is still possible, and is still required of us, so to live that 'in that little Goshen there will be light'.

[1] 'A Free Man's Worship', in the volume *Mysticism and Logic*.

(6)

I find myself, then, constrained to believe that the moral demand derives none of its authority for us from a supposition of the friendliness of the universe even in the sense intended by the best of those who would thus buttress it. Yet the contrary opinion deserves to be treated with some care and respect. For not only is the pessimistic hypothesis, as I have admitted, depressing to our feelings, a source of dismay, but there is besides a haunting sense, which only the less thoughtful are likely altogether to escape, that our situation on this hypothesis is absurd. It is indeed only for this reason that morally serious people are even tempted, as certainly they are sometimes tempted, to think that duty may be just an empty name.

Nevertheless I think we can recognize on reflection that it is not the reality or the intrinsic authority of the claim of duty that is in dispute; it is the universe as pessimistically conceived, the *context* of the claim, that is being judged. And that is a very different matter. We are indeed in rebellion against the pessimistic hypothesis not only in our feelings but with our minds; but we are in rebellion against it with our minds just because we *cannot* doubt the absoluteness of the moral demand. The seeming absurdity of which we are conscious is the absurdity of the misfit between the unconditional character of the claim upon us and the indifference, if not worse, on the part of everything but ourselves to what we do about it. So far are we from seeking a contextual justification of the moral claim that in truth the conviction that it needs and admits of no such justification is presupposed in this sense of absurdity itself.

Nor will it do to suggest that while the moral demand is not to be supported by the hypothesis of a friendly universe it can at least be illuminated, made more intelligible, by it. To make the demand more intelligible would surely be to tell us something either about its nature or about its 'credentials'. But talk about the character of the world-*context* in which the demand presents itself is plainly not the former; and if it is interpreted as providing 'credentials' we are back at the vain attempt at justification that we were considering a moment ago. Of course it is true that the hypothesis of a friendly universe would be 'illuminating' in the sense that it would remove the supposed *situational* absurdity of the occurrence of unconditional obligation in a neutral or hostile world. But to say this is not only irrelevant: it is an irrelevant tautology.

And what, we may ask, is our warrant for speaking even of a situational absurdity here? What is it after all that strikes us as absurd in the pessimistic world-picture? In calling it 'absurd' are we not really first supposing the universe to be the work of mind and then affirming that it would be a lunatic mind that would create it thus? And what right have we to the prior supposition? I do not deny that it may be possible to establish a right to it; but until we do so we are, in strictness, only entitled to speak of the pessimists' universe as *hateful*. And this, without absurdity, the universe might actually be. It would of course be the merest *petitio principii* to describe this hatefulness as absurdity and then to infer to creative mind on the strength of the description. If, as I suspect, the fallacy is not infrequently committed, it testifies to the naturalness and vigour of a prior theistic conviction, but it does nothing at all to support it.

Yet this I think we may allow, that in the experience of duty, and in the effort to respond aright, a man may be moved to say not merely that the pessimistic hypothesis *ought* not to be true (since, it seems to him, the universe is then as though a lunatic had created it) but also that it *cannot* be true (meaning that he 'feels in his bones' that in fact it isn't). A conviction of the friendliness of the universe, that in a sense its ways are as our ways, that it is not simply our place but our home, may then take possession of him. It will not come to him as the conclusion of an argument, but rather as an integral part of the very experience of demand and attempted response. And coming in this form it may truly possess a man even though he himself is not prepared to use in the description of it the terms I have employed. No doubt it will not do so, whether articulately or inarticulately, on every occasion on which, with honesty and truth, we say 'This is my duty: I must do this'; for such occasions vary greatly in their depth and quality. But it may do so whenever the difficulty of loyalty is intense and what it means to stand under obligation is most fully realized. And it should be observed that the pessimistic hypothesis itself, with the strain it imposes on our moral energies if we deeply feel it, is well adapted to stimulate this realization. At such a time, I am suggesting, a man's moral experience can take on a sort of religious quality; for it seems not improper to speak so of the vital sense that one is at once challenged and sustained by 'ultimate reality'. It may incorporate something for which Spinoza's *sentimus experimurque nos aeternos esse* would be no inept expression.[1] But it is necessary to insist that this conviction will be the fruit, and not the root, of a moral concern that has asked for no such assurance.

(7)

The conclusion of the matter, so far, is that the moral demand neither needs nor abides extraneous support from what I have called contextual considerations; neither do such considerations illuminate its nature. It must be left to stand on its own, and to make sense of itself. If, but only if, it is accepted in this way the moral experience may then reveal itself as more than it is ordinarily acknowledged to be, as having a character such that in, and not by any transcendence of, its nature as moral it is also religious, and could perhaps itself be called experience of God. If this be granted, then the moral experience is, of course, one index of what we mean when we speak of 'God'. But to say this is something very different from saying that an independent concept of God and of His ways can be used to interpret the moral experience.

(8)

I turn now to what I have called the aetiological explanation of duty; that is to say, to the line of thought that sees the authority of duty as somehow derived from, or illuminated by, the fact that it is God's command or will for us. This is a view at once imaginatively natural—hence its persistence—and conceptually indefensible. It can be formulated, of course, in a variety of ways,

---

[1] Up to this point, save for his reference to the sense of confrontation by a personal will, I am heartily in agreement with what Professor H. H. Farmer has said about the consciousness of obligation in his *Revelation and Religion*, pp. 142–5. I may also suitably refer here to Professor L. Arnaud Reid's book *Creative Morality*, to which I am much indebted. I should observe that what I have virtually called 'religious morality' corresponds, I think, very closely to what Professor Reid speaks of as 'sacred morality' and distinguishes from 'religious morality' (*op. cit.* Chapter 12, esp. pp. 192–7). I do not wish to deny that there is point in Professor Reid's distinction, but I should hesitate to accept it just as it stands as being *for experience* a sharp one.

with a wide range of nuances. But I think it is possible, without
going into much detail, to exhibit its weakness in principle. It is
indeed just this that causes me some embarrassment; for though
because of its persistence we cannot ignore it, I can hardly hope
at this date to be able to find any but the tritest terms in which
to criticize it.

First, however, I must note and dispose of one complication
that does not affect the essence of the command theory, although
that theory, like any other theory of obligation, must, of course,
be able to find house-room for it. It might be asked in which of
two ways we should conceive of the content of the Divine
command—whether as coincident with duty in the 'objective'
sense, in which we may try, and fail, to discover it; or as coincident
with duty in the sense of 'what we *take* for objective duty'.
Obviously these may differ; and it is no part of a sensible religion
to evade the issue by pretending that, no matter how we interpret
its terms, the question what God's will is can be answered out of
hand and without risk of error. Yet whichever of the two suggested interpretations of the Divine command we adopt there
will seem to be something rather odd about it.

But surely what we must do is to reject the idea that a mere
'either—or' is here in place. We should say, rather, that God's
command includes *both* senses of duty, and endeavour to understand how it may do so by reflection on ordinary human command-
situations. After all, in ordinary human experience commands
may be misunderstood, but misunderstanding is not itself dis-
obedience. Thus if a mother asks her rather silly little daughter
to pour out the tea while she herself arranges some flowers in
another room she is asking, no doubt, without distinguishing the
two, both for obedience from her daughter and for the cups to be
filled. But, if the silly little daughter is silly enough, her mother
may come back to find that the tea has been taken away and poured
down the kitchen sink. Has the child fulfilled her command? In
one sense manifestly not. None the less the mother will have
received obedience in a sense in which the less disastrous 'No I
won't!' would have withheld it. The question whether in such a
case the child has acted as her mother asked her to act is complicated just as is the question whether a man who follows a misguided
conscience has done as he ought. Correspondingly, the question
whether, on the Divine command theory of duty, God commands

E

'objective' or 'subjective' duty differs only in words and not in substance from a question that confronts also every 'non-theological' or 'secular' moralist: the difficulty, if it is a difficulty, is no greater in the one case than in the other, and it has no bearing on the truth or falsity of the command theory as such.

(9)

But however we understand the expression 'what we ought to do', the doctrine that what we ought to do is made such by the fact that God commands it is inept. This is true even of the less radical of the two forms the doctrine might assume. On this less radical view each of us has just one fundamental and *underived* duty, to do whatever God wills; and all the *detail* of our duty is determined, accordingly, and made duty for us simply and solely by His will. God's will is the source of every specific 'norm' of conduct; and precisely because this is so it itself cannot, like human commands, be assessed and judged by reference to any 'norm' but must be represented as an utterly arbitrary fiat. To the suggestion that this conception is really dishonouring to God the retort is ready that it seems so only because we are thinking of God in purely human terms.

As regards the last point, I should indeed allow that it is fair enough to invite us to an adoring silence before God's mysterious 'otherness' were it not that the doctrine we are considering is itself the product of no such silence, but springs rather from a cheerful initial confidence in the appropriateness of the very language, that of human relationships, which we are now instructed to discard. But let that pass. The position I have described is in any case one that could be maintained only if it were true, as it is not, that we have a properly *moral* awareness of a duty to obey God and no other *moral* awareness whatsoever—judgments of the form 'This is what God commands' being, of course, not themselves moral judgments. If it is not true that our moral consciousness is thus restricted—and in fact with many men it will not even include as a component the sense of obligation to God, through their lack of a belief in God's existence—then we must allow that something can at least be thought of as morally required of us independently of our thinking it to be what God wills or commands. But this is to think of it as *intrinsically* binding on us.

And if at the same time we are to suppose, as the command theory asks us to suppose, that whatever is morally binding is *made* so always and only by God's commanding it, we find ourselves baffled by the collision between the suggestion of contingency involved in the concept of 'making' and the seemingly intrinsic authority of the specific obligation that is supposed to be thus 'made'.

It goes naturally enough with this sense of collision that we should even be in danger of ceasing to regard our specific moral obligations as constituted such by God's will and should regard them instead (while still speaking of them as obligations) as being conceivably *opposed* to it, and, when thus opposed, as less authoritative than it. The command theory of the nature of morality will then be transformed into a theory, and a derogatory one at that, of its status. So we may reach such an interpretation of the story of Abraham and Isaac as the one Kierkegaard offers us in *Fear and Trembling*. There (in the section entitled 'Can there be a teleological suspension of ethics?') Abraham's conduct is approved precisely because he was willing to trample on his ethical convictions in order to obey the command of God. 'Ordinarily speaking' (I quote from the translation by Robert Payne) 'a temptation is something which tries to stop a man from doing his duty, but in this case it is ethics itself which tries to prevent him from doing God's will.' It is true that when Kierkegaard immediately goes on to say 'But what then is duty? Duty is quite simply the expression of the will of God' his position may appear less unacceptable to the moralist, inasmuch as Abraham is after all, it would seem, not going against *duty*. But it would be a mistake to draw any comfort from these words. All they indicate is that, with an added increment of confusion, Kierkegaard has torn apart and opposed 'duty' and morality, so that 'duty' itself is no longer an ethical term. It is pointless to debate whether its absurdity or its offensiveness is the more striking feature of such a view.

So far I have been criticizing what I described as the less radical form of the command theory, that namely which allows one solitary underived moral obligation, the obligation to obey God. What of the more radical form, the form that admits no obligation at all that is not a product of the Divine Will? We must concede that this latter view possesses one distinctive merit; it has at least a consistency that the other lacks. It has the courage, so to say, of its conviction that moral obligation cannot be left to stand on its own feet. If the conviction is erroneous, why the command theory at all? If the conviction is sound, why exempt *any* obligation from its scope? It may indeed be asked how we are to view the specific obligation to obey God if it is not to be taken as an ultimate moral fact. Obviously *this* obligation cannot bind simply because God commands it. To suppose so would be circular, like supposing that God's existence can be explained by saying that He created Himself. But to this the reply might be offered that in a sense there is no such obligation at all: obedience to God is not *a* duty but simply the abstracted common relational character of all duties. There is no reason why we should not say this. Duty, then, would be without qualification or remainder what God commands; and this, as I have said, is an improvement in point of consistency on the less radical version.

But I cannot see that it is an improvement in any other respect. It is true that it now becomes possible to regard the proposition that 'duty is what God commands' as a definition. But whether we take it for a definition or not it remains unsatisfactory. If it is not a definition, then either it means that God commands what is our duty (which whether or not it be the case is not the issue we are at present considering) or it means that what is our duty *becomes* such through God's command, and we are then faced by just the same objections to which the less radical version of the theory lies open. If, however, to say that 'duty is what God commands' is to offer a definition, we must point out that it is a definition that does not elucidate, but on the contrary simply denies, the characteristic quality of the experience with which our problem began. The 'normative' has been elided and what can be stated in the language of positive fact alone remains. Is there any way of reversing this verdict? The only hope lies, I think, in the appeal, to which I earlier referred, to the 'otherness' of God; not as something enabling us to suppose that He can, by way of command as that is ordinarily understood, do what human commanders cannot, but as requiring us to acknowledge that the concept of command itself is to be taken 'non-anthropomorphically'. But what sort of hope is this? At the point at which the contention would suffice to silence objection it would suffice also to empty the command theory of all significance. The fact is that if we are not to use anthropomorphic concepts the theory cannot be stated,

and if we are to use them it cannot be defended; and one or other
we must do. There seems no escape from this dilemma.

(10)

It is not surprising, in view of all this, that we should be offered,
as an alternative form of the doctrine of the will of God, the view
that God commands the right as being right—right, that is to say,
independently of His command. There is nothing in this form
of the doctrine to affront the moralist, but something undoubtedly
to perplex. For presumably the theological language is thought by
those who employ it to be important, and important not simply
as a statement about God (an affirmation, that is to say, of His
righteousness) but as a statement about our moral situation. But
what can be its importance from this latter point of view? What
work does the command-hypothesis now do? It appears that it
does absolutely no work unless we can suppose one or other of
two things. Either we must suppose that we can recognize an act
to be wrong without recognizing any obligation to refrain from
it until we conceive of it as also prohibited by God, or we must
suppose that we can recognize the obligation without regarding it
as authoritative for us until we conceive of it as also God's will.
But in fact neither supposition is possible. At neither point—
neither between perceived wrongness and perceived duty of
abstention nor between acknowledgment of duty and acknowledgment of its authority—is there a gap that the authority of
God is required to, and might serve to, bridge.

It is, however, not only the moral theorist who has reason to
be perplexed by the suggestion that it is both true and ethically
important that God commands what is right. The theologian too
should pause to reflect. For is this view consistent with the dignity
of God? Are we not now suggesting that an 'order of values' or a
'moral law' (it does not matter which language we use) has its
being not merely apart from but above God, in that to its authority
God Himself must bow? God, it would seem, is in relation to it
much like the Platonic demiurge in relation to the eternal and
immutable Forms. And the Platonic demiurge is not the God of
theism.

It is of course precisely this consideration that gives force to
the original, or 'high', form of the command theory. 'God is He

for Whose will no cause or ground may be laid down as its rule and standard; for nothing is on a level with it or above it, but it is itself the rule for all things. If any rule or standard, or cause or ground, existed for it, it could no longer be the will of God.'[1] But there are ways of doing justice in words at least to the absolute 'freedom' of God that do not involve us in a doctrine of arbitrary will. God's action, it could be said, ceases to appear arbitrary without being conditioned by anything other than Himself if moral distinctions are regarded neither as the product of His will nor as altogether independent of Him, but as constitutive of His understanding, and as 'having reality' only thus.

But really this will not do. For now we are employing the word 'understanding' in a way that violates its meaning in those human contexts from which it derives such meaning as it has. The criticisms long ago urged by Russell against Leibniz's endeavour to improve on Descartes are, I believe, cogent and of general application. What we know and our knowing it are from the human point of view never the same thing, and to claim knowledge that something is the case includes the affirmation that it is the case apart from our knowledge. On this analogy we should suppose either that God has no understanding or else that moral distinctions, like all that 'enters into' His understanding, in the sense of being its objects, are what they are independently of it. To suppose the first takes us back to arbitrary will, while to suppose the second is again to suppose an externally conditioned divine activity. But to employ the language of 'God's understanding' in the quite empty way required to circumvent this dilemma is rather less helpful, to my mind, than the description that was once offered me of the colour of someone's hair. 'Mouse-coloured,' my friend said; and then musingly added 'but a very queer sort of mouse.'[2]

What I have said is not to be taken as signifying that God *can* have the status only of a Platonic demiurge, or, what would I

---

[1] Luther, *The Bondage of the Will* (Eng. tr. of *De Servo Arbitrio* by J. I. Packer and O. R. Johnston), p. 209.

[2] The views discussed in the foregoing paragraphs are of course (as I have hinted in the text) no more than a simplified version of the classic seventeenth-century positions of Descartes (as interpreted by Leibniz and others) and of Leibniz himself. But Descartes at least was aware of the inadequacies of anthropomorphism, and any fair assessment of his thought must take due account of this. For Russell's comments on Leibniz, to which I have referred, see *A Critical Exposition of the Philosophy of Leibniz*, Chapter XV, Sections 112–13.

think be the franker form of the same position, that 'God' cannot name any real being at all. I am not excluding the possibility that theism is true; and if theism is true then certainly, by definition as I suppose, nothing, be it the 'moral law' or what you will, can be more ultimate than God or even co-ultimate with God. What account is positively to be given of the 'moral law' consistently with this I need not for the moment enquire. For the moment my concern is only with negations; I am concerned, that is to say, only to insist that attempts to explain the moral law or its authority as being God-derived are ineffective. The condition of their being significant and informative is at the same time the condition of their being unsuccessful.

And yet I should not be doing justice to those who employ the language of divine command and will in their account of morality were I to say no more than this. What they set them-selves to do cannot indeed be done; but we should note certain considerations that may suggest that it can, because it must, be done. Those who are moved by these considerations may be quite well aware that it is as impossible as it is needless to find extraneous *support* for the claim of duty in some theological account of its source. They may be well aware also that, in one sense anyhow, such an account does not even *illuminate* our moral experience—in the sense that the concept of the Divine will, except in a form that is both theologically inadequate and ethically inept, is more perplexing and obscure than that on which its opaque rays are shed. One might complain to them that they were no better than the old colonel of C. E. Montague's *Disenchantment* who tried to expound to his troops 'that terse and luminous masterpiece of instruction' (to wit, *Infantry Training 1914*) 'bringing his laboured jets of darkness to show the way through sunlight', and they might feel at least a measure of sympathy with the complaint. And still they might maintain that the story cannot be ended at the point at which the secular moralist would end it, without any reference to God whatsoever. They might feel that even considered as ethical theory it is incomplete without the theological supplement; that, precarious and unsatisfactory though this supplement must be, ethical fact itself testifies to the need of it, so that it would be yet more unsatisfactory to omit it.

What then are the considerations that invite or possibly compel us to affirm, however blankly, the God-originated character of the moral claim? There may be others, but let me take note of three.

(II)

The first of these considerations is very familiar. Ethics itself speaks of a 'moral law': but a law, we are told, implies a law-giver, and who but God could be the giver of *this* law? An alternative, and surely the only plausible one, would be the doctrine that the moral agent is his own law-giver, the thesis of what might be called unqualified moral autonomy. This is plausible because in a sense it is even true that every agent gives the law to himself, that the law has authority for him only because he does so. To say this is simply to express in different words our recognition of the fact that a man can never be justified in going against his own conscience. But then this vital element of autonomy is not exclusive of, but complementary to, a sort of heteronomy that is every whit as important. The man who 'gives the law to himself' certainly does not regard himself as inventing it, or as free to do so. It is what he, more or less adequately, discovers. And it is only as and because it is something discovered and not something invented that he can then *authoritatively* impose it on himself, not by creation but by adoption. And this is just a way of saying that he necessarily takes what he regards as the discovered *content* of the law to be authoritative for him in virtue of its being that content. It is this authoritativeness of the content, without regard to the question '*Who* says so?' that is the mark of the morally binding as contrasted with the positively commanded; and it is because of this authoritativeness of the content that the formula of autonomy fails us. If, then, we are to seek to account for it in terms of a lawgiver at all it must undoubtedly be in terms of a lawgiving *God*.

'*If* we are to seek to account for it in terms of a lawgiver': yes, but this is precisely what we should not do. Not only are we unable, as I have already said, to operate significantly with the concept of a lawgiver in this connection, but we have in fact no need of that concept. Indeed there is even a self-contradiction involved in the manner of its introduction at this point. If the peculiarity of the moral law in what I have called its heteronomous aspect is precisely that the relevant consideration is not *whose* law it is, *who* issues or

prescribes it, but *what* law it is, the *content* of the prescription, it
is self-contradictory to proceed, just as though the content were
not of itself authoritative, to look for an imponent as the source
of its authority; and then, because of the very peculiarity that
forbids us to make this first move, to finish the game by a second
move to the conclusion that in this case the imponent must be
God. What we have to say is, rather, that the moral law is a law
without a lawgiver: and to the objection that this is absurd the
answer is that it is just a way of saying that to call it 'law' at all is
only inadequate metaphor for something that is *sui generis*. The
argument to God as imponent of the moral law is as good an
example as could be desired of thought allowing language to lead
it by the nose. Not of course that we should austerely reject all
employment of the metaphor on account of this danger. But we
must be careful not to take it for more than it is.[1]

(12)

A somewhat less obvious argument for a theistic interpretation
of the moral demand has been developed by Mr L. A. Garrard
on the basis of a suggestion in Martineau.[2] Like the previous
argument it no doubt represents a widely held, though not always
very articulate, belief; but it is convenient to consider it with
reference to a specific formulation that is both compact and
competent. Garrard speaks of the moral law as consisting in
certain 'claims' upon us, our obligations being correlative with
these claims; and a claim supposes a claimant. In Martineau's
words: 'Obligation is a relative term, implying somewhere a
corresponding claim of right: i.e., it takes two to establish an
obligation.' Garrard then points out that the second party to the
relationship cannot in all cases be identified with some fellow-
creature. At least as regards our obligation 'to bring into existence
as much as possible of what, if it existed, would be valuable' the
corresponding claim of right cannot possibly be that of any human
person or society. It is, then, God's claim upon us. And Garrard
goes on to say (and I do not quarrel with this) that 'if this view is
to be adopted at all' (the view namely that our obligation has
God's claim as its correlate), 'it must no doubt be applied in every

---

[1] For a comment on Kant's position see Note A in the Appendix.
[2] Garrard, *Duty and the Will of God*, Chapter V.

case. Not only the claims that are otherwise left hanging in the air, but all claims must ultimately be referred to God as their source.'

Garrard is well aware that his argument may appear to be purely verbal, like the 'every law must have a lawgiver' of the argument just considered. Both alike call to mind the classic 'every effect must have a cause', with which Hume dealt with such elegant economy. Let it be allowed that we speak of 'moral claims' upon us and you have only to press the *word* 'claims' to find yourself confessing a claimant; but might this not show merely that we had been careless and question-begging in our choice of language? Garrard's contention, however, is that it would show no such thing: the use of the word 'claims' is no accident, and 'the implication is present in our thought, whatever terms we use'. The issue, and it is not a verbal one, is whether this is a true account of our thought.

To this I can only reply by reporting the contrary conviction. It seems to me untrue that we cannot think of an obligation as being obligation *simpliciter* but must always conceive of it as obligation *to* someone or other. There is of course a duality of a sort involved in the very concept of obligation, the duality of an ideal on the one hand and of an actual that may or may not become conformed to it on the other. But this is not a duality of inter-personal character, true though it is that we *can* think of the ideal as something to which we owe the boon of realization, as I suppose a man might regard himself as owing to his children *in posse* to beget them. Obligation is not the less what I mean by 'obligation *simpliciter*' because of it. That the obligation 'to bring into existence as much as possible of what, if it existed, would be valuable' is, phenomenologically considered, a case of obligation *simpliciter*, including no thought of a claimant, seems to me to be the fact. Support can be found for this view even in the work of a thinker who like Garrard does regard every obligation as having its corresponding claim. This is Dr Raphael's position; but Raphael is also 'inclined to deny that there is a strict obligation to realize goodness as such'.[1] It is only because he denies this that he thinks the obligation-claim correlation can be maintained; the denial is not an inference from the correlation, but is the condition precedent of his asserting it. Raphael thus testifies to his sense

[1] *Moral Judgement*, p. 50.

that if that particular obligation did exist it would be one that lacked the 'overtone' that Garrard believes himself to discern in it. I myself agree with Garrard and differ from Raphael in holding that there is an obligation to realize goodness as such, but this is not the time for arguing that point. What signifies here is simply that, on the phenomenological question, it would seem that Raphael is at one with me in holding that our 'concern' to realize goodness, whether properly to be called sense of obligation or not, incorporates no consciousness of an other to whom the realization is owed.

I think then that Garrard is mistaken. The language of claims, when extended to apply to the field of obligation generally, is, like the language of law, metaphorical; just as, of course, the language of demand, which I am myself employing throughout, is metaphor. It seems to me neither surprising nor, so long as we do not suppose them to be philosophical analyses, at all improper that we should employ these metaphors. The mistake lies in regarding them as more than metaphors. It is a mistake that it is no doubt very natural for a theist to make; for if already and on other grounds one believes in a God conceived as personal then either our obligations stand in no intelligible relationship to Him or the relationship must surely be such as Garrard supposes. But I maintain that there is no awareness of any such relationship inherent in the duty-consciousness itself, and I suggest that those who think there is do so precisely because they are not successfully abstracting from their independent theistic conviction. Their moral phenomenology has, so to put it, been vitiated by infection from beliefs at which they have arrived by a quite different route.

(13)

It may be held that even if the concept of the Divine Claimant cannot be derived from a scrutiny of moral experience it is a perfectly valid concept none the less. The moral experience itself may not witness to God as owner of a right corresponding to each obligation and yet it may be the case that He is so, and that this is the final philosophical truth about our duties. But this also I should deny, and for the following reasons.

I should accept and insist on the distinction, which I regard as of the highest importance for ethical thinking generally, between a man's *good* and his *goodness*.[1] A man's goodness, I should say, so far as it is strictly moral goodness, consists in his practical concern, be it 'dispositional' or 'occurrent', to live as he ought. But human goodness or excellence is of course by no means restricted to moral goodness whether thus or otherwise defined. In its wider significance it will consist in 'values' of whatever sort in so far as these are 'realized' in man and constitute his nature. Of a man who thus 'has goodness' it is proper to say that he 'is good' (and to say this is to commend), although in ordinary English usage the latter expression, when used without qualification, has the narrower reference to moral goodness specifically. (Compare the common English use of 'virtue' with the Greek ἀρετή.) A man's good, on the other hand, I take to be his interest or advantage: this is what 'good' when used with the possessive pronoun means.[2] And in the end, I should further say, this signifies 'happiness' or 'felicity', which may be described as a man's 'true' good, or his 'real' felicity, if it attends a way of life that fully and finally, or at least more adequately and enduringly than any other that is possible to him, satisfies the longings of his soul. Of a man who has achieved his good, or even his true good, we should not say that he *is* thereby good in any manner or degree: we do not commend but rather felicitate him. And the distinction holds even if it be the case, as many believe, that none can attain his true good unless he also is good, that is to say unless he has achieved goodness. This difference to which I have been calling attention, between one's good and one's goodness, is indicated by the contrast between such expressions as '*Be* a good man' and '*Have* a good time' (that is, 'Enjoy yourself'); and it is what gives its point to the Shakespearian jest: ' "Would you have a love-song, or a song of good life?" "A love-song, a love-song." "Ay, ay: I care not for good life." '

Now in strictness, I incline to believe, it is only because there is a possible good for man, as well as a possibility of goodness, that we can think of men as having, otherwise than simply as a

---

[1] For this distinction see Carritt, *An Ambiguity of the Word 'Good'* (British Academy Annual Philosophical Lecture, 1937). I owe my own appreciation of the point to this paper, but it was, of course, insisted on also by Prichard, whose most adequate statement of it is in *Moral Obligation*, pp. 98–103.

[2] Perhaps this is not its meaning in an expression like Milton's 'Evil be thou my Good'; but, if not, then correspondingly 'my' is not really possessive, but means 'in my estimation'.

matter of law, rights that are in a 'final' sense their rights and are not better to be called 'trusts'. If a man ought to be granted some power or liberty merely because it is a condition of his own happiness, it appears to me that he may properly be said to have a right to it, without any regard to what his obligations are or whether indeed he has any. In this sense, I conceive, animals may have rights, in virtue merely of their sentiency. The case is plainly different where the ground for conceding a power or liberty is not, in the last resort, its relevance to a man's happiness but rather its relevance to his ability to perform some function that, given the ability, he *ought* to perform; as for example when, in a situation of food scarcity, men employed in heavy manual labour must be given a larger ration than other men if they are to be fit to do their work. It is natural enough, no doubt, to speak in such a case of their right to the larger ration, and I suppose this is partly because of the distress that would be caused by compelling them to do their work without it. But, in strictness, the privilege belongs to them not as being themselves the beneficiaries but as being thereby serviceable or instrumental to the achievement of some further good, and they have a title to it only as they use it accordingly. This is what I mean when I say that they may more properly be said to hold it as a trust than as a right. Thus as concerns the 'realization of values'—the achievement of goodness in whatever mode and wherever located —men, being under obligation to endeavour this so far as they can, hold their power not as 'owners' but rather as 'trustees': *mancipio nulli datur, omnibus usu*. In respect of the realization of values only the values themselves, and by a manifest and strained metaphor, could be said to have rights in the strict meaning of the word, as contrasted with trusts.

If we follow this line of thought it would appear that in order to conceive God as having a right correlative with our obligation to realize values we must be able to suppose that this realization of values, including that form of it which is the achievement of our own goodness, would actually constitute His good, His advantage or felicity. 'Would actually *constitute* His good', I say, for it is not enough that we might suppose the one to *conduce* to the other. The two must be the very same thing: the expression 'God's good' must have, or contain, the very same meaning as the expression 'goodness actualized in the world.' To this identification, however, I can attach no significance, any more than I could attach meaning to the suggestion that the words 'the nobility of a son's life' refer to the same fact as might also be described as 'a father's happiness'. These are certainly two different facts, however intimate may be the relation between them. If I have any hesitation in saying that the proposed identification, in the case of God, is a sheer impossibility, it is only because I hesitate over all propositions about God. Yet, given the condition that God is conceived on the analogy of a human person, what else can one say? And if that analogy is discarded, does not any talk of God as having rights lose its meaning?

As I have indicated, it is perfectly intelligible to speak of our achievement of goodness as being the service of God in the sense that it *ministers* to His good. Just so might one speak of a son's nobility of life as a *source* of happiness to his parent. I raise no objection here to the language, with which we are all familiar, of 'so living as to be well-pleasing to God'. But if, employing this language, we were to claim that it explains why we should concern ourselves about goodness we should not any longer be *interpreting* the demand that 'values' make upon us (and this is what we are supposed to be doing) but rather *denying* it. We should be making God's pleasure, considering simply as His pleasure, the overriding consideration. An adequate image of human morality could then be provided by the life of a household— might we say, in nineteenth century Wimpole Street?—whose members were all the time straining to gratify the whims of a parental despot without questions asked, indeed without there being any questions that could be asked, about the reasonableness and propriety of his wishes. This picture ought not to find a purchaser, and I am happy to believe that it will not do so.

It is perhaps here that I may most suitably invite attention to a valuable article by Mr Nicolas Haines.[1] The reference may serve to round off all that I have said regarding the interpretation of the moral law in terms of the will or claim or right of God, brief as is Mr Haines's express discussion of our particular problem. In his article, which bears the title 'Responsibility and Accountability', Mr Haines discusses the distinction and the relation between these two concepts, and convincingly brings

---

[1] *Philosophy*, April 1955. My quotation is from p. 141. The reference to 'theological' ethics comes on p. 160.

out that the second of them, accountability, is 'by no means the whole, and for moralists not even the most significant meaning of the former, that is to say of responsibility'. Using Mr Haines's distinction, I might put my view, and if I correctly understand him Mr Haines's view also, of the theological positions I have been examining, in this way: that they are vain attempts to interpret responsibility in terms of accountability merely. If this statement is not altogether self-explanatory I hope it will send some readers to Mr Haines himself for an elucidation; and if it does so I think they will agree that it indicates, with convenient brevity, the essence of the matter.

(14)

I pass now to the third and last of the arguments I undertook to consider for the view that the nature of the moral demand is not adequately described unless the language of ethics is supplemented by that of theology. Kant spoke of the reverence that we feel in face of the moral demand, and I do not think that he overstressed or in any essential point misdescribed the experience. But it is widely held that only a person, or what at least includes the character of being personal, is a possible object of reverence. Accordingly, it is said, our experience when we are conscious of 'the moral law' is, at least implicitly, the experience of confrontation by a *personal* Holiness; that is to say, by God. The sanctity of 'the moral law' is its 'irradiation' by the sanctity of a God who is its Author.[1]

Again I must be content with the mere denial of what others, after all, merely affirm; and again I do so with the suspicion that their affirmation rests on an 'infection' of their analysis of the moral experience by theistic convictions arrived at independently. But I should add (since the contrary is, I think, sometimes strangely supposed to be true) that Kant himself gives no support,

[1] The view is too widespread for specific references to be either necessary or altogether appropriate. But it should be noted that it is to be distinguished from that represented in Rashdall's *Theory of Good and Evil*, Vol. II, p. 259. Rashdall's contention in this passage is only that reverence for a person is a stronger and more efficacious motive than reverence for the moral law, so that 'it is not easy to exaggerate the increment of emotional intensity' which the latter gains from fusion with the former. Rashdall may well be right in this, though the question of the legitimacy of the fusion is obviously not settled thereby.

even by implication, to the 'personal' reading of the object of our reverence. It is of course the case that Kant tells us that reverence or respect (Achtung) is only for persons, never for things—animals being included among things.[1] But his concern, in saying this, is with the contrast of person and thing, not with that of person and moral law. It is quite clear that as regards the relation between person and moral law he finds the explanation of our ability to reverence persons in the fact that a person can be, as it were, the law itself made manifest in an example: our reverence is strictly not for the person but for the law.[2] To find in the nature of the personal the explanation, or inner truth, of our reverence for the law is thus precisely to reverse Kant's position. Garrard may be right in thinking that what he calls 'Kant's peculiar horror of anthropomorphism'[3] would make it difficult for him anyhow to regard the opposite view with sympathy. But as one who, in some measure at least, shares this horror, I myself naturally look on it as pointing to, and safeguarding, the truth rather than as a stumbling-block and occasion of error.

Nothing that I have said is to be understood as denying (whether or not Kant denied it) that there may be a proper and distinctive reverence or respect for persons as persons that is not reducible to respect for the moral law. Whether this is so is not now the question. The relevant point at the moment is that there is a distinctive reverence for the moral law that is not reducible to reverence for a person. If we are inclined to mock at the idea of reverence for a *law* we are so, I think, because we have in mind what are more properly (i.e. literally) to be called 'laws', whereas the 'moral law' is, as I have said, 'law' only by metaphor. And we only go still further astray if, to match this first error, we deny to Kant's 'Achtung' the weight and dignity of meaning that he plainly intended that curiously mild term to possess. It is strange indeed, in the light of the third chapter of the 'Analytic

[1] *Kr. der Prakt. Vernunft*, p. 99 of the Vorländer (Felix Meiner) edition = Abbott *Kant's Theory of Ethics*, p. 169.

[2] *Op. cit.*, pp. 100–1 = Abbott, pp. 169–70. Cf. *Grundlegung*, footnote on pp. 19–20 of the Vorländer (Felix Meiner) edition = Paton, *The Moral Law*, second footnote on p. 69. England, *Kant's Conception of God*, p. 179, is sound on this point.

[3] *Duty and the Will of God*, pp. 22–3. But Kant's attitude to anthropomorphism is not one of unqualified repudiation of the use of anthropomorphic concepts. See, e.g., for a brief indication of his position, Paton, *The Categorical Imperative*, pp. 159–60.

of Pure Practical Reason', that any one should speak, in reference
to Kant, of 'the reduction of the spiritual life of mankind to the
mere respectful acceptance of a formula'.[1] We can avoid such
parodies if we will attend not to words but to experience. The
sense of an absolute obligation—call it the recognition of moral
law or not, as you please—is, as to at least part of its nature as
feeling, a reverence or respect; and moreover this is a fact, it
seems to me, behind which we cannot go. The theological language
that purports to go behind it does not really take us a single step
in that direction.

(15)

It is with all these negative conclusions in mind that I face the
question how, positively, a theist is to relate in his thought the
concepts of God and of moral law. For relate them in some way
he must. It is unsatisfactory to view the moral law as something
independent of God, and it is also unsatisfactory to view it as
dependent upon Him. What then can we say but that it *is* God?
I think it is sometimes felt that Kant made himself an object of
pity or ridicule by saying, in effect at least, just this. But whether
or not Kant is really to be interpreted so (and it is far from true
that his *words* consistently suggest it) I must confess that I can
see only one ground on which objection could fairly be made to
the use of such language; namely, if the intention of it were to
treat the terms 'God' and 'moral law' as precisely equivalent, to
assert that there is nothing in the meaning of the former that is
not included in the meaning of the latter. There is, however,
nothing at all in our argument to compel us to go so far as this,
nor do I wish to be so understood. The term 'God' may well
mean a great deal more than is meant by 'moral law' and the
more may be of the utmost significance for our lives. To say
this is to say (and I cannot be too emphatic about it) that whatever
may be the case with Kant, I at least am not claiming that
'true religion' can be reduced to 'nothing but morality', nor
even that in the sense in which it is other than morality it can
have no sort of relevance to morality. What I do affirm is simply
that, in so far as the consciousness of moral demand is considered

---

[1] Baillie, *Our Knowledge of God*, p. 158. Baillie himself treats 'Achtung' very
differently at a later point in the same work (p. 242).

F

in and by itself, 'God' can mean nothing different from 'moral law', and that the theological term renames without elucidating. We understand what the new name means through understanding the meaning of the non-theological expression; that is to say, the moral experience in its very character as moral is, as I have earlier suggested,[1] an *index* to what we mean by 'God'. This, I repeat, is very different from saying that our thought about God throws light upon our moral experience.

My position here is of course quite consistent with holding that in another sense moral experience *is* illuminated by religion. If, as I believe, there is a legitimate overplus of meaning attaching to the term 'God', additional to what is signified by 'moral law' or 'moral demand', it will derive from elements or 'moments' in experience other than that of confrontation by the moral demand itself; what may be termed the 'objective correlate' of these other 'moments' being supposed (and, let us assume, correctly supposed) to be somehow ontologically one with the moral law, one that is to say with the very same Being to which we also refer under the name of 'moral law'. It seems proper to claim that in a sense the moral law would be illuminated if it were rightly seen as an aspect of this richer totality of Divine Being and were not considered simply in and by itself. And a theologian might perhaps say that illumination in this sense, by lateral enrichment, so to call it, and not by vertical grounding, is all that he ever looked for. It may be so: but if it is so, the fact is certainly not faithfully reflected in the theological interpretations of morality that are commonly put forward. These seem to me at best to waver between identifying the moral law with God and deriving it from Him; to waver in a way that would not be possible if the point I have been endeavouring to make had really been grasped. We must altogether repudiate the language of derivation. And theology as well as ethics has, I believe, an interest in this. For whatever degree of validity the concept of personality may possess as 'a way of thinking God', mere anthropomorphism must be held in with bit and bridle. But anthropomorphism is on the contrary ridden with a very loose rein in all speculation that would go behind the moral law and seek a source for it in a Being other than itself.

[1] See above, p. 64.

(16)

It will be recalled that I drew a distinction between the problem
of giving an account of the authority of the moral demand (its
formal aspect) and the problem of giving an account of the
'objective order of values' that was, in my view, implied in the
content of this demand (its material aspect).[1] In the end, I said,
these problems may coalesce, but *prima facie* they are different
problems; and hitherto we have been engaged only with the
first of them. I turn now to the second problem, and the view
I am to discuss in connection with it may again be described
as 'aetiological'. Its broad character is conveniently indicated
in words taken from a religious article addressed to the general
reader which appeared some years ago. 'Values are real because
God is real. Truth and justice, fidelity and mercy, are not insubstantial "ideals". They are grounded in the nature of God
Himself.'[2]

A minor question of interpretation arises in regard to this
passage. It is not altogether clear whether 'ideals' and 'values'
are here being used as equivalent terms, two words with one
and the same meaning, the point then being that whichever
term we use we are speaking of something that must be described
as quite insubstantial if it is considered in abstraction from God's
nature: or whether, though 'values' and 'ideals' do indeed have
the same *reference*, that to which they refer is properly called
'value' only when considered as having 'substance' or real being
through its being 'grounded' in God, so that to speak of 'insubstantial "ideals"' is an innocent pleonasm: or whether, finally,
'values' and 'ideals' refer to two quite different sorts of things of
which only those of the first sort possess, through God, what
can be called 'substantial being'. But whatever precisely the
author of the article may have intended (and I am inclined to
think that the second interpretation best catches the derogatory
tone in which he speaks of ideals) it is, in my view, the third
position that comes nearest to the truth, though still falling short
of it. Ideals and values really are, I suggest, two different sorts
of things: or, since I cannot pretend that in ordinary speech the
words 'ideal' and 'value' are employed with any such exactitude,

[1] See above, p. 55.   [2] *The Times*, November 7, 1953.

it might be better to say that there are two different sorts of
things which these two terms may very suitably be used to discriminate, and I shall so use them here. Of values as thus distinguished from ideals it may quite intelligibly be said that they
do have a substantial being which ideals lack, although even
ideals are still not insubstantial in any sense that creates an
ontological problem. But this 'substantiality' of values is, I
should hold, intrinsic to them; they can quite properly be thought
of as 'self-supporting', and cannot indeed be helpfully envisaged
in any other way. I must now elaborate this contention, beginning
with the distinction between values and ideals.

When we speak of an ideal, what we are referring to may,
quite properly, be some more or less defined picture in our mind's
eye of an individual situation thought capable, and deserving, of
realization: or at least (for this use of 'ideal' is also legitimate
and even necessary) capable and deserving of partial and approximate realization. This is what I propose to mean by the word in
the present context. It is important to stress that the picture
may be very indefinite indeed without ceasing to be a picture of
an individual situation on that account; and in no case will it be
precise and determinate in every detail in advance of the ideal's
realization. Now ideals, in this sense, are just as much and just
as little 'insubstantial' as are our imaginations generally. That
is to say, they will appear so in a vicious and disturbing way
only if we try to treat the content of our thought, taken apart
from our thinking it, as a being in itself; in Cartesian terms, if we
abstract the 'objective' reality of an idea from its 'formal' reality
and then speak as though the 'objective' reality itself were a
'formal' reality. Certainly if we do take the content of an idea
in abstraction from its actual being as psychological occurrence
and then suppose it to claim for itself the status of actual being,
our verdict must be that the claim fails. And if we are misguided
enough to go through this procedure seriously we can only end
by feeling that we are up against a puzzling wraith-like entity.
But the recipe for avoiding being worried is simple: it is merely
that we should refrain from making these contradictory moves.

But although these individualized, pictorial ideals are not in
any vicious sense insubstantial, they are none the less dependent,
even considered in their full being not as pictures but as pictur-
ings, on a reality other than themselves. I mean by this not simply

that as occurrences they have causes and that as representations they refer beyond themselves to some actual or possible counterpart, all of which is true of every imagining. I mean that in their distinctive and specific character as being *ideal*-imaginings they presuppose a different order of being, that of *values*. What gives them the mandatory character for us that the term 'ideal', as contrasted with the neutral term 'project', conveys is that they picture, or are thought to picture, a situation that somehow 'incarnates' in the living tissue of historical process certain values that in different modes and measures may over and over again be thus 'incarnated' without their potentialities being thereby exhausted. Platonic idioms, however inadequate in the end, are here almost unavoidable at the beginning. 'Mercy' and 'Truth', we know, are not names of historical particulars; but neither, in so far as they belong to the language of value, are they names merely of certain aspects or features of these. Nor again are they just ways of referring to the whole class (whatever 'whole' could signify) of those particulars whose possession of these characters is the basis of our classification. Our articulate understanding of what such valuational words mean, and most generally of the word 'goodness',[1] may come only by reflection on particular instances. But we *refer* this meaning, as perhaps we should not do with factual abstractions like 'redness' or 'painfulness', to something other than the instances. We refer it, I should say, to that which, through the imperfect mediation of our thought, is the inexhaustible source and control of our ability to construct the concrete 'picture-ideals', whose realization, if and as they are realized, can then be spoken of as good. It is, I suggest, this source and control of our ideal-framing activity that should be described as an 'order of values', in distinction from a 'set of ideals'. Whatever force there may be in recent criticisms of the language of 'non-natural qualities' as a way of stating the truth about what we call moral judgment or value judgment, there is I think a yet more fundamental complaint that might be made both against that doctrine and against at least very many of its critics. It could be complained that they concentrate attention

[1] It is arguable that instead of an 'order of values' I should speak *only* of 'goodness', the specific *modes* of this being even at their most general not 'value' but schematic forms of the 'valuable', into the very constitution of which factual elements already enter. But I do not think it essential to my exposition to insist on this.

too exclusively on formulated ideals and on actual achievements, and are insufficiently concerned with the nature of our power to create ideals; a power in the exercise of which we may, I believe, be justly described, in Shelley's words, as 'the hierophants of an unapprehended inspiration'. An order of values, I am maintaining, is implied in any genuine and valid exercise of this power; in any exercise of it, that is to say, that, unlike the arbitrary work of fancy, yields designs for living that are not just indifferently contemplated, nor even simply attractive, but are, whether attractive or not, *authoritative* for us. And the real point of the theological view I am considering is this: that these values which I have distinguished from ideals, and which in a manner of speaking give ideals *their* substance, are themselves, by themselves, *without* substance and are real only as being 'grounded in the nature of God'.

(17)

But what are we to mean by 'grounded in the nature of God?' Suppose, as is plainly the intention, that we are to think of God as a Person, two possibilities then seem open to us.[1] The first is that values are to be identified with the content of the divine purpose (the divine thought, that is, conceived as purposive), our several ideals being our various and successive, but not necessarily successful, interpretations of this purpose as it bears on the various and successive situations of history. This is as much as to say that values are to be distinguished from human ideals but identified with a divine ideal. Now if the view we are considering really holds that ideals as such are 'mere' and 'insubstantial', it might be asked how the identification of values with even a *divine* ideal could accord them substantiality; unless it be combined with such insistence on the disparity between divine and human purposes as will empty the language of purpose of all its meaning in the case of the former, and thereby frustrate

[1] These alternatives are not always clearly distinguished by those who adopt this general line of thought. Thus in Rashdall, *Theory of Good and Evil*, Vol. II, pp. 211–13, the language on the whole is that of the first alternative but the thought, I am inclined to believe, is as much, or more, that of the second. I feel something of the same uncertainty about the interpretation of Sorley's position in his *Moral Values and the Idea of God* and of Ewing's remarks in his 'Ethics and Belief in God'. (See pp. 386–8 of *Hibbert Journal*, XXXIX, 1940–1.)

our attempt at explanation in a different but no less effective manner. But more important, because not simply an *ad hominem* argument, is my second point. This is that the proposal in any case lies open to the very same objections as have already been encountered in connection with the derivation of moral authority from the will of God. The propriety, or enlightenment, of a human purpose, on the view now being offered us, has to be defined in terms of its conformity with the purpose of God: but as regards God Himself we must say either that His purpose has to be thought of as 'blind'—what we call 'values' being no more than its *de facto* content—or else (and quite unintelligibly) that His understanding, which 'gives eyes' to His purpose, is creative of values as its 'objects' in its very nature as understanding.[1]

The truth is that it is impossible to treat values as in any way a dependent function of any purpose whatsoever. It is perhaps worth reflecting at this point on the problem of the status of values in the Sartrian form of existentialism. What Sartre does, in effect, is just to take the concept of God as creator of values and, as an atheist, to transfer it to the human individual. 'If I have excluded God the Father, there must be somebody to invent values.'[2] What can we say of this but that it is simply a misleading way of denying values altogether? For though it is sensible enough to speak of 'making a *valuation*' it is as absurd and incomprehensible to talk of 'inventing a *value*' as it is to talk of 'inventing a truth'. Theists, I have no doubt, would agree on the absurdity of Sartre's humanist 'value-theory'. But with what right can they do so and at the same time offer as a substitute for it what is only another, a theological, version of the very same story? If there really are to be values at all we must represent them as independent of all actual purposes, though implied as the objective control and standard for those purposes.

The second way in which values might be taken to be 'grounded in the nature of God'—and it is, I think, what the use of the word 'nature' more readily suggests—would be this: that values in their being as values constitute the *character* of God. He possesses, fully and exhaustively, that goodness, in all its modes, that we endeavour by the pursuit of our fragmentary and distorted ideals to realize in historical process. The merit of this view as

[1] Compare pp. 66–70 above.
[2] *Existentialism and Humanism*, p. 54.

compared with the former is that character, unlike the content of a thought, does not involve in the very concept of it a reference to an order of being beyond its own. There is therefore, at first glance, nothing unintelligible in the suggestion that values *are* God's nature and not something different from and implied by it.

Nevertheless this is no more than the first look of the doctrine, and on closer inspection it too reveals a fatal flaw. The objection to which it lies open has been indicated in words once used by Professor J. N. Findlay which are worth repeating here.[1] 'I don't like to attribute *existence*', Professor Findlay observed, 'to the ideal[2] in terms of which my life and action tends to be organized. For by an existent *numen* I can at best understand a *particular case or instance* of worshipful properties. . . . Now it seems to me that such an existent *numen* would be worshipful only *on account of* the properties it manifested, and *to the extent* that it manifested them, which means that it wouldn't really be worshipful *in its own right*, and so not really be a *numen* at all.' I take Professor Findlay to be supposing that nothing but 'concrete' individuals can properly be said to be, that whatever has real being at all must have it in that mode. (No distinction between 'being' and 'existence' seems to be in his mind.) This supposition is, in my view, a mistaken one, but I do not think Findlay is mistaken about the consequences that flow from making it. If you do attempt to envisage your *numen* as an individual you will find that the attempt fails, and that the real *numen*, if there is to be a real *numen* at all, will have to be 'located' elsewhere, and defined in terms of the *properties* of the original alleged *numen*. Now this is just what happens if we represent God as being personal, with values as His 'character', for persons are individual existents. We shall be representing Him not as *being* the order of values but as fully and perfectly *exemplifying* it. He will be, so to say, the Great Exemplar, so that the spiritual striving of men could very properly be described as a ὁμοίωσις τῷ θεῷ, a becoming like God so far as we can. But the order of values as such if (as I and my theistic opponents, unlike Findlay, would maintain) it is

---

[1] *University*, Vol. I, p. 98. Cf. Findlay's papers in *Mind*, Vols. LVII–LVIII (1948–9), reprinted in *New Essays in Philosophical Theology* (ed. Flew and MacIntyre).

[2] Findlay of course is not distinguishing, as I have done, 'ideal' and 'value'. 'Ideal' here must be understood as having something of the force of both my terms.

to be allowed objective reality at all, must still be said to have being, in its own characteristic mode of being, as something other than and apart from Him, and it, rather than He, will be the true Deity.

The dualism and the tension in such a view as this are unmistakably Platonic. And if both sides of it, both the order of values and the perfect existent, are alike insisted on and alike to be regarded as divine, we must no doubt try to achieve some sort of integration of the two. This, we might say, is the distinctive problem of theism properly so called and therewith of Christian theology in its general character as theistic and apart from its special trinitarian features.[1] A verbal formula for such integration might be that which speaks of God not as good but as self-existent Goodness, holding that in 'Him' essence and existence are one. Although I cannot claim that in my own case any positive understanding attends the use of such language I can admit that one might feel driven to employ it. But what it is important to observe is that the employment of it is really a way of suggesting that values are after all to be conceived as somehow substantial in their very being as values, rather than a way of explaining how values which, as mere values, are 'flimsy' can be provided with a sort of 'solidity' with the help of an extrinsic ontological backing. It is the pretence of doing the latter that has been the target of my criticism, the pretence that values themselves can be taken for something less than Deity and that they then both must and can be given a 'ground' of such sort as would be properly described in terms of an independent, and personalistic, concept of God. We may say if we wish (and, if we are to use theological language at all, I think we must say it) that the order of values *is* God.[2] But we must be clear that to say this is not to interpret the meaning of 'order of values' but once again to suggest a meaning for the term 'God'. If theistic beliefs otherwise acquired throw any light on the concept of an order of values it will be, as I put it before, by a sort of lateral, not a vertical, illumination.

[1] See C. C. J. Webb, *God and Personality*, Lecture IX, pp. 234–40, where the point is made with express reference to Plato. I differ from Webb in so far as he maintains that impersonal Goodness is inherently 'incomplete and abstract'. The motive to integration in my case would be not this but simply the unsatisfactoriness of the dualism as such.

[2] So Fichte, as quoted by Sorley, *Moral Values and the Idea of God*, p. 351.

(18)

Many will doubtless still feel that something for which we can find no better designation than 'the order of values' must be of too thin and shadowy a nature to rival, let alone surpass, in 'ontological solidity', such things as houses or trees or atoms or human beings. They may then be moved, like Professor Findlay (in the continuation of the passage from which I have quoted), to reject the notion outright and to maintain instead simply 'that there really *is* a deep-set *trend* or *nisus* in the things of this world towards a consummation which could properly be called worshipful or numinous if it ever could be brought to pass'. Professor Findlay adds, 'If anyone cares to say that this involves believing in God the Holy Spirit, I should not deny that it did. Such a faith seems to me to sustain one's courage (to the extent that one has a right to demand that it should be sustained)[1] while providing one also with an inexhaustible object of aspiration, something which κινεῖ ὡς ἐρώμενον precisely because it is free from the one-sidedness and particularity of existence.'

I have a use, as will appear in due course, for the κινεῖ ὡς ἐρώμενον formula, the concept of that which moves us as an object of our love, in my own account of moral endeavour. But I do not think Professor Findlay's version will quite do. The 'trend' or 'nisus' he speaks of must be a cosmic one, no mere idiosyncrasy of the individual. This is clearly Professor Findlay's meaning, but in any case it would not even be plausible, on any other terms, to claim that the 'nisus' can give objectivity to our purposes in a sense that contrasts with the subjectivism of such a position as Sartre's. Grant, then, this cosmic 'nisus': but are we to conceive of it as authority for, or as constraint upon, or (like 'the force that through the green fuse drives the flower') as the indwelling or constitutive energy of the individual human will? It may seem so obvious that Professor Findlay means the last of these that the question is hardly worth asking. But in that case, whatever story we tell about the emergence of a *sense* of obligation, must not obligation itself be analysed in terms of *power*? And if nevertheless in the business of living a man represents this compulsiveness of the cosmic 'nisus' as moral *authority*, must we not say, from

[1] One would like to know what account Professor Findlay would give of this 'right'.

the standpoint of the view here supposed, that the representation is mistaken? If men cannot help representing it thus the illusion from which they suffer may be called transcendental illusion, but it will be none the less illusion for that. The fact is that what, whether deludedly or not, we mean by authority in morals cannot be stated in terms of power, even if the power be cosmic.

If what is distinctively moral experience is not thus to be falsified or negated the significant thing about the cosmic 'nisus' must be not that it *is* but, so to say, that it *is as it ought to be*. But to use language of this sort is to treat the nature of the 'nisus', specified in terms of its *de facto* direction, as the functional equivalent in the 'nisus'-theory of what, in an orthodox theistic view, would be the content of a Divine will, authoritative not as willed but as content. And is not this as much as to say that, in any form in which it leaves the reality of moral experience unimpaired, the 'nisus'-theory is open to the same objection to which the theological theory it replaces was exposed? We can no more avoid a reference to an order of values independent of the *de facto* direction of the 'nisus' than we could avoid a reference to an order of values independent of the actual divine purpose. In one respect, indeed, our position might be said to be even worse than on the theistic alternative; for as Professor Findlay's own language indicates, we shall be here and now without a real object of our worship at all; the subject of the κινεῖ in Professor Findlay's κινεῖ ὡς ἐρώμενον has simply no actual being whatsoever. And certainly this strikes me as a most unsatisfactory feature of the view. It would, however, be unfair to censure it as retrogression, so far as the life of religion is concerned, if it be the case that the 'actual being' of orthodox theism, though actual, is not truly worshipful.[1]

I readily concede that to speak of an order of values is not to carry our thought to a point at which it may complacently rest. The concept is obscure and problematic in the highest degree. It challenges further enquiry which, if fruitful, might alter our language and thought almost beyond recognition—I wish I

[1] I hope it will not be thought that I have been unjust to Professor Findlay in giving such prominence to a short article not designed for a professional philosophical journal, and not perhaps as carefully worded as an article so designed would have been. But I have done so *honoris causa*. Disagreement is here very far from disrespect: the article seems to me a most valuable one.

knew whether and how. But in default of this enquiry, in which I cannot claim to have made any headway myself, it appears to me that we can neither dispense with the concept—it must be taken as having anyhow a provisional validity—nor yet relate values in any helpful way to some other Being supposedly more fundamental. The beginning of wisdom may here lie simply in getting used to the concept of values as a concept of what *is*, though not as temporal existents are.[1] It may no doubt take some getting used to. We perhaps all suffer from an initial prejudice in favour of 'matter of fact' as the paradigm of the real. And this prejudice may assert itself even in those who try to cast it off, in the form of an interpretation of the reality that is *not* 'matter of fact' as though it were 'matter of fact' with a (somehow) ontologically different 'locus'. Again (to take up a point already touched on), we may have a positive bias against the view that values are independently real, springing from a mistaken belief that what people call 'values', if they have any being distinct from 'valuations' at all, can only be a sort of qualities—'non-natural' qualities.[2] Even those who do not blench at the very concept of 'non-natural qualities' would reasonably object to the idea that qualities could somehow exist on their own and as it were 'floating in the void', in abstraction from what they qualify. This would be too much like asking us to take seriously the Cheshire Cat's grin, or that Worried Look of Mr Abney's (in Mr Wodehouse's story)—'To say that Mr Abney wore it would be to create a false impression. Mr Abney simply followed in its wake.' Surely in real life value-qualities, like worried looks, need a wearer? But values, I must repeat, are not themselves qualities (of acts or situations) even though they are the condition of our ability to use language about acts and situations that suggests that that is precisely what they are. The order of values lies, so to say, behind all value-*qualities*; but we can specify nothing that lies behind it in its turn.[3]

[1] Cf. Plato's remark about the 'battle of Gods and Giants' (*Sophist*, 246A).

[2] I think this mistake underlies, for example, the contention of 'Logician' in Professor A. N. Prior's paper 'Can Religion be discussed?' See *New Essays in Philosophical Theology* (ed. Flew and MacIntyre), p. 5.

[3] For the question whether on this view we might not equally well postulate an 'order of *dis*values' see Note B in the Appendix.

(19)

It may be as well, before leaving this topic, to deal briefly and parenthetically with one possible misconception of the hypothesis of an objective order of values. It might perhaps be supposed that this hypothesis is equivalent to or entails the hypothesis that the universe is friendly to moral purpose in a sense that goes beyond the jejune one in which I earlier allowed this 'friendliness' to be an empirical fact.[1] This, however, is not the case. Naturally there is a harmony between our moral purposes, supposing them to be fully enlightened, and the order of values itself; but this is a merely analytic truth, for 'enlightened purpose' is to be *defined* in terms of this harmony. And the order of values is anyhow not the same thing as the universe. It is of course possible that if we were able to work out an adequate ontology of value it would be found to carry with it an acknowledgment of the friendliness of the universe in the richer sense desiderated, but nothing in our argument as so far developed entitles us either to affirm or to deny that this is so. At the point that the argument has reached, and at which I have perforce halted it, the supposition that there are objective values is perfectly compatible with the admission that the attempt to 'realize' them in historical process may be doomed to frustration by the other forces at work in the world, up to any extent to which experience does not show the contrary.

(20)

I conclude this part of my discussion with a simple reiteration of its central contention. Moral experience in the form of our consciousness of moral demand (the awareness of categorical obligation, with the valuations inseparable therefrom) does indeed, I believe, in opposition to the tendency of much recent ethical thinking, require for its interpretation reference to an order of being other than the natural, or matter-of-fact, order of spatio-temporal existence. Again, the quality of the experience itself may be such that we cannot adequately and convincingly describe it except in language of a religious character, language that has a quality, a 'timbre', at least akin to that of the language

[1] See above, p. 60.

in which religion speaks of God. But all this belongs properly to
moral experience in its nature as moral. This is not to say, nor do
I in fact believe, that religion can be replaced by, or reduced to,
morality; it is simply to say that the moral consciousness itself
is, as such, already a mode of religious consciousness. But, in so
far at least as we restrict our attention, as I have been restricting
it, to the awareness of moral demand, I cannot find that the
introduction of the theistic concept of God as personal does
anything to explain or validate this moral consciousness—does
anything at all, indeed, save create difficulties. It is the moral
experience that interprets to us (that is to say, that contributes to
the interpretation of) the term 'God', not the other way round.
And the God to which it testifies (as consciousness, I repeat,
merely of moral demand) is a God that not only need not but
cannot be conceived under the form of a person.

Such is the contention. But now I must add a footnote to it,
which some will think to be long overdue and to be worth more than
all that has gone before. I have to acknowledge that it can be
objected to me that I have spoken throughout as though there
were no middle way between simple anthropomorphism and the
sheer denial of divine personality, whereas in fact theism properly
understood takes just such a middle way, and would actually
repudiate mere anthropomorphism as idolatrous. Does not this
admission gravely, even fatally, affect the point and cogency of
my criticisms? The objection is well-conceived and of crucial
importance. It is not because I underrate it that I have taken no
notice of it hitherto. But, believing as I do that such force as it
has does not in fact rob my arguments of their relevance, I have
thought it reasonable, and also in the end clearer, to put these
arguments forward as though the objection did not exist. At a
later stage I shall, of course, endeavour to explain what I conceive
to be the fundamental weakness of the objection. But meantime I
must content myself with the bare mention of it and impose on
my readers likewise a further discipline of patience. I have
first to consider our response to the moral demand and the relevance of theology to the interpretation of that other aspect of
moral experience.

CHAPTER IV

THE MORAL RESPONSE

(1)

In my account of our awareness of moral demand I have taken that element in our consciousness in abstraction from other elements from which it cannot, in a living experience, be actually severed. What I am now to say about our response to that demand will depend on a like, and essentially complementary, abstraction. Just as I defined moral demand in terms of our sense of an absolute claim upon us to do our duty, so now I define moral response in terms of dutifulness, of the willing acceptance, in the practical determination of action, of what duty requires. In what follows, then, we shall be considering the nature and conditions of dutifulness, and essentially nothing more than that.

Of course (the familiar distinction meets us again) what is in one sense required of us may in another sense not be required of us at all—may indeed even be morally prohibited. Whatever difficulties may attach to the concept of 'the objectively right act', at least we must allow its validity in some sense that is compatible with the significance of everyday talk about 'mistaking our duty'. It is certainly the case that, in one meaning of 'duty', we can mistake our duty; and even the most conscientious action, if thus mistaken, is in some sort to be disapproved, as not being without qualification what it ought to be. If there is any duty that we cannot mistake it is surely just the duty, peculiar in status and importance and pervasive of the whole moral life, to endeavour to avoid the all too possible errors, to *inform* ourselves about the facts relevant to any decision we have to take and to *enlighten* our consciences. Whatever precisely this means it undoubtedly means something. But then it has to be added that the endeavour at self-instruction and self-enlightenment is itself one that may be prosecuted unsatisfactorily; and this not only in the sense that 'we didn't take it seriously' but also in the sense that, though we did take it seriously, though we honestly tried to carry it through satisfactorily, in fact we did badly at it. Our retrospective verdicts —'How silly I was! How ignorant! How unperceptive!'—frequently admit this. And since in regard to self-instruction and self-enlightenment it is not in mortals to command success, we have to allow that in an important sense success cannot be required of them. In an important sense nothing can ever be required of them beyond the sincerity of the *endeavour*, first, to determine what it is that (in the objective sense) they ought to do, and then to do it. Which brings us back to the definition of the moral response in terms of dutifulness simply.

Not that dutifulness could ever constitute the whole of any response to the challenge of circumstance for a creature of desires and affections such as man is; nor need it even be all that is commendable in it. That is not my view. What I do say is that dutifulness constitutes a factor of so distinctive and central a nature and worth in the life of a good man that it deserves to be singled out and characterized, in contrast with the remainder, as being peculiarly and strictly the moral element in his conduct. But since even this position may be contested it will be well to say something further at the outset by way of explanation and defence.[1]

(2)

It appears to be widely felt that an ethics that thus concentrates on dutifulness is misguided. Even allowing for the qualifications I have hinted at it is still true (many people would say) that such a view provides a picture of the moral man that is at once unlike-able and wildly unlike our actual experience. It represents the moral life as a grim kill-joy affair, a continual self-conscious battle with temptation. Surely this is neither truth of fact nor acceptable ideal?

I feel bound to say that some of those whose reactions are of this type seem to me merely to want their virtue cheap. The very proper insistence that any moral theory worth ink and paper must take full account of human nature as it *is* too easily degenerates into a failure to pay that regard to the meaning of '*ought*' without which there is no moral theory at all. None the less I fully sympathize with the revulsion these critics experience when they

---

[1] I here take up and develop rather more fully, as I undertook to do, a point already touched on at p. 51 above.

contemplate the image that they themselves conjure up; and if I do not agree with their criticism it is because I think it founded on misconception.

In the first place let us be clear about this; that to insist on dutifulness is not in itself to say anything as to what our specific duties are. Accordingly it carries no implication that they must be such as will involve a bleak repressiveness, a constant thwarting of natural impulse. If a man supposes that they do involve this it will, I should myself hold, not be simply because he takes duty seriously but because he mistakes what it is that duty requires of him. Another man who took duty quite as seriously might recognize that not only does this not require that we should live in an atmosphere of penal servitude but it even requires that we should see to it that we do not. To rule out all happy spontaneity from life in the effort to make sure of the correctness of our conduct is to be guilty of a bigger mistake than any we are seeking to avoid; and a fussy and over-anxious moral 'map-reading' every few paces in life's journey is a neurosis of the spirit and not health. A footnote in Bradley's *Ethical Studies*, whether or not we approve the precise terms of it, surely represents the sane attitude. 'It is right and a duty that the sphere of indifferent detail should exist. It is a duty that I should develop my nature by private choice therein. Therefore, *because* this is a duty, it is a duty *not* to make a duty of every detail.'[1] Let us then, for a start, rid ourselves of the error of supposing that to insist on the importance, even the supreme importance, of dutifulness is the same thing as to recommend a *code* of indefensible austerity. The identification of 'being morally good' with 'being dutiful' commits us to no particular code.

And now as regards this identification itself it must be noted that to speak of a man as 'deciding to do his duty' does not signify that he must have the *word* 'duty' on his tongue, or in his mind. All sorts of more specific expressions, even some whose primary force may seem purely descriptive, will serve: 'Decency demands . . .', 'It would be sheer cowardice not to . . .', 'I should be ashamed of myself if . . .', and so forth; including a host of quite undignified colloquialisms. All that is necessary is that such expressions should be felt to have the force of prescriptions that run counter to my doing 'just as I please'.

But, again (and this is really to come back to my first point),

[1] Bradley, *Ethical Studies* (second edition), p. 216.

G

this does not mean that I must feel constrained to do something *materially* different from what I should do if I acted just as I pleased. The essential opposition is not that of two materially diverse courses of action but that of two sorts of considerations by either of which one's course of action might be determined. In the one case the question taken to be relevant is that of the action's moral propriety, in the other case the question is whether or not it is what I want to do. Naturally a man may quite well want to do, independently of any thought of its propriety, the very same thing that he would also judge it proper to do. In that case he is fortunate in his nature or circumstances, or in both. Yet his good fortune surely does not include, or entail, his forfeiture (*pro hac vice*, so to say) of the status of a moral agent. And if we ask what it is that constitutes his continuing possession of the status must we not say that it is his still 'having a conscience', in the sense that he still thinks in terms of right and wrong, that the question of propriety is somehow still 'alive' for him? But if this question is 'alive', then the man's action is approvable (where it is approvable) not because conscience (falsely supposed dumb) has nothing to do with the matter, still less despite the fact that it was unattended to, but only because the man has waited if not on its command at least on its *nihil obstat*, its permission. And this too is dutifulness.

But is it? Here I must pause for a moment to comment on the distinction that I have just indicated in the words 'if not its command at least its permission'. The point is, of course, that while whatever is wrong is morally prohibited not all that is right is morally commanded, or duty. In fact, 'right', except when used with the definite article, may signify only 'quite all right', a meaning very different from the meaning of 'duty'; and while what is duty must fall within the field of action thus defined it occupies only a part of that field. Now, it may be said, I am supposed to be concerning myself only with what is actually duty and with our response to that; for only there is dutifulness to be found—this being true by definition. The reference to 'permission' that I have brought in in so unemphatic a manner is therefore at best superfluous. But, since the distinction in question is not really an unimportant one, it may be suspected that to speak as casually as I have done betrays an insufficient regard for its significance and is nothing so innocent as mere superfluity. On

the contrary, the complaint may run, I have used the reference
to 'permission' to introduce an illicit extension of the concept of
dutiful action, an extension without which my general position
would not be tenable.

It may be true that I do tend to attach less importance than I
should to the distinction between what is morally commanded and
what is morally allowable merely. I do not know. But on the issue
that is vital in the present context, whether I am improperly
stretching the concept of dutiful action, I claim to be not guilty.
I do not press the question whether there is in fact very much
material, as distinct from *formal* difference between what is right
and what is obligatory;[1] that question does not go to the heart
of the matter anyhow. But I should insist that simply to ask
whether an act is even morally permissible, as a condition of our
licensing ourselves to perform it, is itself a form of morally
responsible action that is not something permitted us merely,
but something enjoined. There is, after all, a duty to avoid wrong-
doing (in the sense in which we speak in general terms of 'justice',
for example, and not specifically of 'A's keeping his bargain *x*
with B' as a duty). Indeed this negative duty of avoidance is in a
sense more fundamental than any features of the moral demand
that can by contrast be called positive, just as, and because,
there is a sort of logical priority attaching to the distinction
between right and wrong as compared with any distinctions we
draw within either of these categories. But if there is a *duty* to
avoid wrong-doing there is correspondingly a *duty* to satisfy
ourselves, so far as we can, that in pursuing a certain course we
shall not be doing wrong. Thus, as I have said, to have the
permission of conscience is itself moral *requirement*, and it is in a
perfectly proper sense of the words that a man may be described
as acting conscientiously or being dutiful who waits for this
permission and thereby, and only thereby, fulfils the requirement.

But (it is by now urgently necessary to stress) the awareness
that conscience commands or at least permits an act need be no
articulate foreground awareness. (It is more especially apt not
to be so in cases of permission merely.) The distinction between

---

[1] Put otherwise, is the sphere of the *per se* morally indifferent ('*per se*' as
contrasted with '*deemed* to be so', on the Bradleian principle mentioned earlier)
a wide and important one or not? This can be debated; though my own inclina-
tion is to agree with (for example) Ross in thinking that it is not.

foreground and background awareness is no doubt a tricky one and raises a number of difficulties. But it does not seem to me open to question that it is valid in the sense that there may be much *in* our thought *to* which we are not expressly attending, although there is of course no more a clean-cut contrast here than in the case of the difference between warm and hot. We may surely say, for example, that a man thinkingly avoids the fallacy of 'undistributed middle'—that is, he is thinking *in* avoiding it— without being thereby committed to the view that, like a self-conscious logician, he was thinking *about* that fallacy and the need to avoid it. Similarly, I suggest, genuine moral thinking, operative thinking in terms of right and wrong, could yet be a background thinking, the thinker not being reflexively conscious of himself as morally aware: although if the moral awareness is there at all it may be trusted (in the absence of insincerity and self-sophistication) to become of itself foreground awareness when, and to the extent that, the temptations of a particular situation require it to do so. But if at any time, and I suppose that in our lives as biological organisms there are many such times, there is not even a background thinking in terms of right and wrong, I really cannot see how it is possible to attribute to a man as he is at that time the status of a moral agent at all.

It is along lines such as these that I should seek to defend the view that conscientiousness or dutifulness is the essence of morally approvable action, in no artificially restricted meaning of the expression 'morally approvable'. It is a defence that involves no denial of the obvious fact that an acute and impressive sense of duty is, in normal experience, a very spasmodic phenomenon, and one, be it noted, whose rarity might quite as well reflect a man's goodness as his degradation. I add, however, that spasmodic in ordinary life though this acute consciousness may be, reflection, I believe, can always generate it.

(3)

But the moral response is not only the dutiful response: it is the *freely* dutiful response. Not that it could be dutiful at all on any other terms; but still the point deserves emphasis. For I must make it clear that the freedom I here mean is that of what is called 'libertarian' doctrine. The contention is that the man who makes his dutiful decision could have failed to make it without there being any reason, in the sense of *causal explanation*, for his failure, and that the man who neglects his duty could have conformed his will to it, in a similarly unqualified meaning of 'could'; in neither case do we have to postulate some antecedent change in his circumstances or in himself. To assert freedom in this sense is of course to assert what would be widely denied; but I do not propose to argue the matter on this occasion. Plenty of argument has been offered by others elsewhere, and by no one more forcibly and persistently than by Professor C. A. Campbell in our own day.[1] In any event Christian thinking, with which I am primarily concerned, has been in general ready enough to give a great deal of serious attention to this position, though certainly it has not always clearly defined it or in the end upheld it. The libertarian view is implicit, for example, in certain attempted solutions of the problem of evil, as a recent criticism of these by Professor Antony Flew sufficiently indicates.[2] Professor Flew considers these attempts ineffective precisely *because* they rely on a libertarian conception of freedom, which he himself rejects. The libertarian view is implicit also in the difficulties theologians have found in some of their own concepts, such as those of predestination and foreknowledge and (which concerns me more nearly) grace. The solutions would not be plausible nor would the difficulties even appear to be baffling unless ideas of a libertarian character were at least silently operative.

(4)

There is, however, something more I must say about our moral freedom before turning to the theological issue. I must emphasize that this freedom is at once a deep and a narrow thing. It may be called deep in that it operates (if the metaphor is permissible) below the 'crust' of phenomenal process, of 'nature' conceived as an

[1] But see further Note C in the Appendix. For Professor Campbell's views see particularly his *In Defence of Free Will*: also, 'The Psychology of Effort of Will', *Proc. Ar. Soc.* Vol. XL (1939–40); 'Is "Freewill" a Pseudo-Problem?' (*Mind*, October 1951); *On Selfhood and Godhood*, Lecture IX and Appendix B.

[2] In his paper 'Divine Omnipotence and Human Freedom' in *New Essays in Philosophical Theology* (ed. Flew and MacIntyre). For a succinct statement see p. 153, the passage beginning 'If it really is logically possible . . .'

interacting system of 'things' whose coming to be and passing away, or the succession of whose states as they endure, is the concern of 'natural' science. Of this system our perceptual consciousness (taken in a very forced abstraction from our active participation in the system's ongoing) might be said to give us a surface-view. In our consciousness of ourselves as actively participating, on the other hand, we become aware, one might say, of the system's third dimension; but, if we abstract from our *moral* experience, it might still be the same order of nature as that which we sensibly perceive. Only in the freedom that goes to constitute moral experience do we break right through this 'crust', and our activity at this level eludes the categories of natural science altogether. The distinction between determinist and libertarian accounts of moral action might, I think, fairly be put in the form that the determinist simply denies this, literally, '*praeter*-natural' (but in no way abnormal) level of action, reducing it to no more than a special case of our participation in natural process.

Our moral freedom thus has a metaphysical depth such that no man can have a living sense of it, as distinct from a mere intellectual acceptance of the proposition that asserts it, without a shuddering like that which marks the presence of the numinous. But moral freedom is also narrow in its scope; and this is the aspect that requires more to be stressed in the present context. And here, before I proceed, let me parenthetically observe that I propose to speak quite freely of 'willing', of the 'will' and its 'acts', despite the suspicion and dislike of such language that reigns in some quarters. Not that I suppose the will to be a 'thing', or even a 'faculty' in some mysterious sense that might be thought to explain, and not simply to signify, the plain fact that we make decisions, and with more or less steadiness and effort hold to them and persist in the execution of them. But the terminology provides a natural and, I am convinced, essentially innocent way of talking about such features in the lives of persons; and I do not myself see how anyone can find it easy and convenient to dispense with it whose real wish is not to dispense with some of the facts themselves.

Allowing myself this mode of speech, then, I say that our moral freedom is narrow in this sense, that all that is essentially involved in the possession of it is that an act of will itself (or failure to will) escapes the net of causal law explanation. This much is a moral postulate: without this measure of freedom we should not be moral agents at all. But what will happen as a *result* of our willing (or our failure) may be, so far as moral postulates take us, explicable in principle wholly in deterministic or causal terms. Our willing we take, of course, to be *one* of the causal factors involved in this explanation: we cannot will at all without this conviction that to will is efficacious. And when we will some particular thing we must believe, or at least we must think it sufficiently likely (again as a necessary psychological condition of our willing) that the only causal factor required for the production of the intended result, the only factor that is not already provided or will not at the appropriate point be provided by 'Nature', is our act of will itself. Experience indicates that we are sometimes over-optimistic in this belief; and it is reasonable to suppose likewise that sometimes we are too pessimistic—that sometimes we do not will what could in fact be achieved, simply from a mistaken supposition of its impracticability.[1] There is no necessary linkage of what can be willed to what can be attained, but only to what it is *believed* can be attained; and the fullest freedom and energy of the will, correspondingly, affords no guarantee of any attainment. In this sense we may agree with Rousseau's Savoyard priest that 'I have always the power to will but not always the strength to do what I will.'[2] But it is the 'power to will' that signifies. So far as morality is concerned the scope of the freedom we *must* possess does not extend beyond the self-direction of our wills.[3]

[1] It is worth observing that over-optimism and over-pessimism alike may be due not simply to factual ignorance, in the usual meaning of the words, or to the temper of our mind (sanguine or otherwise), but to a general belief about the world and the forces at work in it. Thus a belief in what I have called the 'friendliness' of the universe could be of real practical importance, either benignly or disastrously, according as the world really is 'friendly' or not.

[2] Rousseau, *Emile*, Book IV (p. 243 of the Everyman edition).

[3] I have here spoken as though 'ability to will' and 'ability to do what one wills' could be cleanly separated, in principle anyhow: as though, however unlikely, it was at least not sheerly impossible for a genuine willing to be even totally frustrated, altogether inefficacious. This is certainly one view; but it may be a mistaken one, and I find the point far from easy. Cf. Farrer, *Finite and Infinite*, where the whole discussion of will and freedom deserves the most careful attention. On pp. 115–16 of that work Farrer denies the possibility of such a total separation. For my present purpose, however, it is unnecessary to decide the question. What I say is that morality *postulates* no more than 'ability to will', and the truth of this is unaffected even if the willing necessarily carries with it some incipient execution of one's project.

(5)

The moral response, then, is to be identified with a freely dutiful willing, an expression I use for brevity (and with some justice, as I have already shown) to refer to acts conceived as morally permissible as well as to those that are morally commanded. This dutifulness of the free will may be termed *elective*, in contrast with the *dispositional* dutifulness which expresses itself in a more or less strong desire to do one's duty as such and which seems to be what dutifulness should mean for the determinist. But now I must draw a further important distinction. Elective dutifulness itself may be of either of two sorts or qualities, of which only the 'higher' *fully* deserves its name; and it is the difference between these that I wish now to explain and stress.

In one sense—and this is the 'lower' form of dutifulness—a man is dutiful whenever he wills some particular action as being his duty which had he not conceived of it as his duty he would not have willed; as for instance when he decides to make a correct return of income to the Commissioners of Inland Revenue if, but for moral considerations, he would not have done so.[1] Even nowadays a man may surely do this as being something not too much to expect of human nature; and, having set aside any temptation to do otherwise on that occasion, he may go forward prepared to consider each successive challenge similarly, 'on its merits' as we might say. It is true that his will to do the particular thing (the making of the correct return, for instance), as being his duty, is in a way absolute; he is certainly not, with clear and complacent consciousness of the fact, positively restricting the scope of his moral loyalty. That, I think, would be psychologically incompatible with his being dutiful at all. But none the less he is as it were averting his gaze from the possibility of more disturbing demands; he is avoiding positive commitment to an attitude of readiness to do 'anything whatever' at the call of duty. He faces, so to say, '*this*' (whatever it is) which he acknowledges to be duty, not *duty* which, as it happens, is here and now 'this'; and his response is cut to the measure of that view of the challenge. It

---

[1] Note that I say he is dutiful *whenever* this is the case, not *only when* it is the case. Of course he would be equally dutiful where non-moral motives were sufficient to secure the appropriate decision, so long as they were not necessary to secure it. But that situation is less satisfactory to work with as an example.

appears to me that this is a common, perhaps I should say the common, form of what we regard as moral adequacy, or even (in the more difficult cases) as moral victory. And that it deserves to be called 'dutifulness' in some sense I have no wish to deny; what else could we call it?

And yet surely it is morally inadequate. There is indeed a covert contradiction in it which it needs a sort of dishonesty to disguise and which honest reflection is bound to disclose. There is a partial holding back of a loyalty that is not really itself unless it is without reservations. I have said that in these cases a man is prepared to consider each issue on its merits. But what could the phrase 'on its merits' conceivably mean? The issue to which it refers is formulated in the question 'Am I or am I not going to do what I see to be my duty?' But we know perfectly well, if we are sincere, that the merits of the claim of acknowledged duty are the same on every occasion; for on every occasion they are absolute. There is therefore a self-protective deceit at work in the very employment of such an expression as 'considering each case on its merits', and what the use of it evinces is that we are, in a sense, here and now *un*dutiful. We may say 'Don't cross your moral bridges till you come to them: one at a time is enough'. But the truth is that in all strictness there is only one moral bridge, but it is a bridge over a moral Rubicon. (We must not be misled by the nightmarish fact that in human life, if we ever succeed in crossing it at all, we none the less later find ourselves back on the hither bank and required, in endless repetition, to cross it again.) The moral Rubicon is crossed when, and only when, the willing of our particular duties is enclosed within a general and unqualified devotion of the will, for which the formal character of duty as duty is in a sense everything and the particular and variable material content is treated as a matter of indifference.[1] This is the 'higher' mode of dutifulness, and it is, as I said earlier, what alone *fully* deserves the name. It is somewhat as if a man were to make out a number of blank cheques payable to Duty, signing them but leaving it to successive occasions to write in

[1] To avoid misconception I must emphasize that I am speaking here of our attitude towards actions already acknowledged as duties. While it is still a question of whether an action is to be acknowledged as duty or not, the 'particular and variable content' is, of course, precisely what engages our attention. I am far from suggesting that particular duties can be derived from the bare concept of duty.

the amounts, instead of waiting to see what the amount is before he decides whether or not to sign. I am supposing, as a libertarian, that there is no difficulty about the bank balance.[1]

It may be said that this amounts to holding that every morally good man must actually be a moral *hero*. This I do not regard as an objection. It is precisely what I do hold to be involved in his being as good (in respect of the quality of his will, simply) as it is possible for man to be. This does not mean that we are not to speak of 'morally good men', in ordinary life, by reference to some less exalted standard, vaguely defined in 'realistic' terms as 'what might be generally or reasonably *expected* of people'. It only means that we are not to treat that everyday working standard as our utmost ideal. The ideal of dutifulness remains, I believe, as I have stated it. And what I maintain is that mere morality, without need of any appeal to 'para-ethical' or 'supra-moral' considerations, requires that our dutifulness should be of this order.

(6)

I have thought it necessary to explain at some length my conception of the moral response, for it is, I think, more open to misunderstanding than is that of moral demand. Were it misunderstood this might not only obscure the views I wish to maintain, but also render them less plausible than, in the eyes of

[1] Here I differ from Farrer, *Finite and Infinite*, p. 165, where also the figure of the 'blank cheque' is employed. I should grant that there is a considerable problem about the distinction and relation between general resolutions and determinate volitions, which I have not explored. But I could not agree that such a resolution is not really a resolution at all (in the sense of being at least something *like* a volition) but only a sort of 'memorandum' addressed to oneself, as Farrer appears to hold. Of course, however we resolve, there can be no advance guarantee that our determinate volition on any particular occasion will be dutiful even in the 'lower' sense of the word: to suppose otherwise would be to treat the will not as free but as determined by its own past. None the less, if there can be such a resolution or 'set' of the will as I suppose, it seems to me that, given that it is sustained and, so to say, 'suffuses' our determinate volitions, the quality of these is thereby different from the quality of will exhibited in what are, in respect of their content, the same decisions made by a man who is living in what is morally a sort of hand-to-mouth way. But I should stress that if my moral psychology is here at fault, as I am very conscious it may be, any consequential changes I should have to make elsewhere in my discussion would not, I believe, affect the substance of my contention regarding the relation between morality and grace.

theologians at least, they are likely to seem anyhow. Let it be remembered that perfect moral response is here being thought of as *dutiful* willing simply, and simply dutiful *willing* (not acting, or doing things in the common meaning of those words); but as dutiful willing in the higher of the two modes that I have just distinguished.

I propose now to examine two questions. First, I shall ask how far, if at all, an account of the approach to or realization of this ideal requires for its adequacy and completeness the introduction of concepts of a theological order, and how far, if at all, it even permits the employment of such concepts. And secondly, I shall enquire whether the ideal itself can be accepted as an ideal; whether it is not perhaps, as some hold, intrinsically corrupt, or, at the least, defective—something to be supplemented by, or transcended in, a life of religious devotion.

First then, what necessary or permissible employment is there for theological concepts in an account of the dutiful life? It is immediately obvious that the cardinal issue here is that of human freedom in relation to divine grace. Grace is the theological concept centrally involved, grace in the sense in which it concerns the will of man, as distinguished from other aspects of his complex unity, as for instance his understanding. Such relevance as other theological concepts may possess will be peripheral merely or derivative, and any mention I make of them will be so likewise. It is on the problem of grace and freedom that attention will be focused.

This problem is as old as Christianity itself; in substance if not in terms it is even older than that. And I must confess at once that in discussing it I shall lay myself open to the charge that even my errors are not novel. Are they not simply the errors of Pelagianism, which William Temple once described as 'of all heresies spiritually the most pernicious'?[1] If errors they be that certainly is their general colour. But I think it is not without reason that 'English Christianity', as Temple also observes, has 'a perpetual tendency in that direction'.[2] And I cherish the hope that the repeated expression of this tendency will at least, and at

[1] *Doctrine in the Church of England: the Report of the Commission on Christian Doctrine appointed by the Archbishops of Canterbury and York in 1922* (London 1938), p. 5.

[2] *Loc. cit.* 'English', not 'British', is no doubt the proper opposite of 'Continental' in the present context.

last, move those whom it does not persuade to reformulate their alternative doctrine in a way less unsatisfactory to the moralist. Certainly it should not content either ethics or theology, in a matter about which tolerably thoughtful people remain perplexed, simply to say 'We settled all this long ago'.

(7)

I must begin by making it clear how I understand the concept of grace itself in the context of our present problem. And here for the sake of brevity and simplicity I shall borrow the language of the Report of the Commission on Christian Doctrine from Temple's introduction to which I have been quoting. There the primary and essential meaning of 'grace' in Christian theology is given, quite adequately for my purpose, in the words 'the will of God (which is also His love) regarded as active on behalf of and in man'.[1] It is of course possible to complicate this simple formula in a variety of perfectly legitimate ways. For example, the somewhat earlier report of another committee (the Theological Committee of the Faith and Order Movement) recommended the drawing of a distinction between 'Grace' and 'the work of the Spirit', 'Grace' being restricted 'to its original meaning as an attribute of God' and 'the work of the Spirit' signifying 'His activity in man'.[2] If we make use of this distinction our central problem becomes a problem not about 'Grace' but about 'the work of the Spirit', but its substance is not affected. For us the refinement is at least superfluous; and I think it even carries with it a disadvantage in the very fact that it changes the terms from those in which the issue has for the most part been debated.

Contenting ourselves, then, with the simple formula for the primary meaning of 'grace' we must notice and emphasize that the concept of grace, in this sense in which it directly concerns the moral theorist, is the concept of something dynamic and personal. We have to do with the activity of a being thought of in personal terms who, as we might put it (and the antithesis is crucial for my argument), moves us not simply ὡς ἐρώμενον but ὡς ἀγαπῶν, not simply as that for which we yearn but as that which, or rather he who, loves us. It should not be necessary to say that

---

[1] *Doctrine in the Church of England*, p. 52.
[2] *The Doctrine of Grace*, ed. Whitley, pp. 17–18.

the fact that our discussion of the moral demand found no place for God conceived as personal does not entitle me to brush aside a personalist reading of the divine nature in this new context. Whatever the resultant difficulties, the new context must be permitted to disclose its own character and implications to a scrutiny as unprejudiced as we can make it.

Of course in addition to what has been put forward as its primary meaning there are a number of 'secondary' senses of 'grace' in Christian theology. We are told, for instance, that it may signify 'the gift to man of a certain secret and mysterious quality conceived as coming from God apart from personal relationship'; or, again, it may signify 'a state of Grace—that is, the state of a man who has come under the influence of Divine Grace, or who has received the gift of Grace'.[1] It is as well to be aware how partial and simplified our treatment is to be; but I shall not concern myself further with such meanings, except for a word of comment on the phrase 'apart from personal relationship' used in the statement of the first of those here mentioned.

The phrase suggests that the operation of grace in the sense that does concern us is one that is *not* 'apart from personal relationship'. And on one interpretation of the words this is obviously true, true by definition: for it is an operation of God as personal on behalf of and in man as person. But the term 'personal relationship' as applied to a purely human situation would normally indicate a relationship in which each party was *conscious* of the other as person; and moreover a relationship in which the difference made to either by the love and action of the other could, with whatever degree of precision or imprecision, be noticed and recognized for what it was and assigned to its personal source. Now to insist that the work of grace is, or is by way of, a personal relationship in this, which may be called its 'strong', sense would be to restrict the sphere of grace to those who have conscious faith in God, or, some would even say, conscious experience of Him, and to treat grace itself as in some way 'empirical fact'. But without positively denying that such faith, or experience, might have a relevance to God's gracious activity, or that that activity could be empirically observable, must we not allow that the activity could also be real even when it is not recognized (if it ever is recognized) on the human side?

[1] Both quotations are from *The Doctrine of Grace*, ed. Whitley, p. 15.

In what follows I take grace to be essentially a matter of personal relationship only in the 'weak' sense in which, as I have said, it is so by definition. The fundamental problem of grace and freedom is, I think, the same whether the 'subject' of grace be believer or unbeliever and whether the work of grace be empirically manifest or not. What *solution* of the problem of grace is permissible —our right (I mean) to end by denying grace altogether or, short of that, our liberty of interpretation of its character—would of course not be similarly unaffected. What is empirical fact in this matter must be as determinative of what is legitimate theory as are the relevant empirical facts in any other context. My primary interest, however, is ethical not theological, and my primary concern accordingly is not with the grounds, empirical or other, for positively affirming a doctrine of grace. To start with, any-how, I simply assume the doctrine as an integral part of Christian theology, however arrived at: and my question is whether it is a doctrine that can and, given its truth, should be incorporated in our account of the moral response, or whether it is on the contrary incompatible with any account that would be ethically satisfactory.

(8)

The grace that is said to be operative 'on behalf of *and in* man'[1] is held to be operative specifically in his *will*. There are at least two reasons for holding this. One, which may be called theo-logical, is that on any other view man's righteousness, in the sense of the goodness of his will, must, if it is to be possible at all, be something self-wrought, in independence of the action of God; and this, it is believed, is inconsistent perhaps with the majesty of God and certainly with the Christian conception of the nature and conditions of salvation. With this theological reason we are not directly concerned. But there is a second and, which is striking, an ethical reason offered for this position; an ethical reason, that is to say, for insisting on precisely that concep-tion of the work of grace that constitutes the problem for ethics. Such a paradox is not of course without parallel in contexts from which theological considerations are absent. There is in fact a very close parallel to be found in the determinism of a purely secular philosophy. This likewise constitutes an ethical problem,

[1] My italics.

in the eyes even of many determinists; and yet it has also been argued that determinism is required for the very freedom that is characteristic of the moral agent.[1] Just so here, the ethical reason for insisting that grace is operative in the will itself is that this is precisely the condition of its being consistent with our freedom. 'The operation of grace is not opposed to the freedom of the human will, since grace acts through the will and not externally to it.'[2]

Now there is nothing at all to be gained by any beating about the bush in this matter. Even at the risk of seeming to deal cavalierly with a great issue, of seeming content to proffer the stone of crude assertion where what is asked for is the bread of satisfying argument, I must make what is in the end a simple point with simple and emphatic directness. As regards the self-regulation of the will when faced with a moral challenge, the sheer 'making up one's mind' and 'setting oneself' to do what seems required of us, not only is there no observable presence—I cannot conceive how there could be—of any power not our own operating within our will, but to suppose that in some unobserved way such a power is in fact operative is to suppose something that is in contradiction with the very idea of a free willing.[3]

It is surely the case that, unless an act of will is in a quite unqualified sense a man's own work, there is nothing that can be his work even in a qualified sense and in some degree. Whatever can in a loose sense be called a man's act (his act, for instance, of saving another man from drowning) is so only because he 'mixes his labour' with it; that is, with the other factors (of wind and water and bodily endowment, let us say) that go to effect or constitute what is described as his act. And it is a vicious regress that is set up if this that is 'his labour' is itself 'his' only in the same non-absolute sense. Now that men in some sense really act, that their life is no mere series of happenings, is doubtless

---

[1] As for instance by R. E. Hobart in the article provocatively entitled 'Free Will as involving Determination and inconceivable without it'. *Mind*, January 1934.   [2] *Doctrine in the Church of England*, pp. 52–3.

[3] I question whether the supposition makes sense even on a deterministic reading of the will's action, such as Luther's for example. (See *The Bondage of the Will*, pp. 102–4.) But it is at least easier to *imagine* that it does so in that case, where it is not necessity as such that has to be 'imagined away' in picturing ourselves as free, but only 'compulsion'.

among the last things that theology would wish to deny, as it is also the very last thing that moral theory could deny—moral theory in denying it would commit suicide. Granted, then, that a man acts, in some legitimate sense of the word, we must go on to say that it is he and simply and solely he who acts in the minimal sense of 'wills'.

It may be objected that this is the language of a shallow rationalism and that we are dealing with mysteries. Doubtless (the objection might run) to say of some dutiful energy of will 'Not I, but God' would be strictly improper, though it is an impropriety not only natural but innocent in the actual life of religion. But to say 'Not I apart from God, not I alone but also God' is a quite different matter; and it is only this and not the other that the doctrine of grace really stands for. To avoid all risk of prejudicing the issue, therefore, we must (it might be urged) fix that distinction firmly in our minds. Let us be absolutely clear that there is no question at all of denying that the human will really is in action, that it is both genuinely will and genuinely human. All that I then have to set against the assertion of the work of grace in it, since nothing of interest to morality is any longer in danger, is the blank counter-assertion that the action, the willing, cannot be at once both human and divine. Of course (my critic might continue) we cannot understand how it could be both; this is where reason must fall silent. But incomprehensibility is one thing and impossibility another. To affirm the second merely because we must concede the first is cheap; and it is also an impotent gesture in face of the self-sustaining convictions of religion.

Now it is indeed true that I must in the end rely on the 'blank counter-assertion' complained of, commenting merely that it is certainly not to be overthrown by appeals to the general idea of divine 'immanence' but is, rather, something to which our interpretation and use of that idea must itself be adjusted. It should by no means be overlooked that the emphasis on 'immanence' in such a thinker as Bradley[1] can bring no legitimate comfort to a theist; for here, so far from being harmonized with, it is radically antipathetic to the Christian concept (and not only the Christian concept) of divine personality and of the status of the finite individual. But as to the 'counter-assertion' itself let

[1] See the essay 'On God and the Absolute' in *Essays on Truth and Reality*.

me say this. I can, and from time to time (in the study) I do, wonder whether man really has that freedom without which, as it seems to me, he is no moral agent at all. But this is not here in question; I am assuming that theology does not deny that freedom. And what I find I cannot 'wonder' is whether what is involved in the very conception of that freedom might not perhaps be negated without the freedom itself being negated also. To suppose that possible is (what else can I say?) to suppose not mystery but nonsense; and a theology is worth no man's attention that does not submit itself to the same rigorous conditions of self-consistency and good sense as apply to every other reflective activity.

What then are we to think of such language as the following? 'Our religious convictions demand dependence on God; our ethical convictions demand human freedom. *The mistake that has been made has been that theologians have aimed at philosophical consistency.*'[1] If these words are really to be taken at their face value the bridges between philosophers and theologians are down. There can be no communication between them on such terms and, to be frank, no safeguard against any speculative folly and fanaticism on the part of the latter. Yet surely the words must be taken at their face value, and not simply as a very reasonable warning against facile and illusory completeness in our thinking, before a theologian will find warrant in them for saying that our willing is at the same time our act and God's. We are entitled of course, if we can, to suspend judgment on the whole matter. But it will be hard to suspend judgment on the proposition that our willing is *ours*. I hope I am not unappreciative of the motives that induce some thinkers to adopt the position I oppose and to do their utmost to make plausible what seems to me impossible. But it would be a misplaced and a doubtful courtesy to pretend that I did not think their enterprise a vain one.

(9)

The error of the view to which I here object is perhaps disguised from those who hold it (and their adherence to it reinforced

[1] *The Doctrine of Grace*, ed. Whitley, p. 20 (my italics). See also Headlam (and his quotation from Mozley) on pp. 385–6 of the same volume.

H

though doubtless not originated) by the affinity of 'Not I alone
but also God in me' with such an expression as 'I not of myself
but only by God's help'. Certainly the latter form of words is
one that can, though it may not, be given a meaning perfectly
consistent both with good sense and with the claims of morality.
Let me illustrate from a simple human situation.

Suppose a child to enter for a competition governed by the
common rule that the entry (painting, essay or whatever it be)
shall be 'all his own work'. Of course, 'he', in this context, is
very much more than what may be called a 'naked will': a
co-operation of mind, hand, eye and so forth is taken for granted,
and 'his' work is what all these in conjunction effect. (All the
same, we should at once deny that the work was 'his' were we
satisfied that he had made no effort, had not 'tried' in that distinctive and recognizable way that we have in mind when we speak
of 'will': even here, 'he' is *peculiarly* 'he as *willing*'.) Now there
are obvious ways in which he, in this broad natural sense, may
be aided in his performance, and yet not so as to disqualify him
as a competitor. The sort of aid given is not incompatible with
the entry being in the relevant sense 'all his own work'. For
example, pen and ink, or paint-box, may be provided by his
parents, the original suggestion that he should enter may have
come from them, his making the effort required may be encouraged
by them, the sense of their interest in, and sharing of, his hopes
and disappointments may be a stimulus and support. In these
ways, consistently with the work being 'all his own', he is helped.
Indeed in the case supposed one might even say that apart from
such help he just would not be able to initiate and carry through
the undertaking at all. We cannot, of course, go so far as this
where the undertaking consists in a moral response to a moral
demand as I have described these, and is accordingly to be
identified with the exertion of the will itself, 'he' being in effect
now *simply* 'he as willing'. At this point our illustration fails us, as
any other would also. It cannot be correct to say that the will's
response is morally required of us and yet cannot be achieved
save on conditions that are independent of our will. Yet even in
this case there is no need to deny the possibility of our being
helped in ways such as, or analogous to, those that I have supposed
in the case of our child-competitor—so helped that the willing
itself is both easier and more effective. The willing will be 'all

our own work', in the relevant sense, none the less. Promptings and the support of loving sympathy and the benignity of circumstance and disposition—all these may play their very important part; but they will not add up to, or even begin to add up to, what we mean by 'willing'. All the help we can get remains as it were extraneous to the will: relative to the will it is all *environmental*, not *constitutive*, no matter how intimately environmental it may be. But the expression 'Not I of myself, but only by God's help' is not careful to discriminate these alternatives: it does not specify whether the help is to be thought of as environmental or constitutive, let alone how the 'I', by reference to which the antithesis is to be understood, is defined. Accordingly, if we are persuaded of our dependence in some sense on divine help, particularly if it be what I have described as environmental help of the more intimate sort that enters into the constitution of the total *self*, we may easily misread this dependence, notwithstanding that the self is much more than just the will, as a dependence that enters constitutively into our very willing. It is vital for my argument that this distinction between environmental and constitutive grace should be understood. Each term, be it noted, is defined by reference to *will*, not by reference to the richer concept of self or person. And what I deny (in the name of morality) is the constitutive action of grace in this sense of 'constitutive'. Moral theory imposes no restriction on the possible scope of grace apart from this, no restriction on the range or intimacy of its environmental working.

In all that I have here said I have done my best to conform to the demand, so strongly and rightly insisted on by Oman in his *Grace and Personality*, that we should interpet the work of grace not in mechanical terms but in terms of personal relationship; and one could not wish for a more emphatic statement than that which Oman himself provides of the fundamental point that any acceptable version of the doctrine of grace must leave the moral personality of the 'subject' of grace unimpaired. The moralist cannot complain that Oman does not take the measure of the problem: but he may well wonder how he supposes himself to have solved it. What I cannot see is that the paradigm of human relationships gives any support to, or even renders conceivable, a theory that does not draw a boundary to the operation of grace where I have drawn it. 'In a right relation of persons,' Oman

says,[1] 'especially of father and child, the help of the one does not
end where the effort of the other begins.' He says this in criticism
of theories, whether Augustinian or Pelagian in type, that set
'God's grace and man's resolution' in opposition, assigning 'so
much to God and so much to man'. If this were intended to deny
merely that the areas of *concern* of father and child can be treated
as distinct and simply juxtaposed, in such a way that the whole
demand-response complex is a sort of mosaic of 'moments' of
help and 'moments' of effort (as the building of a motor-car
might be regarded as a sort of mosaic of 'now this man's job,
now that man's'); if it affirmed only that the whole enterprise is
at once and throughout the child's concern *and* the father's
(that is, the object of his loving interest, expressing itself in every
possible way), this would be all very well. But that is as far as the
human analogy will take us; and it falls short of illustrating
(what Oman surely intends) a sort of immanence of God in the
will such that the act of will itself is a co-operation. We are left
with a co-operation *between* our will and another than ourselves.
It has indeed been suggested that we cannot speak significantly
even of the influence of one person *on* another, we cannot understand how such a thing could be, unless we view the influence as
involving some kind of immanence of the one *in* the other; that
'just in so far as our action is affected by the influence of others it
seems to become theirs rather than ours'.[2] But this seems to me
simply untrue, unless (which makes it irrelevant) it is taken merely
as a strong figurative expression, or possibly (but this would be in
all its implications deplorable) as signifying a hypnotic relationship. The interest of the suggestion consists, to my mind, primarily
in the evidence it provides of the lengths to which one may be
forced to go in order to defend the thesis of constitutive grace.

It is of course quite consistent with the position I have adopted
to hold that when a human will is of its own election *congruent*
with the divine will (assuming here that the concept of divine
will is a legitimate one) it is then, and then only, energized in a
'frictionless' action, if I may so express myself. 'In His will is
our peace.' A belief, or consciousness, of this may play some
part in persuading us that when we respond as we should to a
moral demand the response is not our own work only but also

[1] *Grace and Personality*, p. 87. (My references are to the fourth edition.)
[2] Goudge, in *The Doctrine of Grace* (ed. Whitley) p. 329.

that of God in us. But we must remember that congruence is not identity (any more than with the two minds we speak of as having but a single thought); nor, in any case, is the achieving of the congruence to be identified with the congruence achieved. And as regards the achieving, it is surely indefensible to treat that as being somehow, in the *constitutive* mode, due to God if the corresponding failure is imputed, as in the utterance of religion it normally would be, wholly to ourselves. It is the same freedom of our will that is manifested in the one and in the other, and we cannot admit a quite different account of the 'inwardness' of its operation in the two cases.[1] To do so would be illogical; and the illogicality is not diminished by a frank avowal, however welcome the frankness itself may be. Sometimes it is very frank. Professor C. H. Dodd, for instance, seems prepared quite openly to desert logic at this crucial point, though he is certainly not in general a misologist. Commenting on *Romans* IX 17–18 he writes: 'The truly religious man knows that any good that is in him is there solely by grace of God, whatever he may make of this in his philosophy. But to attribute one's evil dispositions to God is a sophistication. One may feel driven to it by logic, but the conscience does not corroborate it.'[2] This, however, is perhaps one of those occasions on which we should call to mind McTaggart's saying, that 'none ever went about to break logic, but in the end logic broke him'.[3] The asymmetry, then, of the proposed account of moral failure and moral sucess is as such objectionable. But we may add that, even if it were not, the view would still be open to the criticism that it creates a desperate problem of theodicy. If without prejudice to our freedom our moral loyalties can be ascribed to God, how without prejudice to God are we to explain our disloyalties?

It must be admitted that the objections put forward in the last paragraph would not be appropriate to every form of Christian

[1] There is perhaps a parallel here with the problem presented by Kant's view of the freedom of the moral agent, with the interesting difference (at first sight anyhow) that for Kant it is our evil rather than our good willing that is less than fully and solely ours. What Sidgwick had to say (in the Appendix added in the sixth edition of *The Methods of Ethics*) about Kant's confusion of 'neutral' or 'moral' freedom with 'good' or 'rational' freedom still deserves attention.

[2] *The Epistle of Paul to the Romans*, Fontana Books, p. 170.

[3] The quotation is from the last page of *Studies in Hegelian Cosmology*.

theology. Not every theologian has preferred illogicality to what Dodd calls 'sophistication'. The charge of asymmetry cannot be brought against a view like Luther's, for example (in *The Bondage of the Will*), according to which God is as truly operative in our evil-doing as in our well-doing. On the other hand (apart from the point that in this case self-congratulation and self-reproach would have no worse or better warrant the one than the other) it appears impossible on such a view even to *seem* to maintain a libertarian position; and I am assuming (though of course Luther was far from doing so) that we must be libertarians. Moreover, the view makes more manifest, though not more real, the problem for theodicy as a problem of what looks like divine injustice. Luther we know, would regard the demand for a theodicy as presumptuous folly, but I am not satisfied that he is entitled to evade the difficulty in this way. It is not a question of saying simply that we are in no position to resolve the problem of *evil*, which may be true enough. The problem has here been given a specific form as a problem of the *justice* or *injustice* of God, thanks precisely to the personalistic language of the theological doctrine; and the difficulty is not simply that the fashion of God's justice is obscure but that, within the limits of a thinking tied to such language, the fact of His injustice is plain. We can avoid embarrassment only by giving up the personalistic language altogether. But then where would be Luther's theology?

(10)

Here then is my position. It is a condition of the very being of a moral personality that a man's willing, in its goodness as in its badness, should be absolutely his own, into which in neither case does God's action enter constitutively. To suppose that, in any measure, it does so enter is, indeed, to that extent to reduce man from the status of person to that of a mere mode of the divine being—unless perhaps it is on the contrary to reduce the term 'God' to a mere way of speaking of the goodness of the human good will. These are the Scylla and Charybdis between which we must steer. And even the environmental action of God, though it may be so intimate that we may speak of it as immanent not indeed in our willing but in our lives, and though it may be the secret of such right *discernments* as we have, must yet never be

supposed either a sufficient or a necessary condition of our
willing rightly (when willing rightly means willing the performance
of our duty as we see it). For to suppose this would be in effect
to suppose that though our action was indeed ours it was not,
after all, action.

This conclusion will certainly not commend itself to all. And
yet I should have to confess that in arguing for it I have deliberately
taken the question in the form best calculated to make my answer
plausible. I have spoken as though the issue were simply this:
given some particular occasion of moral demand, can I on that
particular occasion 'measure up' to what is demanded of me,
simply of myself and altogether apart from God's help? I have
not stressed the distinction I earlier drew between the lower
and higher levels of dutiful response and, accordingly, I have not
insisted that 'willing as I ought' should mean 'willing with a
total abandonment of self-concern', as contrasted with merely
'being ready to go as far as this particular situation requires'.
Nor have I asked what is the possibility that a man's dutifulness
should be sustained at this pitch throughout the whole of his
moral life.

I think it must be admitted that even those who may be able
to conceive that a man can, of himself, somehow 'scramble home'
to the attainment of a dutifulness sufficient to overcome one or
another particular temptation are likely to find it beyond belief
that the mere moral will can achieve a total and unreserved
devotion to duty sufficient for every possible occasion, and even
more incredible that it can hold itself continuously at that level.
I may cite in evidence so sane and balanced a theologian as
Dr Leonard Hodgson.[1] For all his emphasis on man's 'libertarian'
freedom (the more significant because, as he tells us, he came to
a conviction of it only after the most strenuous efforts to think
otherwise) Dr Hodgson none the less insists that 'we can do
nothing with sin. We cannot cure ourselves of our love of what
is wrong but pleasant; we cannot overcome the weakness of will
through which we surrender to it . . . This impotence, moreover,
is a characteristic interwoven with the very depths of our being.
It is not a sufficient account of the matter to say that sometimes
some of us fail.' These words may or may not be interpreted as
denying the possibility of even a temporary and local victory of the

---

[1] *Towards a Christian Philosophy*, p. 187.

unaided will, but (and this is why I quote them) they certainly
do deny the possibility of its complete and lasting victory. Whether
or not we can of ourselves win battles we are bound, if left to
ourselves, to lose the war. And who, looking around him or,
perhaps more pertinently, at his own life, will venture to deny
that this has the appearance of truth?

Yet I must not myself take refuge in the illogicality I object
to in others. I am bound to say that I can find no reason, *a priori*
or empirical, for supposing that a man who can 'will to do his
duty' on this or that particular occasion whatever its cost on that
particular occasion may be (and the possibility of this is just
what I have been urging) cannot also on any given occasion 'will
to do the duty whatever the cost'; bringing as it were the disregard
of the cost out of the description of the conditions under which
he wills into the description of the content or quality of the act
of will itself. On the contrary, to affirm the first possibility and
at the same time to deny the second seems to me a quite inco-
herent, and in that sense unintelligible, position. Consider as a
case the suggestion that a man who on every relevant occasion,
and despite the risk to himself (whatever it be), can make up his
mind 'to join a rescue-party' can yet never make up his mind
(that is, resolve) 'to disregard the whole question of risk to
himself when the issue is whether to join a rescue-party or not'.
Of course this last phrase does not mean 'not to *notice* the risk
to himself', nor again 'to experience no *temptation* to take
account of it'. But, misconceptions such as these being set aside,
can the suggestion appear other than gratuitous and foolish? And
at least as foolish, it seems to me, is the suggestion that what
can be willed or resolved on once cannot be willed or resolved on
always—that is to say, whenever the alternative 'to will or not
to will' applies at all. Thus I can find no middle way between
conceding the necessity of constitutive grace on at least some
particular occasions of volition (and abandoning thereby all
objection of principle to conceding it for all) and, on the other
hand, denying the need of it for the attainment of even the
completest and most unbroken dutifulness. I find myself driven
to this denial.

And now perhaps I have reached a point at which not only
theologians, or Christians as such, but anyone who reflects at all
will be likely to regard what I have said as nonsense, and rather

pretentious nonsense too. The unbeliever may indeed be apt to
feel less intensely than does the believer about his moral failures,
to be less humiliated by them: but he will not, I think, be at all
more disposed to regard himself as capable of exemption from
them. The difference between the two relates, I imagine, not to
the existence of the 'disease' but to its importance, and the whether
and how of a remedy.[1] At most, it may relate to the question
whether it is really sense to speak of it as 'disease' at all, instead
of accepting it with resignation as something just natural, like
the body's fatigue after strenuous exercise. But underlying all
such differences there will be a strong, even if confused, sense
shared by all that a measure of imperfection in our moral loyalty
is unavoidable; and history, it would seem, confirms the soundness of this belief. I on the contrary am committed to maintaining
that the belief is mistaken, exceedingly natural though the illusion
of its truth may be. But of course it is not enough just to assert
this, on the basis of the contentions so far put forward. If I am
to carry any conviction I must try to explain the illusion, and
to exhibit at least some of the factors that lead to our acquiescence
in it.

(II)

Now I do not doubt that, in the case of religious people, part
of the explanation is provided by their acceptance of certain
interpretations of elements in our experience other than the
moral element. These interpretations, whether or not they are

[1] I confess to some perplexity regarding the Christian position in this matter.
I do certainly think that it must be 'orthodox' to hold the doctrine of what I
have called 'constitutive grace': I do not see how else the relation between grace
and freedom should have come to be thought of as presenting an insoluble
problem (or impenetrable mystery). Now, given acceptance of that doctrine,
one might expect to find it affirmed that by grace (though not without it) the
human will can become perfect; for what exactly would be the point of urging
so insistently that grace is *needed* for that which grace does not itself supply?
Yet in fact it seems to be allowed that even the work of grace does *not* suffice
for this perfection, that imperfection of will must characterize us all (as no doubt
it actually does) throughout our life *in via* (so that what I claim as a possibility
for 'mere morality' will even exceed what is claimed by Christians as a possibility
for Christian faith). Of course it is quite correct to point out that a necessary
condition is not *eo ipso* a sufficient one; but if appeal is to be made to that
distinction in the present case one must ask what, for Christian thought, can be
that further condition of the will's perfection, for which constitutive grace
must, so to say, wait.

explicit and systematic enough to constitute a 'theology', assert or imply a total dependence of the creature upon the Creator or, in respect of his soul's salvation, of the sinner upon his Saviour, such as excludes the possession by the human will of the power I attribute to it. This I note, but shall not further discuss: not, I need hardly point out, because I consider it unimportant, but because it falls outside my immediate concern and is a great deal too important to be dealt with parenthetically. I restrict my view to that which in the moral experience itself seems to support the doctrine of the insufficiency of the unaided will. And I think it is anyhow safe to say that unless the moral experience itself appeared at least to *admit* of interpretation in terms of that doctrine, tenets deriving from other sources would not avail to render the doctrine convincing.

As regards moral experience itself what we must first notice is this, that it is as good an empirical fact as any that our moral decisions vary in difficulty. They can be so difficult that it is perfectly natural to speak of some of them as being 'next to impossible' to make. I think it is true that we shall never say of any one particular decision, as it actually faces ourselves, that it is '*utterly* impossible' or '*quite* out of the question', unless it be colloquially and by way of more or less conscious exaggeration— like the 'Impossible!' that we might use of some reported fact that astounds us, even though we do not really disbelieve the report. Nevertheless, the exceedingly difficult is, to our minds, also the highly unlikely. We think it more or less probable that a man will in fact decide to do his duty (supposing him to be concerned at all about doing it) according as the decision is more or less easy. It seems plain that we do think so; and we are not to pretend that we do not merely because the thought may at first sight be difficult to reconcile with our libertarian convictions. Now, granted that we do think so, we may from this be led on quite naturally to suppose that since some decisions are harder than others, and correspondingly less likely to be made, it is at least conceivable that a demand on the will should be so exacting that it is, in a quite strict and literal sense, simply impossible for the will to meet it successfully. Indeed it is hard to see what should prevent this 'slide' from occurring except the clear recognition, which is by no means characteristic of our ordinary thinking, that the power to will and the power to effect something by willing (that is, to act, in the common sense of that word) are not at all in like case. For certainly as regards the latter we all believe, and have no ground for doubting, that increasing difficulty terminates in impossibility and that repeated failure after effort is good evidence that we have reached the limit. Now the extreme case of difficult willing is provided, of course, by the demand on the will to maintain its moral integrity abidingly in so unqualified a manner that no cost would be refused. If anything, then, were strictly beyond the capacity of the will in its self-direction this would certainly be so; and without ever expressly disavowing our freedom we might readily enough slip, in the manner already indicated, into supposing it possible that it should be so. This supposition, however, that a sustained integrity of will *might* be beyond our capacity combines with our sense of the historical universality of moral failure; and it then quite naturally acquires the force of a conviction that it actually *is* beyond our capacity. Thus we conclude that man cannot totally avoid moral failure, although the historical evidence by itself, of course, only shows at most that he does not. And having reached this conclusion we shall have abandoned, as I said before, all objection of principle to the hypothesis of the impotence of the unaided will at all points.

We must never forget that if we say that perfect dutifulness (or even some lesser measure of goodness) is *impossible* for the unaided will we are treating the pervasiveness of moral failure not just as a *de facto* phenomenon but as something inseparably connected with our nature as man. Those who are sufficiently reflective to feel a need to integrate this persuasion with a recognition of their moral responsibility and freedom may then be disposed to speak, in the language of Reinhold Niebuhr,[1] of an 'inevitable though not necessary shortcoming'. But this formula, though I can suggest no other that would be better for its purpose, is manifestly unsatisfactory. 'Not necessary' may be capable of meaning a variety of things, but the only meaning that concerns the moralist in the present context is precisely that of 'categorically avoidable'. We may understand well enough how such apparently self-contradictory language should come to be used, but that should not make us any more at ease in this pseudo-Zion of 'paradox'. I confess that there seems to me no reason to

---

[1] *The Nature and Destiny of Man*, Vol. I, p. 161.

prefer Niebuhr's paradox to that opposite one involved in the Sartrian view of human responsibility, though I can allow that both alike express, in however unacceptable a form, the natural 'feel' of the human condition in the characteristic experience of the believer and the unbeliever respectively. Responsible action requires both freedom and objective standards. If Sartre does not see the need for the latter, neither does Niebuhr take the former requirement with sufficient seriousness. The only further difference is that Sartre is franker (to put it in a way that favours him) or less sensitive to the difficulties (to put it in a way that favours Niebuhr). Were it not for this we might have had Sartre assuring us that 'values' though inevitably man-made (for 'if I have excluded God the Father, there must be somebody to invent values')[1] do not necessarily owe their existence to man. Theologians, I believe, would not be impressed by this; yet it has as good a claim to impress us as has Niebuhr's formula.

But desperate linguistic measures of this sort are, I consider, as needless as they are ineffective in each case. Values are simply not at man's disposal and his volitions simply are: and, whatever the plausibility, there is no cogency in the train of thought that leads to the conclusion that even the ideal condition of the will is beyond our unaided powers. We must say no more, though also no less, than that this possibility is of all possibilities the barest; and that since this is so a man has no right to be surprised if the fulfilment of it is also of all achievements the rarest. He need not be astonished even if, to the best of his belief, it has never yet been fulfilled or, perhaps he would wish to say, has been so only once.[2] He might reasonably be vastly more surprised if the facts were otherwise and the achievement a common one. 'Omnia praeclara tam difficilia quam rara sunt.' I quote these final words of Spinoza's *Ethics* not just for themselves but to call to mind their whole context, which is (I think one might say) precisely that in Spinoza's system that corresponds to the problem of 'ideal dutifulness' in our present discussion.

It will be observed that in all this I have only been putting in my own way the thesis argued long ago by F. R. Tennant,

---

[1] See above p. 87 where I have already commented on this Sartrian dictum.
[2] I may here again refer to the Appendix in Grensted's *The Person of Christ* for an indication of the way in which the sinlessness claimed for Jesus may be understood in a manner generally congenial to my argument in this volume.

in a work dismissed by Niebhur in a single sentence as 'the most elaborate of modern Pelagian treatises'.[1] It is the thesis that the universality of sin, supposing it to be a fact, can be no more than a contingent, empirical fact. And, it may be asked, should a Christian not agree, if the full normal humanity of Jesus is not to be questioned, precisely because the Christian *denies* the universality of sin? If we say that what makes Jesus an exception is some 'ontological' difference in status between Him and us, must this not mean that between Him *as human* and ourselves there is an 'ontological' difference, since it is precisely to Him as human that the concept of temptation must apply, and correlatively that of sinlessness likewise? And how then can we assert his normal humanity? Yet unless we affirm some 'ontological' difference between Jesus and other men that has a bearing on his sinlessness how can it be denied that his sinlessness disproves the hypothesis that men as such and inevitably are sinners?[2] I am well aware that questions like these may be accused of theological ingenuousness: but they are questions none the less that it is the business of theological skill to endeavour to answer without disingenuousness and without falling into self-contradiction. Learned ridicule of their simplicity will not do. I could not altogether avoid touching on this point, but it is sufficient here to have thus barely called attention to it. I must return to my argument.

(12)

There is of course much more to the so-powerful illusion that moral failure is inevitable than the consideration suggested in

[1] Tennant, *The Concept of Sin*. The Niebuhr reference is *The Nature and Destiny of Man*, Vol. I, p. 262.

[2] It should further be noted, though it is not my immediate concern, that if the sinlessness asserted of Jesus is *not* to be explained in terms of some 'ontological otherness' then neither can it bear witness to any such otherness, the evidence of which must then be sought elsewhere.

I would add, with reference to the whole question of the sinlessness of Jesus in relation to the sinfulness imputed as inevitable to all mankind, that it ought, of course, to be discussed against the background of a precise discrimination of the various meanings that might be assigned to 'sin' when its unavoidability is maintained. Am I wrong in thinking that 'racial solidarity in sin' is a concept that tends to be ignored, when the sinlessness of Jesus is in question, except as interpreted in such a way as allows us to regard the story of his birth as providing the explanation of his exemption from 'infection'? But this is certainly not the way in which all Christian theologians always interpret the idea of our solidarity in sin.

the preceding section; and I can go at least a little further in accounting for it by facing now an objection that might understandably be urged against my whole procedure. My argument, it might be said, rests on isolating what I term the 'bare will', tearing it away from the total thinking, feeling, striving life of a man. It is of such an abstract discarnate little wraith that I deny that God's grace can be either at work in it or a necessary precondition of its own effective work. And who cares about this? For the thing is not only an abstraction but a vicious abstraction. I myself have allowed as a moral possibility, what it is for religion to affirm (if it must) as actuality, that grace may enter into our lives, into the most intimate environment of this supposed bare will; and this is to say that it may enter into the very constitution of our human actions in the only natural and realistic meaning of those words. This concession, it might be held, concedes all; and my denial relates to a mere figment, a sort of mathematical point in the spiritual world, spoken of as though it had magnitude. Now it is certainly true that my argument depends on my making the abstraction complained of. I do distinguish the sheer act of will from everything else that goes to make up our personal life, including every impulse and appetition, every conative tendency in us that still awaits the decisive fiat or prohibition, the decisive commitment. And certainly in our experience these things are so closely associated that to set them apart in our thought, in the way I have done, is to suggest an absurd distortion of fact. Indeed I should not care to maintain that introspection can empirically disentangle the web or assure us of the propriety of my procedure. I do not know that any 'decisive moment of commitment' can strictly be said to be observed, though it is familiar experience to find ourselves now hesitant and then already 'set' in a certain direction, and somehow we have moved from the one to the other condition. The basis of my distinction, however, and to my mind a perfectly adequate one, is other than this. It is that the libertarian account of moral action requires it, and that the libertarian account is in its turn required by the very concept of moral action. with any who would deny that, in the sense intended, we are moral agents I cannot here argue further; but though some may deny it I hardly expect the Christian theologian to do so. And if once our moral agency is allowed, the abstraction I employ is, it seems to me, legitimate and even unavoidable; and certainly it is not positively inconsistent with anything that introspection can tell us. If my language encourages the idea that the will is here being conceived as a sort of little man sitting inside our total being in merely mechanical relation with the rest—the picture of the pilot in the ship that has sometimes been used to represent the mind-body relationship being thus provided with an even less plausible application—well, I must naturally deplore this. But after all how can analysis *exhibit* the 'geistiger Band' as well as the 'Teile'? The analyst can but affirm it, as I do. To exhibit it, so far as that is possible, is the privilege of the writers of the great spiritual autobiographies, and, in their measure, of those who write of other people, real or feigned, in biography or fiction, with a like perceptiveness. The results of analysis have always to be interpreted by a sort of conflation with such accounts checked, as they must be checked to be even understood, against our awareness of the dynamic complexities of experience in our own case. It should not be necessary to insist on this.

I think, then, that the bafflingly intricate unity of enjoyed consciousness in the diversity of its modes and moments, the 'shot' character, one might say, of its iridescent fabric, does not render illegitimate that concept of the bare will with which I am operating; any more than, in my opinion, the experienced 'confusion' of psychical and physical in a whole too integrated to permit us to speak of its components as merely 'interacting'[1] makes illegitimate the distinction between these. But it does have significance in another way that is important for my argument. It suggests, what further reflection will only confirm, that the hypothesis of the inevitability of the will's imperfection is one the empirical *refutation* of which is impossible; and this not only in the weaker sense that we can produce no quite unquestionable instance of a perfect life but in the stronger sense that we can produce no quite unquestionable instance of a perfect response at any one moment of life. Our plight here, as we attend to the particular moment, is not simply that even were we certain that our will was there and then wholly dutiful we could obviously have no coercive assurance of its continuing so. The complexity of our nature is such that we cannot be fully satisfied of the purity and absoluteness of our dutifulness even on the particular occasion.

[1] Cf. Stout, *Mind and Matter*, p. 92.

Agnosticism on this point does not depend on modern theories of 'the Unconscious', however these may reinforce it. We may recall the doubts long ago expressed by Kant.[1] Kant, in the passage to which I refer, was thinking of the ever-present possibility that the inner principle or motive of the performance of an act might not be morally pure even when to our self-examination it appeared so and when the act, as regards its 'content', was certainly right. But to this we must add that there is likewise an ever-present possibility that our judgment of what is right may itself be perverted by an unacknowledged impurity of our motive, that our incomplete dutifulness may disguise its own imperfection by a self-deceiving 'whittling down' of the claims upon us to the measure of our willingness to respond. And here it may be observed in passing that (to enrich the confusion) it is possible that we should sometimes *feel* ourselves to be guilty of this immoral 'whittling down' when all that in fact we are doing is making a quite honest compromise, adopting a policy that 'ideally' we would rather not adopt but that is none the less truly the best in the untoward circumstances of the case. It is sheer muddle to treat this as impurity of will; but it is a muddle that does seem to play some part in persuading people of the pervasiveness of sin. But, besides such difficulties, or at most *practical* impossibilities, that stand in the way of recognizing the real quality of our volition, does there not seem to be also an impossibility of a different order, that precludes us from ever claiming to establish by self-examination that the will is even momentarily in a state of moral perfection? Consider what seems to me the insuperable doubt whether, even if we are not deceiving ourselves and even if it is a genuine concern to act rightly that moves us, this concern is so absolute that we should still be making the same decision, still be deciding the same way, were the temptation to do otherwise indefinitely increased. How could introspection resolve such a doubt as that? Something, then, that as morally required of us must be taken to be at all times possible is also such that we can never be sure that it is at any time actual. And this very uncertainty, if I am not mistaken, is apt to carry for us the feeling of positive contamination, as though there were an actual and recognized impurity of the will; while at the same

---

[1] See Paton, *The Moral Law*, pp. 74–5 (= Kant, *Grundegung zur Metaphysik der Sitten*, second edition, p. 26).

time the sense that the uncertainty is irremediable is transmuted into the feeling that the impurity is inescapable and therefore universal.

(13)

I have said that, even granting that the abstraction of the bare will is a legitimate one and that our proper concern here is solely with the quality of the will, history and personal experience suggest, though they cannot demonstrate, the inability of the will to achieve even its own perfection. I added that not only is empirical observation impotent positively to disprove the suggestion but this very impotence may actually (psychologically, though not logically) reinforce it. And now, to conclude, I must emphasize that whoever does not operate with this abstraction of the bare will which is in my view so essential can of course hardly be expected to acknowledge our possession even of that narrowly defined capacity for perfection for which I contend. For him the conception of the impotence of the *will* to achieve its own goodness becomes merged in, and will be 'read off' as a mere aspect of, the conception of the impotence (which we may all allow) of the *whole man* to become by means of his will what he, as whole man, should be.

For of course there is an ideal, however vaguely drawn, for the whole man, which if it includes is certainly not exhausted by the ideal of a perfect elective will; and in so far as that richer ideal remains unrealized we must acknowledge that we are in some sort 'polluted'. Allowing that this pollution is not, or is not wholly, moral evil in the narrower sense in which that qualifies the will only, still it is to be distinguished from such subjective and irrational *feelings* of pollution as may accompany our recognition of a baseness in the conduct of our country (say) or of some member of our family for which we cannot properly admit any personal responsibility. It is all the more important to insist on this distinction in principle because in practice the situation is likely to be complicated by the uncertainty any honest man will feel as to what are the limits of this (indirect) responsibility for the conduct of others,[1] and by his realization that he himself might

[1] So-called 'acts of our own' performed under the influence of drugs or hypnosis constitute a difficult intermediate class of cases in which a misplaced feeling of guilt may be peculiarly acute. But here too such difficulty as there is relates to the determination of our responsibility.

I

well have acted just so in a like case—'There, but for the Grace of God . . . '. The sense of pollution is warranted only where the baseness is really ours; but it is perfectly warranted then, if it genuinely is baseness, even if it is not elected baseness. And here I must recall what was said earlier on the subject of sin.[1] There can perfectly well be a baseness that is ours and yet not of our own election. There are dispositions, attitudes, feelings, desires (such as envy and the desire to hurt) that, however we account for them, are already in their own nature evil and not simply as the will, by undutiful acceptance of them into itself, is infected by them. Now the ridding ourselves of this form of evil is not just something that we naturally wish for and would welcome. It is something to be striven for, a practical ideal. Yet it is an ideal to which we certainly cannot attain by any 'direct assault' of will. What the will, wisely exercised, may contribute towards its attainment only experience can reveal. But not merely should we all have to report that as a matter of experience our success is no more than partial—and indeed we can set no limit to the possibilities of failure for even the dutiful man—but it is also plain *a priori* that the will must rely on the co-operation of factors other than itself, whether these are to be described in the language of religion (that environmental work of grace on which my argument has set no restriction) or in the language of a naturalistic psychology.

The will, then, we admit, cannot of itself cleanse the man; and, consequently, unless we clearly distinguish between the cleanness of the man and the cleanness merely of his will, all the considerations already mentioned that suggest a similar incapacity in regard to the latter must draw added vigour from this fact. But it is easy to fail to maintain the necessary distinction even as an element in theory, not to speak again of the difficulty of establishing it empirically in any particular case. This will be readily acknowledged by anyone who still bears in mind a relevant passage in my second chapter. We must remember that we have to include on the side of impurity of will not only what by any standard is a surrendering to evil but also, even if in the end we manage to resist full capitulation to them, those half-hearted evil 'velleities' that I spoke of as a sort of 'savouring' of temptations. We must also remember (and it further complicates the issue) that simply being tempted, taken in itself and apart from all

[1] See p. 37 above.

responsive velleity, belongs, so far as it is impurity at all, only to
the impurity of the whole man.

By ways such as these (and it must not be imagined that I
regard the suggestions I have made as exhausting the topic) men
may come to think it consistent with their experience and therefore *possible* to maintain that theory of grace as actually constitutive of moral effort which they may also believe, less perhaps on
experiential than on dogmatic grounds,[1] to be *necessary*. I have
argued that it is not possible. On the contrary the movement of
the will in response to acknowledged duty, whether it be a movement of acceptance or a movement of evasion, must be conceived
as self-wrought, if we are to talk morality; and if it is self-wrought
then it must be purely self-wrought, if we are to talk sense. This I
hold to, while freely conceding that environmental pressures and
solicitations, in the very wide sense of 'environmental' that I
have been employing, may render the will's action to an indefinite
extent either easier or more difficult.

(14)

But now, even supposing all this to be agreed, there still
remains the second of the two questions concerning the moral
response that I undertook to discuss.[2] Allow it to be possible for
unaided man to look after the dutifulness of his own will, to
safeguard its purity, still, it may be said, it would be a mistake
to regard the achievement of this as constituting the ideal even
of his *volitional* being. Thus, though we may have banished
theology from our account of the moral response, in my narrow
definition of it, we may have to retain it in our account of the
fully adequate, the spiritually perfect response, precisely because
the perfect response goes beyond morality. The ideal of mere
dutifulness, some would say, however total the dutifulness may
be, is a subtly corrupt ideal; and some who would not say this
would hold that it is at least a defective one. And the corruption
or defect, they would continue, can be removed only by passing

---

[1] The operative dogmas themselves doubtless rest, in the end, on what are
taken to be adequate experiential grounds, in some sense of experience: but that
is another matter. It raises the whole problem of 'revelation'; and this though
it is certainly the fundamental problem in regard to the relationship between
theology and philosophy generally, cannot, as I said before (p. 33, n. 1) be
explored here.   [2] See p. 107 above.

from a life of 'mere morality' to life of another quality. This 'life of another quality' may indeed be conceived in either secular, humanistic terms or in religious terms—we must not altogether forget the former possibility.[1] But it is of course the religious interpretation that is my particular concern, the doctrine that in religion we transcend the merely moral, and that it is in a life thus inspired and not in simple dutifulness that the proper excellence of the will itself is truly to be found.

This is the suggestion I must now consider; and it will be found that in considering it we shall in the end be brought back once more to the very threshold of that doctrine of constitutive grace on which I might be supposed by now to have said my last word. We shall be brought up against an argument in support of that doctrine that I have not as yet faced and that merits, in my own opinion, the most respectful attention. And since that is so I have to conclude the present chapter with the admission that the issue that has engaged us in it has not been settled even for myself, but must in all strictness be regarded as still *sub judice*.

[1] See below, Chapter V, Section 6.

CHAPTER V

DUTY, LOVE AND PRAYER

(1)

I have claimed that a self-achieved dutifulness, if only it be total and unreserved, is the ideal quality or form of the human will, than which no better can be conceived. (It should be obvious, of course, that I am speaking throughout only of the will of man *in via*: what might be the case with a life *in patria* we cannot know.) But I have to face the criticism that this conception of the ideal condition of the will is a mistaken one; first, because the attempt to realize it is self-defeating and tends rather to a corruption than to a perfection of our being, and secondly, because even were this not so the ideal itself is inadequate. In each respect, it is argued, religion is required as a corrective of 'mere morality'. This contention I must try to answer. My belief is that both parts of it, though they may not be acceptable in the form in which they are stated, are concerned to affirm important truths. Yet as criticisms I think they miss the mark; for the view I defend is in fact consistent with the truths they assert.

I take first the charge that the 'merely moral' ideal of self-achieved dutifulness is positively misconceived, since the endeavour to attain it frustrates itself. What the critics have in mind is that, although the ideal is stated in terms that negate self-centredness, 'mere moralism', as it is called, is in practice incurably self-centred. This appears to be a very widely held view. To cite but three distinguished British theologians of the present century, it is insisted on by Oman,[1] it is pervasive of Kirk's attitude in *The Vision of God*,[2] and it could not be more trenchantly expressed than in the words of Donald Baillie:[3] 'It is Christianity that has discovered and exposed what we may call the "paradox of moralism",—that the attempt to be moral defeats itself, leads

[1] *Grace and Personality*, Part III, Chapter 5 ('The Will of God').

[2] See pp. xii–xiii of the second edition of the unabridged version, and the references there given. See also the same writer's *The Threshold of Ethics*, p. 152 and following.　　　　　　　　　　　　[3] *God was in Christ*, p. 121.

to "Pharisaism" instead of real goodness.' Here is a characteristic sentence from Kirk:[1] 'A system of thought which is primarily moralistic, in so far as it sets before men a rule of conduct by which it is their first duty to measure themselves, is in essence egocentric. It is only one of the many forms which selfishness can take, even though its rule appear superficially altruistic.' And here is Oman:[2] 'Under no guise is self-reverence the right moral motive or self-development the right moral end. Our task is to concern ourselves about doing good, and not about being good,[3] and we must do good for the sake of the good itself and not for our own moral improvement.' But unfortunately (Oman continues) we find 'an insistent moral contradiction which is by no means confined to theory, for what causes more practical distress than the way in which mere moral effort leaves us with our eyes directed towards ourselves that we may approve our own virtue, yet, at the same moment, stirs in us a conviction that our eye should be upon our duty, in utter forgetfulness of the whole question of our merit or our perfection?'

(2)

It is, of course, perfectly true that the distress of which Oman speaks is a genuine, and perhaps even a not uncommon, experience. The question is, what precisely is its root, and how is it to be eradicated? If the attack on 'mere moralism' is to be successful the root must lie in the essential nature of the moral attitude itself. We must certainly allow that if the moral attitude really is at war with itself we shall be able to achieve coherence and 'singleness' of mind only by relinquishing or passing beyond it, only by replacing it by another and (it is suggested) a religious attitude—what Kirk would call the attitude of worship. But what is the fatal defect of the moral attitude as such? As Oman states it, it is this: that 'every moral law, whatsoever its form, is the law of our moral worth, and, the more it is strictly ethical, the more it disallows every motive save reverence for our moral worth'.[4] Were this true, the charge of self-contradiction would be made out. But it is not true. On the contrary, it represents

---

[1] *The Vision of God*, p. 449.   [2] *Op. cit.*, p. 233.
[3] Cf. Kirk's statement of Fénelon's view, *The Vision of God*, p. 463.
[4] *Op. cit.*, p. 232.

a complete misconception, although Kant's language (which Oman clearly has in mind) may be thought to provide some measure of excuse for it.[1]

Let us consider what we really mean when we insist, in terms that no doubt can suggest egocentricity, that a man must above all be dutiful. We do not mean that he is to set the achievement of that quality of will before himself as his supreme objective. True, I have spoken of dutifulness as the ideal quality of the human will, and we certainly use the word 'ideal' with reference to what we approve as an objective. But we also use it in a more general way to signify no more than that something, be it an objective or not, is the best possible of its kind. And that in fact is all that I intend when I describe dutifulness as the ideal condition of the will. Let us not be misled by words. When we say that a man 'must above all be dutiful' we should of course be quite clear that he can be so only in so far as he is looking *outward*, with a pure concern for the doing of what seems to him right, and, it is to be remarked, with a corresponding unconcern, on each particular occasion, about the existence and quality of such desires as may assist him to do what seems to him right.[2] Were we to shift the emphasis to the latter we might indeed fall into absurdity; the absurdity, for instance, of hesitating to do what appears right because it is also what malice, or even mere selfish prudence, suggests;[3] or the absurdity of refusing to use every legitimate device to ease the strain of dutifulness, in order that the triumph of will might, by reason of its very difficulty, be the more remarkable. But these absurdities do not spring from our being dutiful, but from our being undutiful; that is to

[1] Oman's position has long ago been criticized by L. A. Reid. (*Creative Morality*, pp. 197–201.) I echo his protest, but I hope add a little to it also.

[2] I say 'on each particular occasion' to allow for the fact that self-discipline and character-building must of course be included *among* our duties, although on any occasion when that is our primary concern we should still be 'outward-looking' in the sense that *that*, and not the 'then and there' quality of our will in endeavouring it, *is* our concern.

[3] There is an excellent illustration of this sort of situation in Gottfried Keller, *Der grüne Heinrich*, Part II, Chapter 11, where, be it noted, the obstructive thought is that the act in question will earn favour with God (which can hardly be said to be a characteristic idea of 'mere morality'). I have in mind the passage beginning: 'Es ist mir begegnet, dass ich einen armen Mann auf der Strasse abwies, weil ich, während ich ihm eben etwas geben wollte, zugleich an das Wohlgefallen Gottes dachte und nicht aus Eigennutz handeln mochte.' The whole paragraph should be read.

say, they spring from a kind of moral frivolity, from our not being in dead earnest about the various duties, the various things that ought to be done, themselves. It may be a drunkard's duty to try to reform himself and, on a particular occasion, to refuse the drink that he so badly wants to have. If he is in earnest he will do everything he can think of that will help him to refuse it. Can anyone seriously imagine that if, in such a case, we insist that the morally vital thing is that he should be dutiful we mean that so far from letting his friend remove the bottle he should ask that it be set on the table with the glasses ready, and should lovingly contemplate its seductions in order that nothing should stand between him and his liquor but sheer will-power? Manifestly not. When therefore we urge dutifulness as an ideal it is simply the outward-looking concern with the presented duty that we are prescribing, but adding, not as injunction but as simple statement of fact, that if and only if a man is absorbed in this concern will he also be inwardly 'ideally constituted'. 'Be dutiful' is thus not to be taken for an injunction distinct from, and in conflict with 'Do the right'. It is to be considered, in its character as *injunction*, as only another way of saying the same thing. The moral motive, accordingly, is not the motive of 'reverence for our moral worth'; it is the motive of 'concern that what is right should be done'. Our moral worth, consisting as it does in the operation of this latter motive, will then, as it were, look after itself. It is surely not necessary to go a hair's breadth beyond the limits of merely ethical thinking to see and say all this.

If this is understood, it will be seen that there is nothing self-contradictory in the description of the 'merely moral' attitude, and the question before us reduces to one of fact. It is now the question whether a 'concern for the right' can actually sustain itself in a life of 'mere morality' or whether, in the absence of religion, it will inevitably degenerate into a 'concern *for one's concern* for the right'. Without prejudice to the possibility that specifically religious attitudes and practices are helpful for truly moral living, I must say that I can see no justification whatsoever for supposing that this degeneration is bound to occur. The belief that it is bound to occur is, I suspect, the not very logical product of a conviction (which itself may be sound enough) of the prophylactic powers of religion combined with the misrepresentation of the character of the moral motive against which I have just been protesting. I say 'the not very logical product' of this combination, since the moral motive as thus misrepresented is already and by definition degenerate.

(3)

But there are other factors that may nourish, though they do not require, a belief that the 'merely moral' motive, even though not degenerate by definition, is bound to degenerate in fact. First of all, this: that if a man asks himself (as a *moral philosopher* quite properly will) what is the nature of moral goodness, he precisely thereby transfers his attention from the will's objective to its quality. Now it really is the case, I think, that persistence in this emphasis makes it easier than it would otherwise be for a concern for the quality of the will to usurp the position of what should be the operative consideration, ousting the concern to do the right as we see it. Still, it remains perfectly possible to identify this failing for what it is and to correct it by a refocusing of our mind upon objective claims. In any case the danger here is, so to say, an 'occupational risk' of the reflective moralist; it is not incident to all moral living as such. And certainly it is sheer muddle to suppose that, because a moral philosopher, for his particular purposes, stresses the quality of the moral will in his *theory*, therefore he is stressing it, or is insisting that people generally should stress it, in his, or their, *practical attitudes*. I surmise that this muddle has played some part in the building-up of the anti-moralistic contention.[1]

But there is another source of the temptation to adopt an egocentric attitude that is by no means the unwelcome prerogative of the philosopher but, on the contrary, is a feature of all moral experience. What is our duty is sometimes very repugnant to our wishes and feelings, and the will to perform it has need to be strenuously effortful. In such a case it seems to me very natural, and not in itself in the slightest degree reprehensible, that a man should become conscious that in failing to respond as he should he will, besides doing what he considers wrong, be acting in a

[1] Some remarks by J. W. Harvey, in *Proc. Ar. Soc.*, Suppl., Vol. XXIX (1955) p. 22, deserve notice in this connection; though I should not myself wish to attack, on this ground anyhow, the emphasis laid in philosophy upon agent-goodness.

manner unworthy of himself. It seems to me mere psychological matter of fact that this thought is likely to occur to him; and it seems to me mere psychological matter of fact that, when it does, it will have incentive value. (We may recall, as providing at least an analogy, Plato's doctrine that the θυμοειδές is the 'natural ally' of the λογιστικόν.) 'Moral self-forgetfulness' will then, in a sense, be replaced by 'moral self-respect', and this has an egocentric sound. But we must not be hasty in drawing conclusions: let us ask what is the harm in it. The motive of self-respect, so far, is still one of *moral* self-respect: that is to say, the total motive-complex still includes as the *governing* factor a concern to do right as such. The particular sort of humiliation one is seeking to avoid is defined by reference to that outward-looking concern. The motive becomes corrupted into what we might condemn as 'spiritual pride' only when our interest in our self-respect ceases to be adjectival to the essential moral motive, when it becomes detached from it and is erected into a substantive motive on its own account. Of course this can happen; it can happen notwithstanding the self-contradictoriness of the resultant attitude. But it seems to me clear that it is not bound to happen.

(4)

And at this point I must add that the *fear* of spiritual pride may sometimes be so exaggerated as to resemble, I think, a neurosis rather than the health of the soul; and the exaggeration may be numbered among the factors that encourage the denial that our morally good decisions are 'our own work'. If I may say so with the utmost respect, this seems to me to be the case with Donald Baillie when he writes: 'When I make the wrong choice, I am entirely responsible, and my conscience condemns me. And yet (here is the paradox) when I make the right choice, my conscience does not applaud or congratulate me. I do not feel meritorious or glow with self-esteem—if and in so far as I am a Christian.'[1] It may of course be simply a symptom of my not being a Christian if I say that what is here suggested is just not true; as indeed I said earlier that it *could* not be true, even as a 'paradox', that my wrong decisions are blameable and my right ones not laudable. Anyhow if I am to be honest I do not know what else I can say.

[1] *God was in Christ*, p. 116.

I do in a sense, when I overcome a temptation, approve not only my act but myself as willing it: I do reckon the achievement, just as I should the failure, as mine.

But I say I approve myself 'in a sense', for it is certainly not in the particular manner that Baillie's language describes. And I must protest that those who do not positively disclaim all merit are not thereby committed to anything that could fairly be spoken of as indulging in self-applause or glowing with self-esteem. I entirely agree that to glow with self-esteem would be unfitting. But why would it be unfitting? For two reasons, neither of which in the slightest degree supports the view that my achievement is not fully and wholly mine.

In the first place, to overcome even the most difficult temptation is still not to do better than I ought, whereas every failure is a doing worse than I ought. It is evident, then, that from a purely moral point of view there is an ineptitude about the language of self-laudation and glowing self-esteem which there is not about the language of self-reproach and remorse. A man who does not see this has not understood the rigour of the moral demand. It would be better to speak of a feeling of *relief* when we do not fail than to speak of self-laudation; but the relief is that of someone who has not 'fallen down on his job', not that of someone who has been snatched from danger by another's arm.

But in the second place, Baillie's language summons up the idea of a man who has 'taken his eye off' the work to be done and is letting it rest enjoyingly on himself, the doer. Now this too, as I have argued already, is wrong from a purely moral point of view, and it is still a mere, and in principle perfectly attainable, moral attitude that reprehends and overcomes the fault. Even if our feeling is the quite proper one of relief we cannot allow ourselves complacently to rest in it, for the work to be done is continual and the next 'job' is always immediately upon us. For this reason there can be danger even in remorse; there too to be obsessed by the *feeling* is a form of corruption—the feeling is healthy only as it is harnessed to *resolution*. The difference in this connection between the case of moral failure and that of moral success is that the dynamic value of moral success is fully secured by the mere attendant sense of happiness, and is obstructed rather than reinforced by dwelling in thought upon our achievement; whereas, so long as we do not allow our feelings to obsess us, an explicit, attentive recognition of our failure is necessary if its power to stimulate is to be fully actualized.

(5)

To come back to the main point. An egocentric emphasis is certainly to be deplored; and there are factors that constitute an ever-present threat that it will develop. But I do not admit that it is more than a threat, to which we may succumb but need not. And, as Kirk very fairly points out,[1] the threat exists even for the life of worship; even that can corrupt and degenerate into self-centred 'religiosity'. The presence of a religious, as distinct from a moral, element in our attitude towards the moral demand may not then be sufficient to remove the danger of egocentric corruption, any more than it is necessary as a defence against it. Kirk, again very fairly, notices that 'there are those who—though they make little if any use of the time-honoured forms of worship—yet serve their fellows with a humility which puts the ordinary Christian to shame'. He adds, indeed, that 'their unselfish service is in itself proof that—whether by accident or natural gift—they are already in the attitude of worship towards their ideal'.[2] But if 'attitude of worship' here means something other than the properly moral attitude itself, then (save on a misconception, such as Kirk, like Oman, does in fact evince, of the nature of the properly moral attitude) this is mere dogmatism. I suspect, however, that in substance I am really in agreement with Kirk. I suspect that what he calls 'the attitude of worship towards their ideal' is the very same thing that I might more clumsily describe as 'the responsive sense of the absolute claim upon me of an objective order of values'. And this I regard not as an alternative to the 'merely moral' sense of obligation but as the sense of obligation itself when most adequately realized and when, without becoming other or more than moral, it has in its very nature as moral a quality of reverential abasement that may not improperly be termed 'religious'.

(6)

From this conclusion there is a natural transition to the discussion of the second of the two criticisms of the 'moralistic' ideal of

[1] Op. cit., p. 448.   [2] Op. cit., pp. 448–9.

dutifulness to which I have referred. This was to the effect that even if 'merely moral' endeavour is not positively self-defeating yet the 'merely moral' life is a defective one. There is a better life than that of the dutiful will; the life, namely, whose motive or spring or dynamic is *love*.

In proceeding to the examination of this suggestion let us be clear in the first place that we are not concerned with the concept of a *holy* will, in the sense in which that involves *non posse peccare*. By definition such a will would transcend the sphere of temptation altogether, and therewith of our human life. I do not know what it would be like to have such a will; but I do know that it is irrelevant to the context of moral experience—Christian thought, if I correctly interpret it, does not ascribe it even to Christ. The love that is said to be better than even the completest dutifulness must, in the present connection, be something that can be meaningfully ascribed to, something that is available to, tempted and struggling mankind.

On the other hand, it cannot be the all too human love of natural affection for our fellows. Not that the heart's affections are to be despised: far otherwise, and, for myself, I strongly resent it when the emphasis put upon duty in moral theory is mistaken for a denial of their worth. Human friendship and love have their own glory. They have, too, their moral *use*, though no one who delights in them can possibly think primarily of that—it will occur to him only in grateful reflection. 'Even much stronger mortals than Fred Vincy', says George Eliot in *Middlemarch*, 'hold half their rectitude in the mind of the being they love best.'[1] This is undoubtedly true. It would be an endless, and I hope superfluous, undertaking to enlarge upon the ways in which the natural affections enrich life and assist the sanity and energy of the moral will. Yet it is also true that the promptings of our affections, though no thought of duty can generate them and though no conscientiousness is a substitute for them, must approve themselves in the court of conscience. They cannot authorize their own enactment.[2] This is certainly not the love of which we could say *Dilige et quod vis fac*. But of a love that, as a motive, is *superior* to dutifulness must it not be possible to say that?

[1] See p. 256 of the 'World's Classics' edition.
[2] We could indeed, personifying duty, represent it as speaking of the affections in the language of Matthew x. 35–7.

But, we have learned to believe, there is a love of man for man that is not one of mere natural affection; and it may be a peculiar merit of Christianity to have taught us this, or at least to have taught it most effectively. It is that Agape which, in its sober-coloured dress, presents itself to us as a *respect* for our fellows *simply as persons*. Many would say that the claim this makes on our allegiance needs no such anxious scrutiny as do the impulses of the natural affections, and admits no refusal. Yet this again cannot be the love that replaces dutifulness as being a higher motive. It can, it is true, put on a brighter garment of vivid feeling, and it may be that in the life of religion, and there alone, it does so. But however completely the sense of constraint, of moral requirement and effort, may then vanish from Agape itself, so that for the first time, perhaps, it fully deserves its name, this will not meet the essential difficulty. Be it bright or drab it has the same function and the same limitations. Its requirement may be absolute but it is not exhaustive. Whatever we do we should do it with a deep concern for the free spiritual life and growth of others, as members one of another in a spiritual community, as working with them and never merely, even with the best intentions, on them, let alone using them solely as instruments. Yet a man may be set to act thus and still not know what he is to do in this temper of mind. He must discover that in some other way; and to discover it is to discover a moral claim the meeting of which requires that practical respect for the claim, which is dutifulness, and not simply that concern for the other as person, which is love. Once again, *Dilige et quod vis fac* cannot be the self-sufficient last word; not this time because the love itself may need restraint or check but because it does not of itself supply the whole of what is required to constitute an adequate rule of life.[1] Let anyone but examine his own experience and he will discover, I think, how a loving concern can even accentuate the sense of perplexity as to how to act for the best.

(7)

It may be said that no matter how these considerations may bear on the comparative estimates of love and dutifulness in a secular

---

[1] Cf. Lindsay, *The Two Moralities*, pp. 55–7. I should observe that I have here spoken of 'love' as though it were *simply* a spirit or attitude and did not of itself in any measure determine the content of moral action. And this, I incline

or humanistic ethic they do not impugn the theological version of the preference for the motive of love. The love that is to be ranked above sense of duty on this view is not any love of man for man but man's love for God, and that makes all the difference.

Whether it makes all the difference or not, however, we surely cannot say until we know how the expression 'man's love for God' is to be understood. And once again the fundamental issue is that of the employment or non-employment of the human analogy. If we are to think of love for God as love for a *person* what we have already urged is by no means beside the mark. For in that case either natural affection or Agape must be our model; and, whichever we select, the difficulties that confronted us before confront us again.

It might indeed be thought by some, and not least by some of a religious temper of mind, that it is impossible seriously to intend by 'love for God' anything analogous to the natural human affections. But at least as regards Christianity the supposition would be mistaken. Those for whom Christ is not simply man but God and man at once, both an historic human person and an abiding divine Friend, can feel towards *Him* (as the literature of Christianity clearly shows) and *in that sense* towards the Divine, both as Son and even as the Father whom the Son reveals, a love of affection. The feeling, which will incorporate the desire to *please* God, is certainly possible. But just as certainly it does not provide a motive for action that can be preferred to dutifulness. True, in the case of God (unlike any human object of our love) we must suppose that what would please Him coincides materially with what would be right. None the less, just as a human father should wish his child to be governed by the thought of what is right and not by the thought of pleasing his parent (grieved though he would naturally be had his child no wish to please him), so, if we are to represent God as person at all, we

to believe, is not strictly true; or at least it involves a very misleading abstraction. (See my discussion in *Philosophy*, October 1960.) But even if *some* of the moral claims upon us are themselves just specific modes of Agape I should still maintain that Agape is not *all*-sufficient. And Agape itself, as thus interpreted and become determinate, appears rather as a part of dutifulness than as a possible alternative to it; so that now not only may it too need a certain restraint or check, but the question whether 'love' can supersede 'dutifulness' must take another form, related to a different sense of 'love'. It is this new question that is raised in Section 9 of the present chapter and eventually answered in Section 21.

must suppose Him to disapprove of any subordination of our sense of the moral claim as such to our love, our grateful affection (if we may so speak), for Himself. In fact, until we represent God as person we cannot give a *meaning* to the words 'love for God' on the analogy of human affection; and when we view God as person we cannot give the *primacy* to the motive of love thus understood except by contradicting what we believe to be true of the best in human relationships and speaking of God as though he fell short of the ideal of human fatherhood.

Of course, given the material coincidence of what is right with what pleases God, it might be contended that 'pleasing God' is for practical purposes a most simple, safe and efficacious way of *representing* to ourselves the ideal of right living. But what alone will make this representation safe is that we have first defined 'what pleases God' in terms of 'what would be right'. Our doing so is precisely why we cannot envisage a conflict between the two. Now we have only to recognize that this is the position in order to recognize also that even while we speak of love for God as our motive we still regard the claim of the right as such as the paramount consideration; there can be no question of subordinating that consideration to a (supposedly distinguishable) motive of love.[1]

As for the love that is Agape, little need be said about that. It seems to me obvious that even if it is fitting to apply this concept to our relationship to God, even if to do so does not carry (as some may feel it does) a suggestion of blasphemous effrontery, still the very nature of the concept is such as to debar it from being a substitute for the concept of duty, in its God-ward as in its man-ward reference, and for the same reason in each case.

(8)

Is there then no truth in the doctrine that love for God is the supreme motive? I should not say so. I am not recommending that we should remove from its pre-eminent position what we have

---

[1] With the suggestion put forward in the foregoing argument that it is through the idea of the dual nature of Christ that we can *seem* to achieve the concept of God as object of a love of affection that is yet not subject to the claims of duty as ordinary human affections are, compare a somewhat similar line of thought in C. B. Martin, 'The Perfect Good' (in *New Essays in Philosophical Theology*, ed. Flew and MacIntyre).

been told is the first and greatest commandment. The question
is how, if it is to retain that position, it must be understood. And
here I would appeal to a valuable discussion by Clement Webb.[1]
Asking what the words of Jesus could have meant to those to whom
they were immediately addressed, Webb concludes that 'the love
of God described in the first great commandment is . . . to be
understood primarily after the analogy of the love which one may
bear to one's country or one's cause';[2] although, he adds, 'in
Christianity it is presented with the additional "warmth and
intimacy"[3] . . . which belongs to what we call a *personal* relation'.
Let us think then of love for God in terms of love for a 'cause',
and consider what 'cause' that could be that is worthy of an
absolute and comprehensive devotion. In answering this question
I should accept as true what Webb offers as Kantian exegesis;
as explanation, that is, of how Kant could and probably did
interpret the first commandment in its distinction from the
second. What the first commandment enjoins would be, in Webb's
words, 'the general surrender of our wills to the moral law,
whatever that law may command';[4] that is to say, it enjoins
precisely what I have called the higher mode of dutifulness. The
second commandment on the other hand is concerned with the
'specification' of this absolute and general dutifulness into the
determinate obligations of social relationship. The 'cause' we are
to love, then, our love for which is love for God, is simply the
'cause' of morality itself, or 'the moral law'. Thus we recur to
the idea that the moral law is to be identified with God, in the
sense and with the qualifications, of course, that I indicated when
I first put forward this suggestion.[5] And just as God *is* that law
and not a being different from and ontologically superior to it
(or, perhaps we might better say, not superior to that 'objective
order of values' whose pressure upon our wills is *represented* as
law) so our love for God is not a principle of action superior to
dutifulness but is dutifulness itself. 'Conscientiousness is the sum
and substance of the love of God.'[6]

[1] *The Contribution of Christianity to Ethics*, pp. 18–22. See also pp. 64–8.
[2] *Op. cit.*, p. 22.
[3] These words are an acknowledged borrowing from William James.
[4] *Op. cit.*, p. 68.   [5] *Supra*, p. 81.
[6] Tyrrell, *Essays on Faith and Immortality*, p. 26.

K

(9)

But surely dutifulness, as we know it in ordinary experience, is something very different from the kind of glowing loyalty that it would be natural to speak of as love? I am bound to agree. And, of course, so long as we are prepared to allow a place at all to the thought of God as personal (and I have not denied that we may do so) there is no reason why there should not be *associated* with our dutifulness the 'warmth and intimacy' of a personal relationship. How, indeed, could it be otherwise for anyone whose theistic faith is more than a theological formula? To say that such a compounded attitude is better than mere dutifulness might well be true; and still we should not be saying that the personal component in it constitutes a motive higher than anything that is 'merely moral'.

Perhaps this concedes to the religious claim all that is its due. But I am not satisfied that it does. I think it is felt, and I think it is reasonably felt, that the moment of dutifulness itself should be capable of assuming a quality not unworthy of the name of love. The question is, how this could possibly be. And it is at this point that I must consider that fundamental element in the argument for grace as constitutively operative in the will to which I alluded earlier.[1] It is, in fact, through the very forces that seem to threaten me with retreat that the line of advance lies.

But while the ultimate purpose of the sections that follow is the one I have just indicated, I must warn the reader that only a very few pages will be expressly devoted to it. I propose to spend a considerable part of my time in 'stage-setting'; that is to say, in explaining the context in which the problem that will eventually concern us arises. And again, having stated the problem I shall not immediately offer my solution but shall first direct my attention to a different point, though one that provides in my opinion a helpful analogy. The whole treatment may well seem over-elaborate: from one point of view it no doubt really is so. The logical structure of the main argument would not suffer were what I have to say at least very considerably compressed. On the other hand, the leisurely and expansive procedure I shall employ will assist, I hope, to protect me, as nothing else would, against what

[1] *Supra*, p. 132.

could be a fatal suspicion. It may do something to mitigate the feeling that I am dismissing on altogether too slight and cursory a survey a conception with which, it might be said, I am just so totally out of sympathy as to be incapable of doing justice to it. Looked at in this way the elaboration is less irrelevant in fact to my proclaimed purpose than it is in appearance. I must, however, admit that I indulge in it also for the sake of a wider interest. I am glad of the opportunity that the context affords, even if it does not positively demand this, of laying some stress on an aspect of our experience, and of our thought about God, that the limited scope of this essay compels me for the most part to pass by or seemingly to depreciate. There can of course be no question in any case of my pretending to provide a comprehensive and balanced picture of the religious life. But it is right that I should do what I conveniently can to correct a onesideness that is a mere accident of my theme, to guard against a misconception of my own total outlook that my silence and my vociferations alike might create were they left uncompensated. And I shall have no occasion for this more suitable than the present.

(10)

I begin, then, a long way off from my avowed goal, with the reminder that in our earlier discussion of grace and freedom I was in effect asking what moral theory can *tolerate* in a doctrine of grace. I wish now to look at the matter from the other side, from the side not of morality but of religion, and to ask what religion *requires* by way of a doctrine of grace. Certainly for the particular purposes of this essay, taking as it does the standpoint of the moralist, this is a secondary question; yet even by the moralist it ought not to be simply ignored. Suppose the answer to it were such that we had to conclude that moral and religious convictions were inevitably in conflict, could any man reasonably say that that was of no interest to him, simply because he had already decided that, in the event of such a conflict, he must undoubtedly side with morality? At least he could not reasonably expect a patient hearing from those to whom religion is a matter of prime importance and deep personal persuasion, and to whom just for that reason an enquiry such as the present one is particularly addressed.

This question of the legitimate claims of religion did not need specific attention when the nature of the moral demand was under consideration, for the good reason that there the issue was altogether clearer and less complicated and could be disposed of in passing. So far as concerns the moral demand, what religion plainly requires, but also, plainly, all that it requires, is that God should be acknowledged as ultimate authority and not be represented as subject to, or even set merely 'alongside of' the moral law. And this requirement can easily enough be met so long as we do not insist on thinking of God as a person. Now though there is here a problem, no doubt, for religion regarding the nature of God (on which I shall later have a little to say) it is not a problem internal to the context of moral demand itself. So long as we restrict our attention to that context there is no question of how far morality can employ the concept of a personal God, or how far religion requires that it should do so. To both questions the answer is simply 'Not at all.' As regards grace and the moral response the position is very different. Our account of the moment of response *can* make room, as I have argued, for the concept of God as gracious and in that manner personal; and if we once admit the concept of God as personal at all the question how much room to allow it is a real one, the moral and religious answers to which are not necessarily in agreement. I have already indicated what I think is the answer of morality. But what has religion to say? It is not perhaps immediately obvious that to deny the fact of grace is to deny God altogether; and it is certainly not immediately obvious that if religion does require a doctrine of grace it can be satisfied with one whose scope is confined within the limits I have set for it. Both these propositions I believe to be in fact true; but whether they are so or not needs consideration. To this, then, let us turn.

(11)

The question of what religion requires by way of a doctrine of grace has both an *a priori* and an empirical side to it. I take it first in its *a priori* aspect. It is to be understood, of course, that, though I abstract from the distinctive tenets of Christian theism, I assume the identity of religion with theistic religion in some form or other, since only for theism can the concept of grace, as we are here interpreting it, have any significance at all. I do not stay to ask whether this identification has a more general warrant.[1] Neither, I must add, am I concerned to argue for the actual truth of theism, though certain of the things I shall be saying later have a bearing on that. I simply take theism for granted and ask about the relation in which the very concept of it stands to the concept of grace.

Theism we may reasonably define in terms of the belief in one God, the Creator, conceived of as a Being to whom the concept of 'person' *somehow* applies, and as perfect in wisdom, love and power. (Skirting the abyss of the problem of evil, I leave undetermined what is to be understood here by 'perfection'.) And grace, we may remind ourselves, has earlier been defined for us as 'the will of God (which is also His love) regarded as active on behalf of and in man'.[2] But if this is what 'grace' means, then surely for a theist a doctrine of grace in some form is *analytically* involved in his basic belief. He is bound to suppose the operation of grace *everywhere*, subject only to such limitations (whether or not he describes these as voluntary self-limitations) as he must, or without prejudice to the divine perfection can, assign to the power of God. No particular view of the status of man in creation is implied in this. A god such as the theist affirms who did not help all his creatures to the utmost—whether through the pattern of circumstance, or by insights (the whole sphere of illuminative grace) and by impulses and promptings—would be a contradiction in terms. And it is clear, too, that the possibility of 'special', no less than 'general', providence must be in principle admitted. How can this be denied if there is to be any validity at all in the representation of God as personal? At this point, however, we must be content with admitting it in principle merely, for we can have no assurance *a priori* that God's best possible care for us individually may not take the form of subjecting us wholly to the discipline and constraints of general laws.

Thus far the theist must go, and only so far may he go, in his affirmation independently of the appeal to experience. And nothing in this raises problems for ethical thought. Nothing in it forbids our holding that God's 'utmost' is bounded not only by the fact of incompossibles but by the free volitions of finite spirits, whose

[1] But see, for example, Campbell, *Selfhood and Godhood*, Lecture XII.
[2] See above, p. 108.

freedom is none the less real because they, as creatures endowed with it, are ontologically through and through dependent upon God.[1] Nothing, that is to say, that belongs to the concept of grace as a postulate of theism rules out the restriction of the province of grace to what is environmental to, not constitutive of, the human will.

(12)

So much for *a priori* considerations. But what of the evidence of experience? My concern here is not with the question whether experience may indirectly support a doctrine of grace by directly supporting the theistic position that, in the sense already explained, entails it. The point at issue is whether the operation of grace is itself an empirical fact. Thus all experiences are to be put aside as irrelevant that, however amenable they may be to description in terms of the operation of grace, do not actually bear the impress of that character upon them.

In using this phrase I do not wish to suggest that such an 'impress' could ever be quite unquestionable datum. Without committing myself as to whether any matter of fact is datum of this kind I may, I think, safely affirm that at least the operation of grace is not so. What I envisage is rather this: that the 'gracious' character of an experience, though in a sense it is affirmed as *interpretation*, is yet perhaps not affirmed as the conclusion of an argument, any more than a perceptual judgment is inferred from sensation or than in the face-to-face encounter of persons in living communication, the recognition that I am encountering another *person* is an inference from what is primarily an 'I—it' experience. That I am the recipient of grace will, I am supposing, be a matter of direct awareness, if it ever is so, in a mode analogous to that in which I directly apprehend not sense-data but the pen with which I write, or again not vocables and gestures but the man who speaks to me. It will be correspondingly open, on reflection, to analogous sceptical doubts, and liable analogously to error in the particular case. I must not of course suggest that there is a perfect resemblance between these different situations:

[1] It is important to distinguish between (1) a restriction put on God by the incompossibility of A's being a moral personality with A's being devoid of freedom and (2) a restriction put on God by A's actual possession of the freedom that is essential to his moral personality.

I must speak only of analogy, and in doing so hint at a large problem that it would take me far beyond my limited purpose to explore. Obviously, were only precisely similar doubts and possibilities of error involved in our knowledge of other selves on the one hand and in any supposed *specific* experiences of God on the other, then reticence in regard to the work of God in our lives would be, as it plainly is not, as strained and artificial as the pretence of not knowing that here or here I meet as person *this* friend and not someone else or even some impersonal constituent of the world. God is certainly not an identifiable Thou in just the way in which finite beings are. When I ask therefore, whether the operation of grace may be an empirical fact, and remind myself that grace has been defined in personalist terms, it is to be understood that I am asking whether there are occasions in experience that carry with them *some* kind of assurance of an 'I—thou' relationship that at once resembles our consciousness of our fellow human beings as persons and differs from it in a way that leaves it peculiarly liable to sceptical infections.

(13)

What then is the answer to this question? I do not think that any particular pattern of circumstance ('circumstance' being used to cover even such intimately personal factors as our involuntary ideas and impulses) can, simply in its own nature as such or such a pattern, be identified as bearing in some special way the 'signature' of God. That is to say, if, as is commonly done, we distinguish providence from grace (though according to the letter of our definition it will strictly be itself a mode of grace) I do not think we have empirical justification for asserting of any particular pattern of circumstance that it is peculiarly providential. *All* circumstances, of course, will be held by a theist to be providential, except in so far as he lapses into an unacknowledged dualism; and I am not questioning his right to view them so. What I question is his title to identify *particular* circumstances as the manifestation of a *special* providence. There may of course be particular occasions on which one has a peculiarly lively sense of God as Lord of all circumstances, but that is another matter. And even this lively sense of God will be, I believe, no better than superstitious in so far as it depends (as it may never wholly do) on the nature of the circumstances in the particular case, whether that be our 'providential' presence on the pavement just where and when the child was about to run out in front of the oncoming car or our 'providential' missing of the train that was later derailed. If he is not to pretend to have searched the divine understanding a theist should endeavour to combine his general assurance that he is in the hands of God with a refusal to particularize. To the question 'Where does Circumstance end and Providence where begins it'?[1] he will attempt no answer save in terms of that meaning of 'Providence' which will justify him in claiming that the two perfectly coincide; no answer, that is to say, that takes him a step beyond the position to which his theism commits him *a priori*. With Professor Paton's observations on this subject[2] I am so far in complete agreement. I would only add two comments. First, it does not seem to me to follow that, as Paton appears to suggest, the very concept of special providence must be abandoned as illegitimate—my agnosticism cuts both ways. It is only our ability to give it determinate application that is denied. And secondly, necessary though it is, when general and special providence have once been distinguished, to be thus agnostic about the latter, still there is something unsatisfactory about the term 'general providence' itself. It has a chilly deistic sound; and if we cannot improve on it we must at least correct the impression it conveys by insisting that any providence, to be worthy of the name at all, however 'general' in the sense intended it may be, must at the same time be 'special' in that its concern throughout is with the individual person and not simply with men in the mass.

If there is ever any valid immediate awareness of ourselves as subjects of grace this is likely to be found, I should suppose, not in the recognition of some peculiar sign of God in our presented or, so to say, 'incoming' circumstances, but as an aspect of, and embedded in, the active 'outgoing' experience which is *prayer*. In saying this I do not restrict the term 'prayer' to signify only deliberate and articulate petition. As to articulateness, I can believe that the old woman's 'Oh!' of which

---

[1] A. H. Clough, in Part IX of the *Bothie of Tober-na-Vuolich*.
[2] Paton, *The Modern Predicament*, Chapter XXIII, Section 4. Cf. Kant, *Lectures on Ethics*, trans. Infield, pp. 94–5.

Rousseau writes *could* be a good prayer.[1] And as to petition, I question if it makes a material difference whether we treat that only as prayer or extend the meaning of the word to embrace in the end the whole range of worship: whichever we do, it surely is the fact that petition and worship cannot, for the theist, be dissevered. There can indeed be petition addressed to beings whom we do not worship, but this is not what religion means by prayer. What there cannot be, I think, is worship without petition where the object of worship is thought of as in any sense a person.[2] Finite and needy creatures are simply unable to abstain from petition in such a case. It is of the essence of their self-consciousness to be, so to say, full of 'optatives', and where the fulfilment of these is thought to depend upon another to whom appeal is possible they pass naturally into 'petitives'. But I must point out that to say this is not to say that everything that appears as petition, every utterance that uses the *form* of petition, is the petition it appears to be. It will become clear in due course why it is important to insist on this.

(14)

If, then, it is asked whether grace is an empirical fact, the testimony that is most relevant, however troubled others may be about accepting it, is surely the testimony of those whose lives are peculiarly lives of prayer. And the tenor of this testimony seems plainly to be such as to support the view that in prayer we may establish a relationship in which grace is revealed as operative in the sense that God is 'met' as personal.

I must of course go on to insist that this testimony of prayer to the fact of grace should not be too readily taken at its face value. It is true, and not always sufficiently attended to, that those who lack the experience that is relevant, if any experience

---

[1] Rousseau, *Confessions* Book XII (Vol. II, p. 281 of the 'Everyman' translation): 'I remember reading of a wise bishop, who, during a visit to his diocese, came upon an old woman who, by way of prayer, could say nothing but "Oh!" "Good mother," said the bishop, "continue to pray in this manner; your prayer is better than ours." This better prayer is also mine.'

[2] The connection is affirmed of course only under this condition. The worship of a Spinozistic 'Deus sive Natura' so far from embracing, or generating, petitionary prayer would exclude it. It may be asked whether we should be willing to speak of the *worship* of such a being if the experience were not coloured (or discoloured) by personalist concepts. But this question, though it is relevant to that of the propriety of equating religion with *theistic* religion, is no part of my present concern, which is simply with the implications of theism.

is so, can hardly claim to dictate a theory to those who have it. But even those who have it must, as philosophers, scrutinize it with all possible scepticism. Here is where it is necessary to remember that the alleged fact is not datum in any unquestionable sense; and that, as interpretation even, it does not have the kind of security that we enjoy in regard to the reality of our human friends. It is not simply gratuitous to question whether the theistic faith postulated by the attitude and activity of prayer is well-founded, or whether the experience itself is delusive or at best (if I may put it thus) accidentally valid, as an ill-founded belief might be accidently true. We must ask if it might not be the case that in petitionary prayer we are simply conforming our thought and practice to a use of interpretative concepts—the personalist concepts of theism—that comes naturally to us and is subjectively satisfying, and of which we are only entitled to say further that against their application nothing in the experience to which they are referred positively rebels. '*Man never knows how anthropomorphic he is*, says Goethe; and so man tends always to represent everything under his own figure.'[1] Perhaps that is the root of the matter. Nor have we necessarily to do merely with a primitive or 'innate' tendency of the mind: habituation to explicit conceptual schemes may similarly determine our reading of the facts in a way that the facts themselves in their psychological character do not compel.[2] And thus, so far as the evidence of prayer can take us, there would be no more than an 'as if' status to our theism and to the 'encounter with God' to which we lay claim.[3] Certainly we cannot rely on any quite simple pragmatic test, in terms of the efficacy of prayer 'informed' by the concepts of theistic faith, to carry us further. Apart from and prior to the question whether the test is passed there are the very perplexing questions of the precise form it should take and of the evidential value of any test of this type.[4]

[1] Matthew Arnold, *Literature and Dogma*, Chapter 1.

[2] Thinkers occupying such different standpoints as Broad and Mascall can so far agree. See Broad in his paper on 'The Validity of Belief in a Personal God', *Religion, Philosophy and Psychical Research*, p. 173; Mascall, *He Who Is*, p. 22, n. 1.

[3] 'So far as the evidence of prayer can take us'; I am of course abstracting from other possible grounds for a reasonable belief in a personal God.

[4] For the possibility, and difficulty, of such a test see, for instance, Basil Mitchell's remarks on 'the witness of the saints' in his essay 'The Grace of God'. (*Faith and Logic*, ed. Basil Mitchell.)

All these are obvious difficulties which, however, I have no intention of trying to resolve here. They concern the credentials of theism rather than the nature of the convictions intrinsic to the theistic standpoint. Yet I should like to say just a little more by way of affirming and explaining my own belief that the evidence of prayer must be taken seriously.

I would observe that we must be careful not to look for the wrong sort of certitude in this connection, and not to conclude, if we cannot attain it, that we do not have all possible assurance in the appropriate mode. We must remember that we do not and cannot have a 'Cartesian' or 'mathematical' certainty even of the existence of other finite selves, and that such certainty as we do have in that connection provides at least the closest analogue to the experiential certainty we should expect in regard to a personal God. The question then is whether it is reasonable to doubt, against the testimony to the contrary, that the man of prayer has a certainty somewhat of this sort that he stands in a real 'I—Thou' relationship to the Being whom he addresses. And here I would mention two considerations that might, I think, suitably be borne in mind by those who are disposed to reply to this question with a very confident 'Yes'.

The first is this. Not only is it true, I believe, that the continuous avoidance of the 'I—Thou' prayerful attitude is what really demands effort on our part, rather than the intermittent achievement of it; it is also true that this effort of avoidance, so far as it is successful, creates not so much a sense of release from shackling superstitions as the sense that a native freedom of the spirit has been shackled. We are, as it were, 'strenuously not using' a part of our natures. Perhaps this is not the common experience: I report on my own case in the hope that some may recognize a likeness to theirs.

But, secondly, is it not perhaps rather more intelligible that there should be a doubt of the reality of a 'thou' where there really is a 'thou' than that there should be a persuasion of it in its absence? (We are speaking, we must remember, of the persuasions of people who are perfectly sane and balanced, judged by other criteria.) For it is surely true that our living sense of another human being as a person, as distinguished from an habitual and unfelt thinking of him so, depends on our adopting an attitude of receptiveness; so that even when it is we who talk, our talking is a moment in a colloquy—we are talking listeningly. Now without this living sense of the other as 'thou' there is no security that even our habituated thinking of persons as persons will remain effective and will not (despite a continuing lip-service to their personal status) degenerate into regarding them for all practical purposes as things, as the physical organisms that in part, and for perception and its scientific interpretation, they manifestly are: that is to say, we shall acknowledge them to be men but, really, men only in a biological sense. The acknowledgment of God, however, since He is not a perceptual object, cannot in this way merely degenerate. It can only, if the living sense be lost, be cancelled altogether. And without the listening utterance of prayer how can the living sense of God fail to be lost? Thus easily might a man come to disbelieve (though not perhaps, if he lacks honesty and self-criticism, to realize that he disbelieves) in a personal God, who none the less not only exists but is, in the appropriate manner, 'experientially accessible'. Would it really be as easy, we must ask ourselves, for the sense of the presence of God that belongs to at least some experiences of prayer, in the lives of some perfectly sensible people, to assert itself in the way it does if God did not exist?

For myself, anyhow, the conclusion to which I incline is this: that if there is to be any empirical warrant for the thought of God as personal and graciously operative it must be found ultimately in the experience of prayer, and that it is reasonable to believe that there in fact it is found. Evelyn Underhill has spoken of, on the one hand, man's 'intuition of a remote unchanging somewhat calling him' and, on the other hand, 'his longing for and as clear intuition of an intimate adorable somewhat, companioning him'.[1] My gloss on this would be that, whereas the 'calling' may or must be treated as metaphor, the 'companioning' may, when referred to the experience of prayer, so resist that treatment that in this case it would be more natural to speak not of 'somewhat' but of 'someone'.

(15)

Now if we take seriously the view that in prayer at least (whether or not in prayer only) a man may be in a personal relationship

[1] *Mysticism* (14th edition), p. 41.

with a God active in love, and if the petitionary form of prayer is as valid as, for a theist, it is natural and indeed unavoidable, then surely we must say in the name of morality itself that the proper practice, whatever that be, of petitionary prayer is a fundamental and standing interest of the honest and wise will. This must be said in the name of morality itself, since the morally devoted will, as I have argued already, is outward-looking: whatever its capacities, it is not ambitious to insist on its own independence, but only to bring into action every available power for good.

We are, then, to make petition, taking petitionary prayer as valid in principle. But if prayer is valid in principle so also, of course, must be the concept of answered prayer. For what then do men rightly, and not merely superstitiously, pray? Whatever it be it must be meaningful to suppose it granted. And now at last we come to what, in the structure of my argument, has been the objective of this whole discussion of prayer. While much that men ask for concerns what is at most environmental to their moral effort they do also ask that their will itself may be 'conformed' to God's will and 'enabled'. However this is to be understood it is at least not crude superstition; it is not, I am sure, something to be lightly dismissed as simple-minded error. But if it is not to be dismissed as error, then it is a quite fundamental factor in the case for the theory of constitutive grace. The prayer for enablement is, in the language of St Augustine, an asking God to 'give what He commands', namely the will's own quality and energy; and this can be gift only in the form of the grace of God immanent in and constitutive of the will. Of course one might enquire how, on this view, a man comes even to pray for this gift: but the question, if intended as criticism, seems to me unprofitable. After all, if constitutive grace is not as such an impossibility, why should we cavil at interpreting the prayer itself in terms of it?

So I find myself confronted by these alternatives: either I must retract the denial of the possibility of constitutive grace, notwithstanding everything I have said on that subject; or else I must hold that, contrary to appearances, the prayer for enablement can be interpreted in terms consistent with that denial. Of these alternatives I adopt the second. And the general principle of my interpretation is this: that without prejudice to the admission of a genuinely and properly petitionary element in prayer, and despite the naturalness and, it may be, the psychological inevitability of the petitionary form of the prayer for enablement itself, that prayer is in substance not petitionary.

But before I develop this interpretation I wish to make what is, on the face of it, a very considerable digression, but one that I hope will justify itself in relation to my argument as a whole. I wish to say something about forgiveness and the prayer for forgiveness. I wish to do so because in this case also what appears to be pure petition is, I believe, not really such; and because in the last analysis the concept of God implicit in the prayer for forgiveness is not the unambiguously personal concept that the language of petition suggests. In both these intimately related respects there is a striking parallel with the prayer for enablement. To exhibit this may help towards gaining acceptance for my interpretation of the latter, supposing it to be in need of such assistance. It may serve to remove a possible suspicion that that interpretation is no more than a desperate expedient devised *ad hoc* by a philosopher at bay.

(16)

It can be allowed that from a dictionary point of view 'forgiveness' means primarily 'the action of forgiving' (or the correlative 'condition or fact of being forgiven') rather than the frame of mind, the 'disposition or willingness to forgive', from which the action proceeds.[1] It is after all a noun formed from a verb that unmistakably suggests the performance of a determinate act on some particular occasion. Nor is the suggestion misleading if by 'forgiving' we mean some overt and formal remitting of a debt or surrender of a claim, even though the *act* of forgiving might in this case consist in no more than a performatory utterance, 'I forgive' functioning in a manner parallel with 'I hereby promise'.

But certainly this is not the meaning of 'forgiveness' and 'to forgive' with which ethical or religious thought should be primarily concerned; and from their point of view the natural suggestion of our language—namely, that we are talking of an act in the first place and only secondarily of an attitude—is a source of confusion. For them, to forgive is essentially to be in a certain

[1] The definitions here quoted are those of the *Shorter Oxford English Dictionary*.

state of mind, which in its positive character is, I should say, love (Agape), though considered as forgiveness it is defined by its negation of resentment in a context in which resentment would be natural. There is here strictly no *act* of forgiving at all, in the ordinary sense of 'act'. Any specific act is not itself the forgiving but the means of conveying to the person forgiven the consciousness that he is forgiven already. 'I forgive' is not now performatory but declaratory. The consciousness of forgiveness is, correspondingly, the consciousness of being the object of this unresentful love. We must, however, distinguish between the bare and precarious *belief* that one is loved and the *experience* of being loved; for I should maintain that our being loved can be an experience—it is not merely that a certain distinctive self-enclosed, purely subjective and 'intransitive', experience may generate the thought that one is loved. When I speak of the consciousness of forgiveness I mean it in this experiential sense. Now in this sense, it may be held, the consciousness of forgiveness cannot arise unless a love on the one side meets a penitence on the other; and it may further be held that sincere penitence in its turn is inseparable from love (Agape) on the side of the wrongdoer for the person wronged. I am disposed to accept both these suggestions, with the comment that the forgiving love itself, as distinguished from its object's consciousness of it, does not wait for penitence, nor of course does the penitence in any way earn or pay for the love.[1] The total perfected transaction, then, in which forgiveness—the freely forgiving and being freely forgiven—is joined with the consciousness of forgiveness, constitutes or restores, it may be with enrichment, a personal relationship that is essentially a meeting of two loves mediated by penitence.

Such I take to be the nature of forgiveness in the sense in which moral and religious thinking are interested in it and can approve it. And nothing in this account goes beyond what can be accepted as an ideal for human relationships. Correspondingly,

[1] What indeed could *earn* forgiveness? Nothing, surely, short of an undoing of the injury done, in the same exact sense in which repayment of a debt abolishes one's indebtedness. But this is 'metaphysically' impossible (though full discussion of the point would have to reckon with such views as that of Scheler, as reported by Stark on p. xxiii of the English translation of *The Nature of Sympathy*), and if it were possible it would no longer be love as *forgiveness* that was earned.

there is nothing in it that cannot be applied to the relationship between man and a God conceived as personal. We may intelligibly say, as people do say, that in this sense men ought to forgive one another as God does forgive them. But it is to be noted that the prayer for forgiveness, to be consistent with this account, must be understood to be something other than the petition that it appears to be—an asking God to change His attitude and action towards us, as though He were not already perfect in love. It is simply, so far as it is not dishonouring to God, the natural form in which the penitent realization of our wrong-doing finds utterance. The realization does of course demand utterance, even though only *voce interna*. It is not here sufficient, any more than in human relationships, to be *conscious* of our fault; we must *confess* it. We do not indeed imagine that God, like our human friends, requires to be informed of our penitence; but the penitence must have an overtone of welcoming recognition of the fact that it is not our secret. This recognition *is* confession in relation to God, and confession in this sense is inseparable from seeking forgiveness. Still it is true that what we have is not penitence *and* petition, but rather penitence expressed *as* petition; and it is by penitence and not by petition that the achievement of the right relationship is conditioned, by a change wrought in us and not by a change wrought in God.

(17)

Here, then, and even while we remain within a context in which we can represent God as person (in a context, therefore, in which the idea of petitionary prayer is appropriate enough), we have a prayer which though petitionary in form is not really petitionary in substance. But all this is still at a very superficial level, and we must go deeper.

For all the parallelism between the concepts of divine and human forgiveness there must surely also be an essential difference; and it is at this point that an internal tension develops within the concept of divine forgiveness. To make clear what the difficulty is I must refer back to the distinction I drew at an earlier point between a man's *good* (his interest or advantage) and *goodness*.[1] If I may assume the distinction to be understood

---

[1] See above, Chapter III, Section 13.

and accepted, I would now observe that, just as we distinguish between goodness and a man's good, so we must correspondingly distinguish between being indifferent to, or outraging, goodness and being indifferent to, or interfering with, a man's good. The first is evil-doing, the second is injury. No doubt consciously and gratuitously to inflict an injury is at the same time to outrage goodness, to do evil. But though the same act may be both these things at once they are none the less two things.

Now in a sense a man has a proprietary right in his own good, his interest or advantage. So far as it is considered simply as his good, and so far as he is considered simply in his character of being its actual or potential possessor, it is entirely his affair how he shall react to unjustified interference with it. This is what makes it proper to speak of him, if he reacts lovingly and not resentfully, as forgiving the injury done to himself; this he *can* forgive,[1] whereas it seems absurd and offensive to suggest that any man is in a position to forgive an injury done to another. When, however, injury is considered not as injury but in its character of wickedness or evil-doing we recognize that, so regarded, it is something that no man, not even the person injured, can properly be said to forgive. Men can forgive injuries; they cannot forgive sins. This is where the parallel between divine and human forgiveness breaks down: for God, unlike man, we are told, can and does forgive sins. The question for us now is, whether at this point at which God's forgiveness is seen as differing in scope from man's we must not also acknowledge that the concept of God as person fails us; and that the very meaning of 'forgiveness', hitherto so completely a concept of personal relationship, suffers a corresponding change though what it changes into may be very unclear.

Look at it this way. The concept of forgiveness has up to now been tied to, explained with reference to, the concept of injury. How then can it be applied to God's attitude to sin? Only, it would seem, by treating sin as injury done to God. I can see no alternative to this except that of defining God's forgiveness of sin in terms of the mere conjunction of the two facts, first that

---

[1] Of course when we bring into the account the fact that we all, besides having a proprietary right in our own good, are subject to the moral requirement to achieve goodness we must add that we not only can but ought to forgive the injuries done us.

L

He loves us, and second, that we whom He loves are sinners. It may be that this alternative is sometimes adopted in effect, though without clear recognition of its character. But it certainly does not do justice to the force of the expression 'forgiveness of sins', which plainly intends something more than the bare compresence of love on the one side and sin on the other. Neither does it preserve that very difference between God and man that we are supposed to be trying to understand; for in this most artificial and inadequate sense of forgiveness there is nothing to prevent any *human* being from 'forgiving sins'.

Consider then the proposition that sin is injury done to God. People do say this, and in one sense, given the concept of God as person, it is proper to say it. For His own holiness and His concern for goodness cannot be separated, and conceiving Him as person we must therefore represent Him as grieved and affronted by evil-doing. This way of thinking is surely familiar enough.

But in all probability no more is really intended by those who speak in this way than that we grieve God *by* our evil-doing. Our evil-doing involves a hurt to God, although the term 'evil-doing' has not the same meaning as the expression 'hurt to God'. We are still left with the distinction between sin considered as sin and sin considered as injury; and we must still ask whether, when we say that God forgives, we are speaking of His attitude towards the sin as such or of His attitude towards the injury. We can indeed form some idea of the latter attitude, but only because it does not transcend its human analogue and is not, distinctively, forgiveness of sin. But it is precisely the concept of forgiveness of sin *as sin* that we want to understand, and from that we are as far away as ever.

If we are not to abandon altogether the clue provided by our human forgiveness of injury, what then can we do but retract, as being too weak, the formula that we injure God by our sin and insist instead on an *identity* of sin with injury to God? That is to say, we define 'sin' as 'injury to God'. Now this will certainly not seem impossible to everyone. On the contrary, it is but fair to point out, it fits admirably with interpretations of the moral demand in terms of a personal divine will. But I have already considered and rejected such interpretations, and I must be permitted here to suppose that they ought to be rejected. On the alternative view that takes as ultimate a non-personal 'law' or 'order of values', however, an identification of sin with injury, as we have been understanding the latter term, is strictly meaningless. Now if this is so, we must also admit that since 'forgiveness' derives its meaning for us from the context of injury, we are in the end unable to attach any positive meaning at all to the expression 'forgiveness of sins'. Consequently, forgiveness of sins is not anything for which we can, really and significantly, make petitionary prayer. Penitence of course is still open to us, and the petitionary form of its *expression* will be as natural, or even unavoidable, as before, in so far as we do not simply discard the concept of a personal God as an irrelevancy. Moreover, we may be experientially entitled to say that repenting of the evil we have done brings a kind of peace to the soul that is qualitatively akin to that which attends forgiveness in human relationships. But that is all. Is it perhaps sufficient? Is it possible that those who look for more than this are really seeking a comfort that no reasonable doctrine can provide, though we may sometimes come by it illegitimately, by not being reasonable enough? Do they seek the comfort of the thought that our wrong-doing has been literally abolished, which is like the comfort that may come in a dream in which things are as if some disaster that has in fact befallen had never taken place?

Let me repeat the sum and substance of these reflections. There is, if I may so describe it, a *metaphysical* ground for denying a straightforward petitionary character to the prayer for forgiveness when what is meant by 'forgiveness' is, as it should be, forgiveness of sin, as distinguished from forgiveness of injury to God. So long as we are thinking in terms of forgiveness of injury merely we remain within the bounds of a personalist reading of the divine nature, and the idea of petition retains its applicability in principle. If it is inappropriate in fact, that is simply because we ought not to represent God as less willing to give than we are to receive; that is to say, the inappropriateness is what may be called a *moral* inappropriateness. When, however, it is forgiveness of sins that is in question the idea of petition seems to be inapplicable in principle. It is true that the petitionary form of our prayer may well be adapted to the pictures of our imagination, and it is true—the possibility is not to be excluded—that there may be associated with it an element of what is really

and properly petition to a God to whom the language of personality does also significantly apply. But the prayer itself, taken in
its essential nature as a prayer for the forgiveness of our sins,
must be understood as a mode of spiritual action on our part,
the 'answer' to which consists in the very condition of soul that
we ourselves thereby constitute, and not in something other that
is granted, as it were, contingently upon our action.

(18)

I may now at last turn to consider the case of prayer for enablement of the will. I have already said that if this is at once valid
prayer and genuinely petitionary in character, then we cannot
suppose its being answered to be anything other than the active
presence of God Himself in the will ὡς ἀγαπῶν, as succouring
love; which is to say that God's grace will be immanently constitutive of the will's very quality. As I pointed out, the *Da quod
iubes* of Augustine represents the frank acceptance of this as the
true account of our situation. But its frankness, to my mind,
simply emphasizes its impossibility. 'To ask him to change my
will', said Rousseau's Savoyard priest, 'is to ask him to do what
he asks of me.'[1] Are we not bound to agree? But if we are to
escape admitting the constitutive operation of grace without at
the same time denying what can be described as the *substantial*
validity of the prayer for enablement, we must deny that the
essential character of that prayer is properly represented by its
petitionary form. And this, as with the prayer for forgiveness,
is just what I should do. As the prayer for forgiveness is essentially the act and expression of contrition, of moral recovery, so,
I hold, what appears as petition for grace to make the resolution
required of us is in fact itself the moral victory, itself the resolution for which it seems to ask.

The prayer, we must remember, is ostensibly for a change in
the quality and efficacy of our will in face of a moral demand.
It is therefore of its essence that we hold, and continue to hold,
that demand before our mind. We are not interested in cases in
which our effort begins as or lapses into the stubbornness of pride,
or that blind stubbornness for which the question whether or not
to go on has really ceased to exist. The point at issue is how,

[1] Rousseau, *Emile* Book IV (p. 257 of the 'Everyman' translation).

when we are conscious of the demand upon us as *moral* requirement, it is always possible for us *of ourselves* to will as we ought.
And in giving my view about this I shall also be answering, so
far as I know how to, the second question that, now a long time
ago, I undertook to consider the question how the moral concern,
which the prayer itself evinces, can become transfigured, and
may at least approximate to the character of strong and eager
desire.

(19)

It is possible to have a genuine and sincere sense, which is yet a
bare and colourless one, that a particular course of action is our
duty. But at moments of serious temptation this will not suffice.
There is then nothing for it but either to 'go backward', so to say,
or else to 'go forward' in respect of our consciousness of the claim
upon us. To succumb to the temptation is to go backward in
respect of this consciousness. I mean by this that we never
succumb except as we lose the sincerity of the initial recognition
of our duty. To this extent, and it is very far from being negligible,
the Socratic contention that moral failure is a matter of ignorance
is to be accepted. 'All yielding is attended with a less vivid consciousness than resistance; it is the partial sleep of thought'.[1] But it
is even more important to notice the inadequacy of the Socratic
view. For in this 'partial sleep of thought' we still in a way know
our duty and know it to be absolute demand; only we are at the
same time refusing, as it were, to see its absoluteness. Insincerity,
after all, is not just ignorance. It is volitional, as is more clearly
indicated if we call it self-deceit; and our failure at this point is
a failure of will. If the failure occurs, still sincerity was equally
possible, equally a matter of our volition. Sincerity is the will
not to lose hold of the recognition of things as they are; in this
case, the recognition of the absoluteness of the demand upon us.
The choice between sincerity and insincerity thus understood
is the very heart of our free action as moral persons.[2] It is essenti-

[1] George Eliot, *The Mill on the Floss*, Book VI, Chapter 13.

[2] I need not say that this is not an original view. But it is worth remarking
that, to the best of my belief, it is Christian thinkers rather than secular moralists
who have most insisted on it. To name but one with whom I am in little sympathy generally, Kierkegaard, *The Sickness unto Death*, Part II, Chapter 2, may
be cited. Among recent English writers see, for example, Farmer, *The World and
God*, pp. 190–4 (who draws on William James), Farrer, *Finite and Infinite*,
Chapter XIII, Section V, Hick, *Faith and Knowledge*, pp. 170–2.

ally *this* choice that, in my view, is always and wholly ours. And to ask *why* we are 'volitionally insincere', when we are so, if it is not merely to ask what tempts us to be so, is to ask a question that admits of no answer, a question the mere putting of which reveals a failure to understand the nature of our case.

Now as it becomes more and more difficult not to avert our gaze from the rigour of the demand, so our resolution not to do so assumes a sometimes almost desperate intensity. Whatever the reason, it then, in point of fact, tends to express itself in the language of petition. With those who are theists it will no doubt actually be fused with what properly is petition for all possible environmental succour from a God conceived as personal: and the naturalness of the petitionary formula in the case of others, if it is not simply imitative, may perhaps reflect an *implicit* theism there also. Anyhow, if our resolve persists so too, as its difficulty increases, does our awareness of the moral demand positively gain in strength, becoming a more and more living sense of its sacredness. It is as though a sort of heat and glow were generated by the friction between moral resolution and our natural desires. This is what I meant when I spoke of 'going forward' in respect of our consciousness of the claim upon us. And I think we are so made that as we more vividly apprehend the nature and quality of the demand so also are we moved to respond to it more eagerly. 'Eagerly' of course does not mean 'easily'; but the difficulty the will experiences in such cases surely is and feels different from that which besets the divided, and therefore uneager, mind. Thus resolution brings an intenser awareness, and the intenser awareness in its turn reinforces resolution with the power of a heightened natural attraction; and so on, in a continued reciprocity of influence. It is in this way that even the barest acknowledgment of duty, if it be genuine and sincere, is the germ from which, if only sincerity is not surrendered, the most ardent loyalty of response can develop as the occasion may demand.[1]

[1] In his valuable paper 'Are there "Degrees" of the Moral Emotion?' (*Mind*, October 1936, pp. 492–7) Professor C. A. Campbell has argued that the question asked in his title should be given a negative answer, and it will be as well that the precise location of the conflict between his view and mine should be identified. I entirely agree with Campbell that 'it is strictly meaningless to speak of *more* or *less* of moral oughtness' and again that the moral feeling is 'just the emotional aspect of' the idea of the moral ought. Where I differ is in supposing that the idea may be more or less vividly *realized*, with corresponding modifications of our feeling. But it should be stressed that I regard these modifications

(20)

To this statement of what I consider to be the core of the matter I must add two footnotes. First, I must lay some stress on the words 'as the occasion may demand'. For of course many occasions do not demand any particularly vivid realization of our duty as the condition of our adequate response to it; just as at some times a man will not need to represent to himself with imaginative concreteness the sufferings of others in order that his natural sympathies should become practical and efficacious, though at other times that is precisely what is required. Now where vivid realization is not needed any attempt artificially to stimulate it is perverse, an expense of spirit in a waste of sentiment. Integrity does not involve a continual living on the stretch, and it positively repels all false dramatization. Yet without artificiality a man may surely help himself to a general attitude of 'readiness', which as it becomes in some sense a 'habit' of the will[1] may be said to give his dutifulness pervasively something of the character of love of the right.

The second comment I have to make is this. I have suggested that a sense of duty might on occasion become so passionate as itself to deserve description in the language of love; and even in circumstances in which it need not, and therefore cannot naturally, attain this quality it might still be of such a sort that it is, as it were, 'set' to do so and, failing intrinsic degeneration, would do so according to the measure of the challenge. But, it might be held, to speak so is just to make an inept transfer to the context of action *sub ratione debiti* of concepts whose appropriate use is with reference to action *sub ratione boni*. Despite Kant, who thought it not improper to speak of 'love of the law' as an ideal, it is the *bonum* alone, not the *debitum*, to which we can respond in any manner that would justify description in terms of 'love'. Now that there is point in this distinction[2] between the *ratio debiti* and the *ratio boni* I have not the slightest wish to

as governed by, not as independent factors governing, the exercise of the moral will. Their occurrence, accordingly, in no way supports a determinist reading of the situation.

[1] The concept of a 'habit' of *will* is certainly a most difficult one. Perhaps it is strictly indefensible. None the less I feel sure that the words I have used point to a real feature of our constitution however unsuitable they are as a description of it.

[2] On which de Burgh laid such stress. See his *From Morality to Religion*.

deny; and it does not adequately meet the criticism to insist (though I think this is true) that a sort of austere passion can accompany even the thought of duty as such. It is more relevant, and more fundamental, to say that, valid though the distinction is, it is still merely a distinction, never a total separation, in any experience that properly deserves to be called moral. In some cases the consciousness may be more one of duty, and in others it may rather be a consciousness of a 'value' in virtue of which we have the duty; but this is a matter of comparative emphasis, to which a variety of factors may be relevant, and it is never more than a matter of emphasis. And here it is particularly important to recall that our concern is with occasions of what is genuinely a consciousness of moral claim, not with occasions of a blind stubborness of will which, though they may have begun with such a consciousness, no longer incorporate it, even if the word duty continues to be used. That word in these latter cases is no more the mark of a duty-*consciousness* than the mechanical or merely expletive repetition of 'O God . . . ' is the mark of prayer. Now a genuine sense of duty cannot possibly be totally disengaged from a sense of the values that are the source of the duty: and on the other hand the sense of these values cannot be totally divorced from a sense of duty—were they so divorced they would at the same time lapse from being *desideranda* to being *desiderata* simply. Values as such may be attractive; but, as values, they are not *merely* attractive, but also are authoritative. 'It is the peculiar characteristic of ideals that in them appeal and constraint, pressure and aspiration are subtly interwoven.'[1] In the light of all this it must be understood that, when I speak of the growing intensity of the sense of duty when it maintains its integrity under strain, I am not talking of sense of duty as opposed to apprehension of value but of sense of duty in association with apprehension of value. And so long as this is clear I do not at all mind admitting that it is primarily by reason of this second feature that the total experience can possess the character indicated by the word 'love', although the language I have used in describing the experience has been, as was natural in the present context, the language of duty.

[1] Morris Ginsberg, *The Diversity of Morals*, p. x. On this 'interweaving' see also Farrer, *Finite and Infinite*, pp. 153–4, though I am not to be taken as agreeing with everything he says about it.

(21)

My conclusion on the two issues with which we are directly concerned—that of constitutive grace and that of love and duty —is then this. A willed attentiveness to the nature of the demand upon us is the substance of what appears as petition for the will's enablement. We may supplement this, but we do not contradict it, by adding (if we feel entitled or bound to do so) that in consciously religious experience the moment of attentiveness is integrated with petition proper made to a God thought of as person. This willed attentiveness is the whole secret of the motive of love, not indeed in every high sense of the term but in that sense in which alone it can plausibly be said to transcend the motive of duty. And, strictly, love in this sense does not transcend duty but is, rather, dutifulness itself in its supreme form—in a kind of incandescence. It is a verbal matter whether or not we elect to speak of this attentiveness as 'prayer'. But if we allow it that title it is a prayer that answers to the injunction 'Be still and know that I am God'; and what we know as God in this way is the law or the goodness that is not conceivable as person. Our devotion to it is, it is true, in one sense not of ourselves: for though our seeing is volitionally sustained it is in virtue of its own nature that the seen so constrains our reverence as to make possible the loyalty we are tempted to abandon. But to say this is to say something like κινεῖ ὡς ἐρώμενον, 'it moves us as the object of our yearning', rather than κινεῖ ὡς ἀγαπῶν, 'he moves in us as actively loving'. Now it is only the latter formula that imports the doctrine of constitutive grace, and the interpretation I have offered is accordingly consistent with my denial of that doctrine. Nor of course is it any criticism of this interpretation to point out that an ardent dutifulness such as I have imagined is nowhere to be found in its completeness, free from all painful shrinking of the flesh and with no 'chains of lead upon its flight of fire'. For so far as human experience goes we could say no more even of the 'grace-given love for God' of a more orthodox, or at least more usual, exposition. Human experience is the same whichever theory we hold; and the theory itself, in each case, points to a limit, a perfection, of which all experience in fact falls short.

CHAPTER VI

THE CONCEPT OF GOD

(1)

The main argument of this essay has now reached its conclusion. But, before I pass to my brief final comment on the thesis of 'morals without religion' from which the whole discussion originated, I must make good an undertaking given earlier, and call attention to a related problem that arises out of what has been said.

In speaking of the moral demand I was insistent that it could not be interpreted in theological terms by reference to a God represented as personal. The concept of God as person, I maintained, is not merely unnecessary in this context; the context positively repels it. But at the end I admitted that my contention might be dismissed as ineffective, so far at least as serious theology is concerned, on the ground that it rests on a crudely anthropomorphic reading of what is meant by divine personality such as no responsible theologian would wish to uphold. At the time I did no more than note this objection, promising to explain later why I did not consider it fatal to my position. This is the promise I have now to redeem.

But to redeem the promise is at the same time to emphasize a difficulty, on which also a few words must be said, though they will scarcely go beyond an indication of its character. For it is, I suppose, a part of theistic belief that there should be in some sense an aptness in using of God the language of personality. Now although I have not made it my business to argue for the truth of theism neither have I supposed it incapable of being true. Far from it. Unless I had regarded the theistic hypothesis as at least deserving of respect I should not have treated the problem of the relation between grace and freedom as a genuine and serious problem. And in fact I have gone beyond allowing that theism is a respectable possibility. I have indicated, in speaking of prayer, my own readiness to accept it as the truth. Yet how can we accept it, how can we claim validity for the concept of God as person and at the same time insist that the term 'God', if our use of it is

not to misrepresent the nature of moral demand, must be understood to refer to some *non*-personal Being? If only I could believe
that the 'impersonalism' of the view I have advocated was needless I should be spared this complication. To that extent, at
least, I have good reason for wishing that its critics were right.
But I remain unpersuaded, and I must try to explain why. When
I have done so I shall add a few observations on the resultant
collision of incompatibles, as it seems to be, the resultant clash
between the personal and the impersonal concepts of Deity.

(2)

The supposed critic of my argument might perhaps put his
complaint as follows. 'Theologians who speak of a personal God
certainly do not intend by this simply magnified man; neither
are they logically committed to meaning just that. There is a
middle way between talking anthropomorphically and talking
emptily. This middle way you have altogether ignored; and it is
only because you ignore it that you are able to put up any case
at all for the impersonal view. Once this is realized, what is
central in your account of the moral demand will be seen to be
without foundation.'

Now I should at once agree that there is a perfectly good sense
in which those who speak of God as a person may not intend, and
need not be taken to imply, that this language should be understood literally; that is to say, as indicating a being who is a person
in the very same sense in which we speak of one another as persons.
Nothing that I have said excludes, to my mind, our having a right,
and perhaps being even obliged, to speak of God as a person in
this non-literal way. I do, however, maintain that there is also a
sense in which we cannot mean anything by the term 'person'
except what we mean by it in those human contexts from which,
after all, the concept is derived; cannot in fact transcend anthropomorphism when we employ such language. It is on this latter
contention that my argument throughout relies.

The distinction I wish to draw is this. We may certainly apply
the concept of 'person', meaning by it just what we ordinarily
mean, as a sort of final and, so to say, despairing 'gesture of
affirmation' regarding a being that we do not think it really fits,
but in the conviction that to deny what is thus affirmed would be

even less appropriate. This, I should allow, is something we may significantly do; though no doubt we must be prepared to offer some reason for doing it. But it is quite another thing to suppose that we can as it were inject the necessary modifications of the anthropomorphic concept into the concept itself, so as to change it into one that does fit. This would be in effect to suppose that we can negate features that are essential to the original and ordinary meaning of the concept and can still, despite our having done so, retain the terms that express it as significant terms, not mere marks or noises. It is this second procedure that I take to be impossible. Yet only if precisely this were possible could we attain to a non-anthropomorphic 'personal' concept of God that was possessed of some positive content. And only such a positive concept could serve as a basis for further argument and provide an instrument for the elucidation of some further fact. After all, to borrow a phrase from George Tyrrell, 'we can deduce nothing from a riddle'.[1] But since we cannot frame the required positive concept, it follows that any actual employment for elucidatory purposes of the thought of God as person must in fact be an employment of it in a purely anthropomorphic sense, no matter what the user's intentions may be. Accordingly, theological interpretations of the moral demand such as I examined will be in fact, and necessarily, all of them anthropomorphic in character, whatever may be claimed to the contrary, and will be legitimate targets for a criticism that treats them as being so. One may still allow, of course, that in so far as there is propriety at all in using of God the language of personality it will be natural and even proper to describe the 'moral law' or 'order of values' as being or expressing the will of God. But it will be vitally important to remember, if we do so describe them, that this is no more than a manner of speaking; a permissible *description* indeed (and even as description no more than permissible, rather as one might be permitted to speak of Scott as 'the author of *Waverley*' even in talking of his work not as novelist but as sheriff), but still in no sense an *explanation* of the moral facts. Explanation, however, is just what has been pretended.

[1] Tyrrell, *Essays on Faith and Immortality*, p. 87.

(3)

It will be noticed that this defence of my position might be challenged on either of two grounds, resting as it does on two assumptions. The first assumption is that the concept of 'person' is derived from experience. The second assumption is that, if it is derived from experience, it can never be used with a positive and at the same time non-empirical *significance* as distinguished from what I have called a 'despairing' non-empirical *reference*. Now of these two propositions the former has been expressly denied, while the latter is presumably false if the theological 'doctrine of analogy' is true. I must therefore at this point say something first about the suggestion that 'person' is not strictly an empirical concept, and then about analogy; observing beforehand that it is perhaps not without significance that each of these doctrines implies a dissatisfaction with the other.

An example of the first of these positions, expressed in terms that have a very Cartesian sound, is provided by Professor John Baillie. In his book *Our Knowledge of God* we read this:[1] 'Personality is not in the first instance something which we find in man, but something which we find somewhere else and desiderate for him. In other words, personality is like all true moral conceptions in that it is not *a posteriori* but *a priori*, describing not the actual but the ideal. . . . Where then do we discover this ideal of personality against which we measure our human selfhood and find it so sadly wanting? . . . The answer can only be that we find it in God. . . . He who knows the poverty of his own personality knows it only because there has first been revealed to him the perfect personality of God.'

Now of course even one who supposes the concept of person to be empirically derived may allow that the term can, and even should, be so defined that 'personality' is something that admits of degrees, of less and more adequate realization. If for instance, with Professor Baillie, we regard psychological integration as entering into the constitution of what we call 'personality' (and perhaps this is not so much an example as the very essence of the matter), then clearly there are degrees of personality. But the fact that personality, thus conceived, is realized in different measures is itself an empirical fact. And the further hypothesis that there is

[1] *Op. cit.*, pp. 250–2.

a perfection towards which the series of less and more adequate realizations tends is one that, here as in other cases, requires for the mere framing of it no appeal to a non-empirical insight. It is doubtless true that experience of our own nature, and of that of our fellows, cannot teach us what is the concrete character of this perfection, what it would be like to be thus perfect; perhaps it is even incompetent to assure us that the thing is a real possibility. But this will only support the view that we derive the concept of person from some non-empirical source if we do in fact know what, concretely, perfect personality is; and that surely is not the case. I do not wish to quarrel here with the idea that there may be in some sense a direct knowledge of God: and if there is any experience, or any feature of our experience generally, that may suitably be so called, its distinctive quality may be supposed in some way to control our efforts to speak of God. But it is consistent with admitting this to hold that the only concepts available to us, which must serve our turn if we set ourselves to be articulate at all, have a different source. Indeed, unless their source is different how shall we explain the fact that in using them of God we fall into such confusions and must plead so anxiously not to be taken too literally? This, which is intelligible enough if we are using concepts derived from our experience of human nature, would be a very perplexing phenomenon in the case of a concept derived from an apprehension of the very Being for the description of whom we then employ it.

(4)

I turn now to the doctrine of analogy. And here I suffer from a painful sense that I may seem to be guilty of impudent folly in pretending to deal with this most difficult and debated question in the space of two or three pages. In fact of course I make no such pretence at all. I am brief because full discussion would be quite out of scale with the rest of my undertaking. And though this disproportion might have to be tolerated had the doctrine not already been carefully examined by others, or had I some cogent novelty of my own to bring forward, neither of these things is the case. What I have to say must be taken for no more, essentially, than an expression of my concurrence with the views of people better qualified than myself to have an opinion, who have before me found the doctrine unsatisfactory and indeed not altogether intelligible. I shall express this concurrence by simply indicating the sort of bewilderment the doctrine creates in me, using as my text some sentences in a fairly recent and very sympathetic treatment of it by Dr E. L. Mascall. My comments, may I say, might perhaps be most profitably read as a supplement to Professor Campbell's short discussion of the topic, which similarly bases itself on Mascall.[1]

The problem is how we may significantly speak of God in language whose original and proper application is to the creature. If we regard our terms as applying univocally to God and the creature, God is, in effect, reduced to creaturely status; this would be what I have called crude anthropomorphism. If, however, our language is purely equivocal, this is as much as to say that we mean nothing by it at all in its reference to Deity. But, it is suggested, we are not restricted to these manifestly unsatisfactory alternatives. In virtue of an analogy, though it is no more, between divine and creaturely being, the terms in which we speak of the latter can have some meaning, though not the same meaning, when we use them of the former.

Now, without going through the whole process of his argument, consider what in the end, in Mascall's own view, this claim amounts to. 'If it were possible,' says Mascall, 'to make a statement about God that bore exclusively on the essential or conceptual order, that statement would collapse into sheer equivocity and agnosticism, for no concept of the essence of God can be formed by a finite mind'. Here, as throughout in the passage from which I quote, Mascall is confessedly adopting and restating Gilson's position, which he has reported a page or two earlier. Gilson's words were: 'On the level of the concept there is no middle way between the univocal and the equivocal.' Nothing so far could be more in harmony with the position to which I am myself committed; and it would clearly be a mistake, with these words before us, to suggest that those who rely on the doctrine of analogy are supposing, any more than I myself suppose, that the 'content' of our empirical concepts can be 'corrected' into something adequate to the divine nature. It is

---

[1] C. A. Campbell, *On Selfhood and Godhood*, Appendix D. The passage in Mascall with which I am particularly concerned is *Existence and Analogy*, pp. 119–20. But the whole of Chapter V must of course be studied.

not by this means that they can be fitted for non-empirical employment. 'Since, however,' (to continue from Mascall) 'God's essence necessarily involves his existence, no statement about him can remain in the essential or conceptual order; it passes over immediately into the order of existence and the judgment.' (In Gilson's words, ' . . . in the case of God, every judgment, even if it has the appearance of a judgment of attribution, is in reality a judgment of existence'.) 'What begins as an attempt to conceive God's goodness', Mascall proceeds, '—an attempt which is doomed to failure—issues in an affirmation that self-existent goodness exists; but even this last statement needs careful interpretation if it is not to be taken as implying that we form a concept of "self-existent goodness". It would perhaps be better to say that goodness exists self-existingly. . . .' And later: 'Analogy does not enable us to *conceive* God's goodness as identical with his essence but to *affirm* it as identical with his existence.'

Now it is by no means clear to me that this contention, even if it were accepted, would enable us to claim that we can speak of God in a way that will be not only true but useful to those who wish to go behind the moral law to an Author of that law; and that is the point of immediate interest to me. But in any case I do not see how the contention can be accepted, for the radical reason that I cannot even make it intelligible to myself. I do not know what it means to say that we can assert 'that goodness exists self-existingly' despite our lacking a concept of self-existent goodness. I do not see how it could be suggested that we could use these words significantly if we had no concept of goodness at all; and I do not see how it can be maintained that we are better off if any concept we do have is (as we are given to understand it must be) a concept of a goodness that is *not* self-existent and is *eo ipso* different, *as goodness*, from a goodness, that is.[1]

Mascall indeed quotes from Gilson,[2] though I cannot make out that in what follows he himself specifically uses it, the thesis

---

[1] To hold as I do that there is an 'order of values' ('values' as distinguished both from 'ideals' and from 'value-qualities') might, I suppose, be described as holding that 'goodness exists self-existingly'. But I cannot say that I have found any employment for a doctrine of analogy either to establish that there is such an order or to clarify its nature. Not that I pretend to have clarified its nature in some other way, of course.

[2] *Op. cit.*, p. 118. Gilson is using Aquinas *S. contra Gentiles*, I, xxix.

that 'since every effect resembles its cause, the creature . . . certainly resembles God'; and this, it is true, indicates a way in which our affirmations about God might possibly be given some 'body'. But, quite apart from any questions that might be raised regarding this doctrine of causality, is the thesis really compatible with the view that we speak neither equivocally *nor univocally* of God and the creature? It appears rather to suggest that we speak univocally. Perhaps the further thesis, put forward by St. Thomas in the passage to which Gilson refers, that we are to distinguish between the legitimate assertion that the creature resembles God and the illegitimate assertion that God resembles the creature, is supposed to meet the point. But it seems to me not really to avail for this purpose. So far as resemblance is concerned the relation can only be reciprocal; and what makes it more proper, as we may allow that it is, to use the one formula rather than the other is simply that there is in addition to the relation of resemblance a relation of derivation. Of course if derivation did not merely co-exist with resemblance but actually modified it there might be some foothold for the view that the resembling characteristics are not univocally predicable of both terms in the relation. But this seems not to be the position. St Thomas takes as his illustration the relation of a man and his portrait. Now of course the painting in the sense of the three-dimensional physical object does not resemble the man at all in any respect that matters to us; it has no nose, it is not bald, and so forth. What significantly resembles the man is the portrait as 'likeness'. Here the *range* of resembling characters is no doubt restricted; for example, the portrait does not resemble the sitter as regards his lisp or stutter. The range is more restricted with a painted canvas than with a coloured statue, and more restricted in each of these cases than in that of the child who is 'the living image of his father', where indeed there is in principle no restriction at all. But whatever the range may be, it is only in so far as the derivative object is capable of duplicating characters possessed by the original, not just of symbolizing and suggesting them, that it is even meaningful to assert a resemblance between the two. And in so far as the copy can duplicate the original (as the painting can duplicate the sitter in respect of looks) everything that we can say of the one can be said of the other also, in words that have precisely the same meaning in each case.

M

Between meaninglessness and univocity we have still found no middle way.

(5)

Let me repeat that these remarks do not purport to be a 'refutation' of the doctrine of analogy: my sense of proportion is not so enfeebled. But I hope they will sufficiently indicate that it is not from mere thoughtlessness that I myself reject the idea that that doctrine can explain how God might be thought or represented as personal and yet not as humanly so. Now if this possibility is excluded, if in interpreting the moral demand we must either conceive of God anthropomorphically or dispense altogether with the thought of a personal Deity, it is, I still maintain, the latter alternative that we must choose.

And at this point it is worth while to remind ourselves that it is not only in the context of the interpretation of moral demand that Deity, if we are to speak of Deity at all, must be represented in non-personal terms. Even in considering prayer, even that is to say in a context in which the thought of a divine Thou is natural and insistent, we have found, in discussing the prayers for forgiveness and for enablement, that the concept of God as non-personal is at least an indispensable *element* in our thinking. It is important that we should remember this, not only because it shows how pervasive and fundamental the non-personal element is, but also because it underlines the fact that if the non-personal element does not (as I hold it does not) actually obliterate the personal element it equally cannot be barely co-existent with it. Personal and impersonal must somehow be *integrated* in Deity, just as on the human side there is an integration, and not merely a juxtaposition, of the moments of experience in which analysis discovers the personal and the impersonal concepts respectively. Now although consciousness of demand on the one hand and movement of response on the other are themselves only distinguishable aspects of an integral experience, still the latter aspect does not unambiguously incorporate the personal concept as the former, in my view, unambiguously requires the impersonal one. It is when, as in the case of prayer, we attend exclusively to the 'outgoing' moment, and notice how within that moment itself personal and impersonal concepts are together operative, that it is really brought home to us that our experience postulates a corresponding objective unity of being in which personal and impersonal features are similarly integrated.

(6)

We must, then, somehow think of God as both personal and impersonal, and in one sense, it would seem, this presents no difficulty. Something very like it is achieved constantly, by all except the most simple-minded, in the very acknowledgment that personality as we know it does not adequately represent the divine nature. Yet when, in reflection, we endeavour to be more explicit, what results seems not to be integration so much as a sort of working conflation of the ideas of the personal and the impersonal, consisting in what remains the blank affirmation of their conjunction together with their use as *alternatives*, according as one or other seems more apt in a particular context. The concept of God (if it can be called a concept) then functions in much the same way as Eddington's notorious concept (if it can be called a concept) of 'wavicle' in the theory of light. Now this procedure may be pragmatically justified; it may be indispensable for the 'practical purposes' of the religious life. Indeed it is, in a manner, preferable even as theory to any one-sided clarity. None the less it is manifestly unsatisfactory. Our working conflation rests on an inattention to the conflict of personal and impersonal conceptions rather than on a transcendence of it. What is needed is that we should, so to put it, replace a 'bi-focal' vision of God by one that is 'uni-focal'. And, of course, if we could achieve this the whole picture, or diptych rather, presented to us at the bi-focal level would be transformed: which is as much as to say that in one sense what I have maintained in these pages cannot possibly be the truth. This is an admission I am perfectly prepared, and indeed eager, to make; and it concedes nothing to the views I have criticized, which I should judge to be still wider of the mark. But I must add that the achievement of this uni-focal vision seems to me something that must forever remain beyond our reach, and in default of it we must be content to assert, without comprehending, the unity of personal and impersonal natures in God. It is this predicament that I am sometimes tempted to describe, in words that are frivolous though my intention is not, by saying that natural theology should consist merely in two 'bracketing' shots followed by a 'Cease fire'.

One way, of course, of asserting this uncomprehended unity is to speak of God as 'supra-personal', and many would so speak. Now it is fair, and important, to insist that if we use this expression we should not allow it to degenerate into just a polite equivalent of 'impersonal'.[1] It is philosophers rather than theologians who need this warning. But a corresponding warning must be addressed to the theologian. Those who speak of God as 'supra-personal' must not allow themselves to understand by that expression merely 'personal *plus* . . . '. The 'supra' in 'supra-personal' does not indicate simply a 'more': it indicates a 'more' such that the 'more' transforms the meaning of the term 'personal' itself. Consider a parallel and related case. The word 'eternal' is abused (intending as it does a supra-temporal mode of being) if it is taken as only the negation of the temporal or, again, as referring to a complex of two factors externally and unintelligibly related, namely endless time, as we conceive of time, and the timeless.[2] In just the same way, the term 'supra-personal' would be abused whether it were taken simply to negate the meaning of 'personal' or to supplement it in a merely additive way.

Thus even granted that for the life of religion, when that is contrasted with 'mere morality', the emphasis must fall on the personal moment in our thought of God, it is also true that theology must not take this moment at its face value. And, it must be added, the very life of religion will itself remain healthy only if the personal concept carries overtones that point to its own transcendence, overtones that at least include a hint of that other, impersonal, way of thinking which, it has been my main concern to insist, is indispensable for any interpretation of moral experience that is not sheerly irreligious. In point of fact, and it need not surprise us, the operative beliefs of the religious life are less apt to be at fault here than the more articulate concepts of theology. To take but one example, Clement Webb has observed

[1] W. R. Matthews, for example (*Studies in Christian Philosophy*, p. 182), very properly makes this protest. But does he sufficiently guard himself against the imputation of the opposite error that I go on to mention?

[2] The popular equation of 'eternity' with, simply and solely, 'endless time' has as its counterpart, of course, a crude anthropomorphic personalism in our thought of God, the idea of transcendence (of time in the one case, and of the humanly personal in the other) being elided altogether.

that however much men 'may tremble at the thought that there is nothing in them but "is naked and open to Him"; "in whose sight the very heavens are not clean" yet not for one moment do they feel the sense of insecurity and outrage which they would feel if they believed their hearts to be exposed to unauthorized prying by a fellow-creature'.[1] This represents just such an over-tone of the personal concept as I have in mind, and perhaps it is as natural to the religious life as breathing is to our life as organisms. But theology, being conscious intellectual construc-tion, cannot be immunized against error in any similarly natural and unselfconscious way. Its self-corrective measures must be con-sciously adopted, and I cannot but think that theologians are insufficiently watchful to apply them. Were this not so they would surely be more reticent, less seeming-informative in reliance on the human analogy, than in general they are.[2]

[1] Webb, *Problems in the Relation of God and Man*, p. 148. But of course degeneration is possible; people *can* get into a 'Thou, God, seest me' state in which they are disconcerted and even terrified just as they would be had they the feeling of being watched by a concealed human observer. In this case there is certainly a sense of insecurity, though perhaps still not precisely of outrage.

[2] If I do not misunderstand him (as I easily may have done) there is much in Tillich, *Systematic Theology*, Vol. I, Chapters IX–X, which is in harmony with what I have said. See especially pp. 268–9, 271 and (on eternity) 304 and following.

CHAPTER VII

MORALS AND RELIGION:
A CONCLUSION

If now we turn back to our original question whether there can be 'morals without religion', how will it appear in the light of all that has been said? Let me give the essentials of my own view without elaboration. There is no need for any formal division into sections in the simple statement of it. There is indeed nothing very striking about it. But at least it will make plain why I personally cannot with any comfort answer the question with a straight yes or no. Whether we affirm or deny the dependence of morality on religion, in either case it is not the formula but its interpretation that signifies.

It is certainly possible to be moral without being religious if morality is defined in terms of what we may call 'the decencies', average respectable conduct, organized and justified (in so far as any justification is offered at all) by reference to some more or less articulate conception of a way of life that we simply take for granted, simply accept. The general way of life itself, in such a case, presents itself rather as datum than as requirement. That morality in this sense is possible without religion is conceded readily enough even by one so critical of 'mere morality' as is Oman; but it is conceded in the significant words 'Never . . . can morality without religion penetrate from good form to goodness, from manners to morals'.[1] Oman's point is that such non-religious morality is not even genuinely morality. And I should agree inasmuch as it is a morality whose 'imperatives', no matter how coercive they *feel*, are all in reality 'hypothetical'. To the extent that the way of life to which they relate is itself simply *de facto* 'given', not evaluated, they are all imperatives of the same order as the 'obligation', for the utterly conventional, in a particular social milieu, to wear a black and not a white tie with a dinner jacket. No doubt they differ very greatly in importance, as regards their material content; but as regards their formal character as 'obligation', that is the category to which they belong. None the

[1] Oman, *Grace and Personality*, p. 62.

less, this is the sum and substance of what many people will have in mind when they speak of 'morality'; and of course I do not deny that it is a good thing as far as it goes, given that the accepted 'decencies' happen to deserve that name.[1]

But though a non-religious morality in this inadequate sense of the term is possible it is also very precarious. Circumstances can easily fail to provide what, at this level of motivation, would be a psychologically satisfying outlet for our passions and energies within the framework of the established *mores*; and, where that is so, mere 'good form' will tend to crack under the pressure. The morality of decency will then either break up or it will maintain itself (with or without some change of content) by transformation into a more genuine morality, no longer uncritically accepting but reflectively approving its code, and drawing strength from a personal recognition of absolute obligation. It must be a matter of common experience that a rule of conduct in obedience to which we have been brought up but which, though never positively questioned by us, has never really approved itself to our 'moral reason', is a weak thing in comparison with one that expresses our own honest conviction.

This genuine morality also, however, can be independent of religion, if religion is here understood to mean something other than and, as it were, extraneously supporting the attitude of moral commitment. On the other hand there is good sense in saying that genuine moral commitment is itself religious in quality whether or not a man so describes it in his own case.[2] And when we look at the matter in this way we shall say that morality is *not* possible without religion. In that sense, but in that sense only, I can allow such language as this that Oman uses in the same paragraph from which I quoted earlier: 'Never, except in the atmosphere of living religion, has morality maintained its absolute demand, penetrated from outward conformity to inward motive, grown sensitive to the deeper requirements of humility and sympathy, and, finally, passed all rigid bounds of law and come face to face with the infinite claim of love, which destroys all idea of merit and leaves men, after they have done

---

[1] But how different from one another in moral quality may be the things one is adjured to do by appeal to such concepts as that of the 'gentleman' or the 'sportsman' ('Be a sport!') needs no stressing.

[2] L. A. Reid's distinction between 'sacred' and 'religious' morality being here ignored. See above, Chapter III, p. 64, note 1.

their utmost, unprofitable servants.' This, in all essentials, I can accept, but (which was not Oman's intention) I accept it as an *analytic* truth: that is to say, I accept it on the understanding that 'religion' in this context *means* in Professor Paton's words,[1] 'the most supreme development of the moral will' and not 'the foundation upon which morality is built'. My complaint against Oman, and others of the same persuasion, is really this: that by an arbitrary and falsifying limitation of the meaning of 'morality' they create, as it were, a vacuum in the description of human experience which has then to be filled by an inrush of distinctively religious language.

But certainly 'the most supreme development of the moral will' does not exhaust the meaning of 'religion': it is a much richer term than that. Those who hold that a truly moral devotion is itself religious are not obliged to deny that religious devotion can be also, and healthily, a great deal besides. And a man for whom the word 'God' means more than the goodness that makes its claim on him in the moral demand, and whose worship accordingly is not simply identical with his moral submission; a man, more particularly, whose practice includes prayer in the sense in which that is addressed to an Other that, in praying, he cannot but think of as personal (with whatever accompanying sense of the inadequacy of this representation)—such a man will draw massive support for his endeavours from his prayer and worship at the same time as his moral attitudes themselves acquire pervasively a distinctive 'flavour' or 'tang'. To call attention to this is not, of course, to maintain that the 'moral utility' of worship constitutes the whole meaning and importance of it. But its 'moral utility' is all that concerns us here. And it must be said that for anyone who does not suppose the act and experience to be merely superstitious and delusive it would be total folly, and worse than that, not to avail himself of the support thus provided, by all the means suggested to him by the experience of mankind, and found to justify themselves when tested in his own experience. Whatever the truth in the doctrine that the moral will is sufficient to itself, it is grotesquely to misunderstand that truth not to make use of all the legitimate resources by the employment of which we can render the doing as we ought easier, happier and perhaps in various ways more effective. Not to do so is indeed to go against

[1] Paton, *The Good Will*, p. 440.

the very nature of dutifulness which, as I have earlier insisted, is an altogether outward-looking concern that what is right should be done, and not in the least a concern for one's own spiritual status as the doer.

I therefore heartily agree that (as it was once put to me) a man who sets himself to get on without religion may be like a man who persists in hopping on one leg along a road on which he might more comfortably and quickly proceed by walking on two. None the less a man who is under the honest impression that he has only the one leg not only must but can, however painfully and slowly, travel that way. That is to say, the dependence upon religion in its richer sense of the sort of morality now in question will never amount to an essential and absolute dependence, inasmuch as the consciousness of an authoritative ideal that characterizes this morality need not be enclosed within any fuller religious consciousness, and inasmuch as the moral will remain its own master whether or not the exercise of its mastery incorporates specifically religious practices.

But for those who do enjoy a fuller religious life that includes a 'moment' for which God is personal that 'moment' is so fundamental, and the person-image—image rather than concept—is so easily and powerfully operable, that this one 'moment' may appear in their *thought* to constitute the whole of religion even when the 'religion of obligation' (to borrow Farmer's phrase[1]) is a vital factor in their *experience*. Thus they may slip into a habit of speaking of God in personal terms without the proper reservations, and be in danger, correspondingly, of passing from a sound to an erroneous conception of the sense in which the Divine Being demands, and supports, our moral allegiance. The danger may be at one and the same time both disguised and increased by the fact that the motive of devotion to God as personal can be so potent that it may secure from a man the 'works' of morality even if the spirit of morality, the genuinely *moral* devotion, is lacking or frail.

If this were to happen, if while the 'works' continued the spirit departed, we should have come back to something of much the same moral status as the conventional 'morality of the decencies'. The new morality would, of course, exhibit characteristic differences of content, deriving from the special religious beliefs of its

[1] Farmer, *Revelation and Religion*, Chapter VII.

practitioner, and it might possess a vitality that a non-religious 'morality of the decencies' (but not perhaps a morality of loyalty to some 'charismatic' secular leader) is unlikely to rival. But its general status would not be affected by this. Such a morality would be *essentially* dependent on religion, and on religion as something *extraneous* to morality itself.

Now it is just such a dependence that attacks on the idea of 'morals without religion' seem commonly to be concerned to maintain, notwithstanding that neither religion nor morality can be accorded its proper dignity in terms of it. There is a genuine danger, then, that insistence on the view that morality cannot exist or sustain itself apart from religion will actually tend to the debasement of both, the replacement of the real thing by the inferior substitute. The substitute may well be easier to provide and cheaper to procure than the real thing, and if this is so the danger will be all the greater. But we should be careful, if there are many who are quite content with it, and if in the end it captures the market, not to misdescribe the character of the achievement. It is no good reason for calling margarine butter that butter is more expensive. And of course there is another danger. What of those to whom religion as they understand it, and as it is so often presented to them, makes no appeal, and for whom, as for all of us, the self-restraint required by any conception of a moral standard is irksome? Is it sufficiently recognized that the formula 'no morality without religion', proclaimed though it is with the design of bringing them to religion, may instead have the effect of divorcing them from morality, seeming to license and encourage them, in view of their unbelief, to abandon all serious moral concern? No doubt some self-deception would also have to be at work; but then it is at work all the time. Men were self-deceivers ever. The danger of the formula is that it makes easier this all too welcome self-deception.

Happily it is true that people are often better than their theories. Those who maintain as a theory that morality is subordinated to religion in the way described may none the less be protected against the evils latent in their position by a blessed inconsistency. They may continue to affirm in their practical attitudes that autonomy of the moral life that they deny with their lips. This seems indeed to be the common case. But reliance on inconsistency is not merely intellectually disreputable but practically unsafe.

Reflective belief does affect operative conviction, to strengthen or corrode; and when the two are in conflict it corrodes. And if a man's operative convictions did get eaten away to the point of thorough consistency with this defective theory there would have been brought about once more that separation of morality from religion, that 'demoralization' of religion, which it is so great an achievement of what we call the 'higher' religions to have overcome. In such a case the very 'works' of morality, the 'decencies' themselves, are threatened; not by men's natural selfishness or sloth but by their fanaticisms. This is no mere speculation: it is a real danger to which, as a matter of history, individuals and groups have at times succumbed. Recent secular movements show plainly how great the danger may be. Unquestioning loyalty to an earthly leader may infuse a remarkable energy into men's practice; but energy to what end? We have but to translate 'leader' into 'Führer' to be reminded how corrupt the practice can become. And the fact that the 'leader', or idol, whom we serve is a figment of our thought bearing the name 'God' provides no safeguard at all, once the construction of his image has escaped the control of an unsurrendered, independent moral judgment. Indeed the contrary is the case. Submission to any particular person as the sole source of authoritative prescription has as its natural accompaniment a certain measure of licentiousness in conduct. But the transcendent non-historical character of this 'God' enables his servants to assume a *limitless* licence such as no earthly potentate could permit. This must be set down to his account in addition to all the evils that ignorance and depravity may feel constrained to enact at his supposed command. Antinomianism is properly a *religious* phenomenon, and one that is positively corrupt in a way in which the laxity that springs from mere insufficiency of moral seriousness is not. It is corrupt somewhat as 'bestiality' in human beings, as distinguished from the bestiality of the brutes, is corrupt.[1]

For all such corruptions of religion, the possibility of which is ever-present however hopeful we may be that their recrudescence in the extremer forms is unlikely, the only competent preventive or cure (all else being at best palliative) is a constantly renewed

---

[1] But not precisely so. There is a difference between an 'insufficiency of moral seriousness' in normal adults and the 'moral innocence' of the very young child; and it is the latter that more resembles the status of the brutes.

realization of the true character and quality of the moral life. What is needed is a continuing conviction of morality's independence of religion save in the sense in which religion is just the fully moral attitude itself, and of the primacy of its authority over any authority that may be claimed by religion otherwise conceived. Only a practical moral sincerity can supply this realization and conviction: argument cannot do so. But in so far as false theory may impede it, argument may remove the impediment. I should like to believe that these pages contribute something towards that argument. And even if, both to those who agree with and to those who dissent from their contentions, they seem to contain little that is new, I may still hope that they have their use. For this perhaps is one of those subjects to which may be applied the observation justly made in a different context: 'Platitudes must be repeated frequently, more for the sake of protest than for the sake of information.'[1]

[1] Plamenatz, *Consent, Freedom and Political Obligation*, p. xi.

APPENDIX

Note A (*Chapter III, p. 73*)

KANT AND THE CONCEPT OF A DIVINE LAWGIVER

Since the position I adopt regarding the ultimacy of the 'moral law' is so largely what it is through my reading of Kant, I must in fairness note that Kant himself sometimes uses language that seems like an assertion of the 'legislative' theory that I have repudiated. In so far as all that he intends is that a theist may rightly, or indeed must, *represent* the status of the moral law to himself in this manner, speaking *as if* it were God's command, there is no occasion to be perplexed and disturbed. But sometimes what he says appears to go beyond this, and to be meant as 'ontological interpretation' and 'underwriting' of the law; which is not the same thing as his postulating God as the condition of the possibility of the *summum bonum*, though the distinction between the two seems to me a difficult one. This is certainly the case with a number of passages in the *Opus Postumum*, and a similar suggestion could be conveyed by some of the language used even in the works that Kant himself published. For example, one or two expressions in the 'Remark' in § 86 of the *Critique of Judgment* might be regarded as open to suspicion.

These, however, are isolated sentences, and it is difficult to believe that Kant ever abandoned the position on this matter that is characteristic of his central ethical writings. As late as the *Critique of Judgment* that position is surely sufficiently safeguarded, by the distinction drawn (on the very last page of the work) between an 'ethical theology' and a 'theological ethics', and the express denial of the possibility of the latter. If the precise status of the former, which is allowed to be possible, is not altogether clear, the difficulty (which is only an aspect of the more general and fundamental problem of the nature and scope of practical, as distinguished from theoretical, 'knowledge') is not directly relevant to my present concern. As to the *Opus Postumum*, though some of the jottings do indeed seem to employ the concept of the Divine Lawgiver in what I should regard as an improper manner, others suggest a very different view. Webb, in Chapter VI of his *Kant's Philosophy of Religion*, provides instances of both kinds of language: contrast the quotations on pp. 192–3 with those on p. 196. If we endeavour to harmonize the two sets of statements, a clue may be found in Kant's conception of moral autonomy which could lead to an interpretation less crude and more interesting than the common theological view of duty as divine command. It might be said that

Kant is so deeply concerned to maintain the autonomy of the will that he does not distinguish, as I have done and as I think must be done, a heteronomous *aspect* of morality from the autonomous aspect which it complements. Adopting, then, an extreme and unqualified doctrine of autonomy, he can avoid a pernicious subjectivism only by viewing practical reason in the human individual not as 'his' reason but rather as Practical Reason (with capitals) immanent *in* him. 'Practical Reason' so conceived is then *equated* with 'God', and to say that I am my own lawgiver (autonomy) and that my duties are commanded me by God, being indeed my duties as being commanded by God (which has an appearance of heteronomy), is really to say one and the same thing with only a shift of emphasis.

Whatever may be urged against a view of this kind, at least it does not yield the sort of theological interpretation of the moral law against which my argument protests. But this I think can be said against it; that it offers a doctrine of divine immanence of such a nature that either the individual is in respect of his moral reason only a mode of God's being or else 'God' is only a dangerously concrete term used to refer to the purely qualitative identity of moral reason in a diversity of persons. (So at least it appears to me, though others would no doubt say that this merely exhibits my own inability to grasp the idea of immanence at all.) In Chapter IV I take note of the necessity to be on guard against a similar conception of the relation between God and man in our account of the moral response.

Perhaps I may take this opportunity of observing that I think there is room and need for a full discussion by some properly equipped scholar of the connection between Kant's ethical and his theological views, with special reference to the *Religion innerhalb der Grenzen der blossen Vernunft* and the *Opus Postumum*. Webb's admirable volume, short though it is, is only partly concerned with this theme; and it is now over thirty years old. The texts are as fascinating as they are difficult, and a competent exposition of them would not only complete, and in some respects transform, the average English student's picture of Kant's mind and thought, but would, I believe, even at this date be a notable contribution to the study of the problems that have prompted me to the writing of the present essay.

Note B (Chapter III, p. 92)

VALUES AND DISVALUES

A critic who would I think disapprove, though in the friendliest way, of the whole idea of an objective 'order of values', has asked why I do not equally allow an objective order of '*dis*values', since we speak of acts and situations as being wrong or evil no less than of their being right or good. This, he correctly surmises, I should find embarrassing. (Of course it would be wrong to suppose that everyone would be similarly worried—there *are* those who would uphold a fundamental dualism in this matter.) The question is, how in reason I am to avoid the embarrassment. My answer to this is implicit in the distinction I draw in the main text between 'values' and 'value-qualities'; and in making it more explicit now I may hope also to clarify in some slight degree what was admittedly a somewhat vague and general statement of my position.

So far as the qualities of actual or envisaged acts and situations are concerned I have no wish whatsoever to distinguish in status between the good and the evil, the right and the wrong. At this level I do not regard evil as less real than good, and certainly not as non-existent or just 'good-in-disguise'. (I need not go into the difficulties that such radical 'optimism' faces from the fact of the apparent evil of there *being* 'merely apparent' evil.) Correspondingly, if a 'value' were simply a class-*character* or 'abstract universal' answering to these qualities, as for example 'sphericity' or 'hardness' might be described as being, 'values' and 'disvalues' would stand on the same footing. But then that is what 'values', as I have used the term, are not.

The suggestion I have made is that 'values', as distinguished both from the good and bad qualities of what is matter of fact and from the 'goodness' and 'badness' that are the corresponding abstract universals (assuming that these 'qualities' and 'universals' really are two different things), are what control our framing of ideals. They could be said to be *postulated* as the condition without which our ideal-framing activity cannot be understood: although I also think there is something that might be called an inarticulate value-apprehension, which to speak merely of postulation fails to indicate. (One may compare the relation between 'experience' and 'proof' of God; and not surprisingly, since on my view 'values' and 'God' present not just parallel problems but rather one and the same problem.) Anyhow, I have myself no *argument* at all for believing in an order of values except that which is founded on our ability to formulate authoritative ideals. Now ideals (as distinct from neutral projects or possibilities that we merely 'entertain') are, it seems clear to me, always formulated under the idea of the good. It is impossible (however we interpret the impossibility) to regard badness as such as having a *claim* on us. Accordingly, it is value only and not disvalue that the ability to frame ideals presupposes. This is why I have no use for the concept of an order of disvalues: at *this* level of being goodness (not to be confused with 'what is good') is alone real.

I do not, then, deny or in any way attempt to 'dissolve by interpretation' the evil that is actual and occurrent (whether in the form of misapprehension of good or in any other form) in the matter of fact and historical order. It is empirically manifest, and must be acknowledged to be so. The position is not that there is no actual evil, but that evil is, so to say, only actual, whereas good is both (on occasion) actual and, as 'value' (goodness), supra-actual also.

It may be suggested that even if these remarks serve to show that there is no positive reason, such as exists in regard to values, for affirming an order of disvalues, it is none the less true that an order of disvalues, no less than an order of values, is conceivable as a possibility. But is this really so? If we abstract from any direct experiential consciousness of values and disvalues (which my critics would deny that we possess in either case and I at least in the latter case) can we be said to have any conception at all of this level of being *except* the relative concept of it as that which constrains our practical thinking and our action? *Operari sequitur esse*, no doubt, and what operates on us must have some intrinsic nature. But can we say anything more specific about it except in terms of its operation? I think not: and since disvalues are not revealed as operative they will therefore not be revealed or be positively conceivable at all. The idea that we can at least 'think' them as bare possibilities rests, I should say, on some sort of mental image in which they are pictured 'alongside' values (though this order of being cannot really, of course, be pictured at all), and which we *mistake* for a thought, helped by the fact that we have the verbal apparatus for expressing the thought, if there were a thought to be expressed. Plato, I do not doubt, would have had something to say about this.

Note C (Chapter IV, p. 101)

' "OUGHT" IMPLIES "CAN" '

A full discussion of the free-will problem is neither necessary nor in place in this volume. But something may appropriately be said here about the principle popularly stated in the form ' "Ought" implies "Can" ', in which the essence of the contention of the libertarian moralist is, to my mind, conveniently summarized.

Since nobody supposes that 'ought' implies 'cannot not', what the principle asserts is that there can be no such thing as moral obligation unless an agent has what Professor Campbell has called 'contra-causal' freedom of decision or choice between acting as he sees he ought to act and not doing so. In the end, as I suggest in Chapter V, Section 19, the relevant decision or choice is that between, on the one hand, facing with sincerity the claim that in any given case confronts us and, on the other hand, a dishonest inattention to it. This is a freedom of negligible scope, it might be thought, but still it is one to which we may apply the words used by Aristotle (E.N. Bk. X. 1178ᵃ 1–2) with reference to the place of reason (nous) in human life. It may not bulk large, but it has pre-eminent worth. On grounds that I indicate in Section V of my discussion in the 1951 Supplementary Volume (Vol. XXV) of the *Proceedings of the Aristotelian Society* I do not think that it is strictly correct to say, as the formula ' "Ought" implies "Can" ' rather suggests, that we argue from the fact of obligation, as something 'given', to the fact of freedom, as something to be established merely inferentially. But it is none the less the case, I should hold, that libertarian freedom is implied by moral obligation, and, whatever their extent may be, they are, I believe, and are of necessity, *co*-extensive.

Now in opposition to a view of this nature it has sometimes been held that our freedom is not restricted to the sphere of our moral obligations, but extends more widely than that; and it has contrariwise sometimes been held that we are not free even within the sphere of moral obligation, that in fact 'ought' does *not* imply 'can'. From my point of view it is this latter doctrine that is the more challenging one; but since I dissent from both, and since even the former is not necessarily as harmless as it may at first appear, I wish to say a little about each in turn.

Consider first the suggestion that our freedom is more extensive than the sphere of moral obligation. It is of course obvious that on some interpretations of the term 'freedom' this suggestion is perfectly correct. No libertarian would wish to deny that freedom in the sense of absence of constraint by forces 'outside' the self's own nature has no essential connection with obligation. A creature altogether incapable of having duties might be free in this sense, which is a proper and important sense, of the term. We need waste no time in arguing that point.

The case is rather less simple when it is said of the ' "Ought" implies "Can" ' formula itself that not only the moral 'ought' but perhaps any 'ought' whatsoever implies 'can'; a position adopted by Mr Hare in the volume of the *Proceedings of the Aristotelian Society* to which I have already referred. But here again we must I think allow that the contention has at least a certain truth. Unless in some sense *x* can be the case, or can be done, there is no propriety in supposing that it ought to be the case or ought to be done. Doubtless we might slip into a habit of *saying* that something or other ought to be when all we really have in mind is that it would be good, or nice, if it were;

N

and we may meaningfully say that it would be good, or nice, if something were the case without any implication that it is possible for it to be so. Optatives are not tied to the possible as a condition of their *meaningfulness*, though the *usefulness* of indulging in them may be. But then 'ought' is not a matter of mere optatives; and when we not only say but really mean 'ought' we do imply the possibility of realization. *Every* genuine 'ought', let us grant accordingly, implies 'can' and not only, as I have suggested, the moral 'ought'. And what harm does it do to allow the 'can' this wider range? Why should I question it? Even if the libertarian moralist has no positive interest in this additional province of the realm of the possible, at least, it may be said, there is equally no positive reason why he should deny its existence. The province that does interest him remains included in the larger whole, and that surely is all that matters.

But of course this will not do at all, and an illustration may help to make clear why. Suppose some severe Cato enters a room where a drunken party is in full swing. He recoils in disgust, which he expresses in very sweeping terms. But, being a fair-minded man, he makes the concession that 'Wimble there, I grant you, is sober enough'. Suppose, then, that one of the celebrants retorts, 'Of course he's sober: we're all sober'. Would Cato be relieved and rejoiced to discover the area of sobriety thus enlarged? Clearly not. He could rightly say either that if this is what sobriety means he is not interested in sobriety and he needs some other word to describe what he *is* interested in, or, alternatively, that anyone who really thinks all these people are sober is plainly in no position to recognize sobriety when he sees it. What purports to be simply the assertion of a more widespread sobriety is, in fact, a denial of sobriety's distinctive nature. And so it is with the assertion that any and every 'ought' implies 'can'. It does not simply affirm an extended range of 'freedom'; it denies, in doing so, the distinctive character of the freedom that the *moral* 'ought' of duty *specifically* requires.

Mr Hare observes (*op. cit.*, p. 201) that 'if I say "Smith ought to have tackled Robinson", it is a sufficient rebuttal to say "But he couldn't; he wasn't fast enough to catch him" '. And of course it is, without question asked whether the 'ought' was a moral 'ought' or not. But now suppose that Smith was fast enough, and yet didn't make the tackle, would it be sufficient rebuttal of the contention that he ought to have done so to say 'But he couldn't; his whole purpose was to prevent the All Reds scoring, and he thought Robinson was about to pass to Jones, who was unmarked, so he turned his attention to Jones'? Or 'But he couldn't; he's no sportsman, you see, and he wanted his crowd to lose because he has a grudge against Atkins who captains the side'? These explanations would surely seem odd, in the latter case especially. And they would seem odd because they certainly would not be denials of the kind of capacity implicit in the normal use of 'ought' in contexts like these. Yet they could be significant denials of capacity in another sense. They could quite conceivably be true (though one would hardly expect the second to be true except with reference to the fiction-world of a school story); and if they were true it really might be the case that this little portion of Smith's life *had* to be the way it was. What we have here, then, is a perfectly natural, but non-moral use of 'ought', which implies indeed a corresponding 'can' but is consistent none the less with our also, and in another respect, affirming a 'can't'. When, however, 'ought' means 'has a moral duty', and *only* when 'ought' means 'has a moral duty', the corresponding 'can' that is implied is an absolute and unqualified 'can' that does not admit of combination, in regard to the particular possibility in question, with any 'can't' at all. The capacity, the freedom, that is postulated is now for the first time a *contra-causal* freedom. Now when the libertarian moralist appeals to the principle that ' "Ought" implies "Can" ' he means, though he has not, I agree, plainly enough said, that this *categorical* 'Ought', and it alone, implies this *absolute and unqualified* 'Can'.

But it has to be acknowledged that even some libertarians who are in no way guilty of confusing absolute and non-absolute uses of 'can', whose conception of the nature of the freedom that is a moral postulate is (from my point of view) beyond reproach, are persuaded that this freedom is not restricted to occasions of action under the idea of duty. They may hold that but for the experience of duty we have no reason to believe in this freedom, but they consider that the concept thus validated can none the less be allowed a more general application. Now here we really do have a view that need cause me no concern; it really does simply extend the scope of my own claim without diluting its strength. In a sense, then, I do not mind whether it is true or not. But in fact I think it is not true, and for the following reason. When a man considers he has a duty to act in a certain way he clearly has, in that thought, a ground for so acting. Likewise, whenever a man wants to act in a certain way it is quite intelligible if he does so act. Accordingly, whenever there is a choice that can be described as one between doing as one thinks one ought and doing as one most wants, whichever way a man actually decides there is a sense in which one can well understand his making that decision. But where this conflict between (as we may briefly put it) 'duty' and 'desire' is absent there do not any longer seem to be practical alternatives open to a man such that it could be said that whichever way he chooses there is some

*

sort of intelligibility about his so choosing. For let us suppose him committed heart and soul to acting as he thinks he morally ought and confronted by a situation in which he must either lie or break a promise; he must of course make up his mind as best he can which of these conflicting claims is, in the particular case, the more important, but once he has done so it would be totally incomprehensible if (so long as nothing but his sense of duty is operative) he chose to satisfy what he judged to be the less important claim. And it would similarly be quite incomprehensible if a man, suppose him concerned only to do what he wants, did not choose to do what he wanted most to do.

I believe, then, that the distinctive type of freedom that is postulated by the distinctively moral 'ought', the 'ought' of duty, does not extend more widely than does the fact of duty itself. And now I must turn to the opposite contention; that of those who would unduly narrow, or altogether abolish, the range of our freedom, not unduly enlarge it. Here I ignore necessitarian views that pay no heed at all to the question of the import of 'ought'. My interest is in views that reckon with the language of obligation but, expressly or in effect, hold that 'ought' does *not* imply 'can'. This is not a position that is at all characteristic of secular ethics. Secular moralists evince no disposition to deny that where we rightly say 'ought' we may rightly say 'can' also; the issue in their case, as I have indicated, is whether it is *only* where we say 'ought' that we may also say 'can', and again what is the meaning of the 'can', what is the nature of the freedom, we affirm. But with theologians it is otherwise. Theologians, concerned to interpret the nature and action of God and compelled to face the problem of the relation between God and man, may quite naturally feel driven to deny man's freedom while still insisting on his responsibility, to hold that the 'can' is abolished even though an 'ought' remains. And some theologians (but, I need hardly say, by no means all) do seem in fact to adopt this course. I propose to comment on one example only, but a classic one, of what appears to be such a view; that namely of Luther as represented by a work to which I have already made some reference in this volume, the *De Servo Arbitrio* of 1525, recently (1957) translated by Dr Packer and Mr Johnston under the title of *The Bondage of the Will*. I shall use their translation.

Let me first observe that my remarks are confined to this one aspect of Luther's argument. I attempt no evaluation of his position as a whole; nor, of course, am I here concerned with the question of the effectiveness of his polemic against the half-hearted attitude of Erasmus. Over and over again Luther insists that Erasmus' arguments, if they proved anything, would establish a more radical freedom than Erasmus himself dares claim; and this may very well be the case. If it is the case it is certainly awkward for Erasmus, but not necessarily for his arguments.

Luther's own view on the point that at present concerns us is in substance this. It is necessary to a man's salvation (which depends absolutely upon God) that he should be utterly humbled. This total humiliation, this recognition that we can do nothing at all for ourselves, this self-despair indeed, is the very condition of the saving gift of grace (*op. cit.*, p. 100). It is in the light of that fundamental truth that we must interpret God's commands to us. For example, when it is said (Deuteronomy xxx. 19.) 'I have set before thee life and death . . . therefore choose life', this injunction does not imply that we have any freedom whatsoever to make the choice. We have in fact no such power, and the command neither implies it nor creates it. Its purpose is quite other. 'Reason thinks that man is shocked by an impossible commandment, whereas I maintain that by this means man is admonished and awakened to see his own impotence' (*op. cit.*, p. 158). It is thus not at all true that either man must have freedom to choose between good and evil or else to command him to choose good is absurd. 'Is it absurd, pray, that a man who has both arms bound, but who proudly maintains or ignorantly assumes that he is wholly competent in either direction, should be commanded to stretch forth his hand in one direction or the other, not in order to make fun of his captivity, but to disprove his false assumption of freedom and power, and to make him realize his ignorance of his own captivity and misery'? (*op. cit.*, p. 161). Now this is precisely our universal human predicament. 'The Scripture sets before us a man who is not only bound, wretched, captive, sick and dead, but who, through the operation of Satan his lord, adds to his other miseries that of blindness, so that he believes himself to be free, happy, possessed of liberty and ability, whole and alive. Satan knows that if men knew their own misery he could keep no man in his kingdom . . . Hence, the work of Satan is to hold men so that they do not recognize their wretchedness, but presume that they could do everything that is stated. But the work of Moses the lawgiver is the opposite of this—namely, through the law to lay open to man his own wretchedness, so that, by thus breaking him down . . . he may make him ready for grace, and send him to Christ to be saved. Therefore the function performed by the law is nothing to laugh at, but is most emphatically serious and necessary' (*op. cit.*, p. 162).

Now there is a great deal of force in this contention. The law, as a schoolmaster, would on this view only be employing a technique that has its place also in the work of those who are teachers in a less metaphorical sense. There are occasions when 'Very well, since you know how, *do* it' may be the best way of making a pupil conscious of his insufficiency and amenable to further instruction. But all that this signifies is that issuing a command, or *saying* 'you ought', indeed even the *usefulness* of doing this, carries no implication of a capacity to perform on the part of the person addressed. Saying 'ought', however, even in the first person form of 'I ought', is not the very same thing as actually having an obligation. This is not the less true if, as I believe, a man cannot *have* a duty (in the philosophically primary and indispensable sense of that word) who does not *also* in some sense affirm to himself that he has it. We may, then, with complete consistency both maintain (as Luther in effect does) that the *assertion* of an obligation does not. imply freedom and yet hold also that the *being* of an obligation does imply freedom. Nothing that Luther says affects in the slightest the claim that the second of these propositions has to be accepted by us; and the cogency of that claim still seems to me perfectly manifest.

What is not, I confess, so clear is whether Luther himself distinguishes, as I have just done, between the mere *assertion* of an 'ought' (or issuing of a command) and its *validity* (or the bindingness of the command). Since for him the relevant assertion is ultimately God's assertion, the command we are required to obey God's command, it would be natural that he should not make the distinction. This is at once a characteristic feature and a grave weakness of the usual theological accounts of the moral claim. If, however, Luther does not draw the distinction the question arises whether we are really entitled to cite him as a representative of the view that 'ought' does not imply 'can', that there are genuine obligations even when there is no capacity to fulfil them, or whether we should say rather that, since 'ought' certainly does imply 'can', Luther is in fact denying that there are real, as distinct from merely seeming, obligations at all. Perhaps we may regard the question as settled by the fact that he did elsewhere say, in so many words, that *a debere ad posse non valet consequentia.* (See Webb, *Problems in the Relation of God and Man*, p. 116.) But even if we were to suppose that there is open to us a choice of interpretations, still one or the other view we must attribute to Luther unless we prefer to say that he has no coherent view at all. And if we attribute the first view to him we must say, as I have already indicated, that his arguments do not establish his conclusion. If, however, we interpret him in the second way, is it not implied that the successful mastering of the lesson of our impotence would abolish the very *belief* of obligation? Now to that there would appear to be two objections. First, the result, were it achieved, would surely not constitute that desperate frame of mind that Luther desiderates for us; for our despair seems to depend on the *conjunction* of a sense of requirement and a sense of incapacity. Secondly, it seems in any case to be true that though, through the recognition of our limitations we do come to modify in a quite radical way our initial views as to what it is that we can properly and strictly be said to have a duty to do, none of us is ever brought to an honest conviction that he has no duties whatsoever, that 'duty' is a *vox nihili*. Correspondingly, on the assumption that Luther is *not* denying that 'ought' implies 'can' it seems that no one will ever attain that conviction of *total* powerlessness without which, on his view, Satan still triumphs and the seats of the elect remain empty.

To sum up. It may be debated whether in the work under consideration Luther is better regarded as holding that there are no genuine moral obligations or alternatively that there are but that their existence does not carry with it any freedom of the will. I think myself that we must impute to him the second of these views; but in any case both alike seem to me untenable. Further, Luther's contentions about the disciplinary functions of 'the law' do nothing to establish either of them; rather these contentions presuppose that one or the other is independently established, on the basis, obviously, of a theological position derived from the text of the Bible.

But I must in conclusion insist again that those who differ from Luther on the crucial issue may still go a long way with him, only not the whole way, in regard to human weakness. Not all libertarians would wish to do so; but nothing in the libertarian position is positively inconsistent with the admission that the most important proposition about our freedom is that 'our wills are ours *to make them thine*', that our effectiveness depends on our according a practical recognition to the truth of that proposition, and that nothing so conduces to this as the insistent demand of an ideal that we feel bound to endeavour after but to which we find ourselves unable to attain by any sheer effort of will. It may be proper—nothing I say in this book excludes this—to surrender every manner of self-confidence except one; except, that is to say, the self-confidence that consists in the conviction of

'this main miracle, that thou art thou
With power on thine own act.'

To surrender this would be self-despair indeed, but the *sin* of despair. It would not be humility at all, for there is no humility in being ignorant of, or in lying about, our proper status. We are to accept our own nature and not pretend either to a higher *or to a lower* one. And our own nature (it does not dishonour God to say) is that of persons, not of puppets or any other sort of things.

INDEX OF PROPER NAMES

GEORGE ALLEN & UNWIN LTD

London: 24 Museum Street, W.C.1

Auckland: 40 Wyndham Street
Sydney, N.S.W.: Bradbury House, 55 York Street
Cape Town: 109 Long Street
Bombay: 15 Graham Road, Ballard Estate, Bombay 1
Calcutta: 17 Chittaranjan Avenue, Calcutta 13
New Delhi: 13–14 Ajmeri Gate Extension, New Delhi 1
Karachi: Meherson's Estate, Wood Street, Karachi 2
Mexico: Villalongin 32–10, Piso, Mexico 5, D.F.
Toronto: 91 Wellington Street West
São Paulo: Avenida 9 de Julho 1138–Ap. 51
Buenos Aires: Escritorio 454–459, Florida 165
Singapore: 36c Princep Street, Singapore 7
Hong Kong: F1/12 Mirador Mansions, Kowloon

REASON AND GOODNESS

Brand Blanshard

In these Gifford Lectures, delivered at St. Andrews, Professor Blanshard surveys a battlefield, the field of recent ethics. The views of Moore and Ross, of the emotivists and the linguistic philosophers, of Westermarck, Dewey and Perry, are critically examined. From this examination there springs a fresh account of what the central terms of morals mean—terms such as 'good', 'right', and 'ought'. The present debates about them, which are often thought to be merely verbal, Professor Blanshard shows to be the results of centuries of slow refinement of the issues. Indeed some of the most acute of ethical conflicts are rooted in a tension between reason and feeling, between Greek and Christian ways of thought, that are some two thousand years old. This book attempts to state the issues clearly, to trace their history, and to make proposals for their solution.

Demy 8vo. About 40s. net

THE RELEVANCE OF WHITEHEAD

Editor, Ivor Leclerc, Ph.D.

This collection of essays marks the centenary of the birth of Alfred North Whitehead. The continuing influence and significance of Whitehead's thought is exemplified in the way in which the various writers, who do not constitute a particular school, approach their chosen topic of enquiry. While a few devote themselves specifically to the assessment or criticism of aspects of Whitehead's work, others develop Whiteheadian themes and suggestions and still others follow their own lines of thought to which Whitehead has been relevant.

In acknowledgement of the importance of Whitehead's achievement for the contemporary philosophical scene, and of the contributors' indebtedness to Whitehead, this volume is entitled *The Relevance of Whitehead.*

Demy 8vo. About 42s. net

GEORGE ALLEN & UNWIN LTD

-2. JUN. 1961